Minds and Persons

ROYAL INSTITUTE OF PHILOSOPHY SUPPLEMENT: 53

EDITED BY

Anthony O'Hear

WITHDRAWN

CAMBRIDGE
UNIVERSITY PRESS

BOWLING GREEN STATE
UNIVERSITY LIBRARY

PUBLISHED BY THE PRESS SYNDICATE OF THE UNIVERSITY OF CAMBRIDGE
The Pitt Building, Trumpington Street, Cambridge, CB2 1RP,
United Kingdom

CAMBRIDGE UNIVERSITY PRESS
The Edinburgh Building, Cambridge CB2 2RU, United Kingdom
40 West 20th Street, New York, NY 10011–4211, USA
477 Williamstown Road, Port Melbourne, VIC 3207, Australia

© The Royal Institute of Philosophy and the contributors 2003

Printed in the United Kingdom at the University Press, Cambridge
Typeset by Michael Heath Ltd, Reigate, Surrey

*A catalogue record for this book is available
from the British Library*

Library of Congress Cataloguing-in-Publication Data applied for

Mind and persons/edited by Anthony O'Hear.
  p. cm.—(Royal Institute of Philosophy supplement,
   ISSN 1358-2461 ; 53)
  Includes bibliographical references and index.
  ISBN 0-521-53733-9 (pb.)
   1. Philosophy of mind—Congresses. I. O'Hear, Anthony. II. Series.

BD418.3.M553 2003
128′.2—dc21

                                        2003053219

ISBN 0 521 53733 9 paperback
ISSN 1358-2461

Contents

Contents

Preface

The papers collected in this volume are based on the lectures given in London as the Royal Institute of Philosophy's annual lecture series for 2001–2 under the title of Minds and Persons. If nothing else, the range and diversity of the lectures demonstrate the complexity of the topics discussed and the multiplicity of approaches to them in current philisophical discussion. It would be fair to say both that some of the leading contributors to that discussion are represented in this volume and also that within it there are some strikingly orginal theses and arguments.

On behalf of the Royal Institute of Philosophy, I would like to thank all the contributors both for their lectures and for the papers based on the lectures. I would also like to thank Sophie Allen once again for her invaluable help in the preparation of the volume and of the index.

Notes on Contributors

Ted Honderich
Grote Professor Emeritus of the Philosophy of Mind and Logic at Univeristy College London.

José Luis Bermúdez
Professor of Philosophy, University of Stirling.

D. Z. Phillips
Professor of Philosophy Emeritus at the University of Wales, Swansea.

Peter Carruthers
Professor of Philosophy and Chair of the Department of Philosophy at the University of Maryland.

Michael Tye
Professor of Philosophy at the University of Texas at Austin.

William Lycan
William Rand Kenan, Jr. Professor of Philosophy at the University of North Carolina at Chapel Hill.

Geoffrey Madell
Formerly Senior Lecturer in Philosophy at the University of Edinburgh.

David Cockburn
Professor of Philosophy at the University of Wales, Lampeter.

David Papineau
Professor of Philosophy at King's College London.

S. R. L. Clark
Professor of Philosophy at the University of Liverpool.

Notes on Contributors

E. J. Lowe
Professor of Philosophy at the University of Durham.

Tim Crane
Professor of Philosophy at University College London.

Frank Jackson
Professor of Philosophy in the Philosophy Program, Research School of Social Sciences, The Australian National University.

Perceptual, Reflective and Affective Consciousness as Existence

TED HONDERICH

1. Criteria of Adequacy for Analyses of Consciousness

One criterion of an adequate analysis of the nature of consciousness has to do with its three parts, sides or elements. These are seeing and the like, thinking and the like, and desiring and the like. The seeming natures of the perceptual, reflective and affective parts or whatever of consciousness are different despite similarity. An adequate analysis of consciousness, even if general, will preserve the differences. It will pass the test of what you can call differential phenomenology.

A second criterion is making consciousness something that exists in the ordinary way, a reality. Certainly we suppose it to be such. Yours came into existence at some stage of your embryonic development and goes out of existence and comes back into existence when you fall into and come out of dreamless sleep. What is it for anything to exist in the ordinary way? To my mind it is for the thing to be physical or of the *same sort* as the physical. What it is to be of the same sort as the physical, and hence what a tolerant naturalism or physicalism comes to, will be clearer later.

As for physical things themselves, they come in two lots. (1) Things that take up space and time and are perceived by all, or maybe all the experts—this truistic point about their being public will be relevant to much that follows. (2) Unperceived things that take up space and time and are in causal or other nomic connection with the first lot of things, the perceived ones. So physical things consist in chairs and the rest of the perceived physical world, and also atoms and the rest of the unperceived physical world.[1]

Thirdly, consciousness is subjective. This third criterion of an adequate analysis of its nature is the most uncertain, obscure and fundamental. All the consciousness we know about—forget the speculative talk about computers and Martians—divides up into sequences such that each of them is different at least in being in a special relation to one organism or subject. Somehow consciousness is not objective.

[1] Cf. Anthony Quinton, *The Nature of Things* (London & Boston: Routledge & Kegan Paul, 1973).

1

Ted Honderich

A too weak version of this condition is simply that facts of consciousness have some *dependency* on only one organism or brain.[2] The version fails, if you do not get immaterialist or spiritual about an organism or brain, because other things than consciousness have such a dependency. Others say about subjectivity that it involves privacy, or, more mysteriously, that neural processes have an 'inside', or that talk of them connotes more than it denotes or has a special sense as well as a reference.[3] The strongest version of subjectivity is that facts of consciousness are out of space and come in sequences that are attached to or are episodes of a subject in the sense of a self or ego out of space. This is an idea of folk psychology, so-called, and maybe of many philosophers not actually struggling with the subject of consciousness. The idea is commonly assigned to Descartes.

Fourthly, an analysis of consciousness must allow for causal relations between events of consciousness, whatever their intrinsic nature, and physical events that precede and follow them. This is the input-output or body-mind criterion. Locations of croquet balls cause ideas and vice versa. Like other criteria, this one has its own implications. One is that an analysis of consciousness with the upshot that there is no mind-body problem at all, that it has all been just an illusion, will be at least suspect.

Can all else worth attention as a criterion be put into these four categories having to do with differential phenomenology, reality or physicality, subjectivity, and input-output? That has been my inclination. It is a mistake to suppose that anything needs to go in about certain doctrines of philosophers having to do with aboutness or intentionality—that is, we do not have to suppose that an adequate account must be in line with any such philosophical doctrine as Franz Brentano's.[4]

---

[2] E.g. John Searle, *The Rediscovery of the Mind* (London & Cambridge MA: MIT Press, 1992).

[3] E.g. Edgar Wilson, *The Mental as Physical* (London: Routledge & Kegan Paul, 1980).

[4] Franz Brentano, *Psychology From an Empirical Standpoint*, ed. Oskar Kraus, Linda L. McAlister (London, Routledge & Kegan Paul, 1973), p. 88. For interpretation see David Bell, *Husserl* (London: Routledge, 1990), Ch. 1. For my rejection of intentionality as a criterion of consciousness, see 'Consciousness as Existence, and the End of Intentionality', in Anthony O'Hear, (ed.), *Philosophy at the New Millenium*, Royal Institute of Philosophy Lectures for 2000–2001 (Cambridge: Cambridge University Press, 2001).

2. Six Analyses of Consciousness

To come now to a second of my short lists, it is of sorts or families of answers to the question of the nature of consciousness generally. Six have been getting attention. Several of them have been getting it for a long time.

Plain or 17th Century materialism, what Donald Davidson calls 'Nothing-But Materialism'[5], allows to events of consciousness only certain physical properties. These are neural properties as we know them—electrical and chemical properties of current neuroscience— or other properties of current science. By way of a useful parody, consciousness is cells. If the idea started with Hobbes, it has gone on being bequeathed. David Papineau in *Introducing Consciousness* seems to be one residuary legatee.[6] A lot of scientific models of consciousness turn up here, including a recent one in terms of the common interpretation of Quantum Theory, this model being inspired sometimes by the wonderful proposition that since consciousness is a mystery you need a mystery to explain it.

A second answer to the question of the nature of consciousness is that conscious events have neural or anyway physical properties, but not of the electrochemical kinds in, say, in Kandel, Schwartz and Jessell's current edition of their splendid *Principles of Neural Science* or even in editions that can be anticipated.[7] Consciousness is not the stuff in current neuroscience, but the stuff of future science. We found the physical reality of magnetism, and one day we will find the physical reality of consciousness. Maybe because of its vagueness, this is a popular view, certainly in the laboratories. It has also had philosophical advocates, such as me in a weak moment.[8]

Thirdly, the pill of plain materialism with respect to our consciousness is coated by adding a proposition about the input and output relations into which our neural events enter. This is one understanding of functionalism and cognitive science with philosophical ambition. Here we start with the truth that desires, say, are items with certain causes and certain effects, and equally banal

[5] Donald Davidson, 'Mental Events', in his *Essays on Actions and Events* (Oxford: Clarendon, 1980).

[6] David Papineau, *Introducing Consciousness* (Cambridge & New York: Icon/Totem Books, 2000). For a review, see my 'Consciousness and Inner Tubes', *Journal of Consciousness Studies*, 7, 7, 2000.

[7] Kandel E. R. R., J. H. Schwartz and T. M. Jessell, *Principles of Neural Science* (New York: Prentice Hall, 1991).

[8] 'Consciousness, Neural Functionalism, Real Subjectivity,' *American Philosophical Quarterly*, 32/4, October, 1995.

truths about computers and computation, as well as forgetfulness about other truths about desires and computers. We leap to the drama that our own conscious events are wholly electrochemical events related to certain other events. The drama is coming to the end of its run philosophically, as behaviourism did before it.[9] It is becoming respectable science—brain science, the science of the basis or a basis of consciousness, not the philosophical issue of its very nature.

A fourth view is another understanding of functionalism and the like. Here the conscious events are identified not with actual events in relations, say electrochemical events, but with whatever events could turn up in the relations—or rather, not even that class of events themselves. Conscious is the relations, not the possible events in them. Consciousness is in this sense abstract. That is what is said, to whatever effect.

A fifth sort of view is that the mind is the brain, or consciousness is identical with neural processes, but in the mere sense that conscious properties are properties of single events that also have neural properties. Davidson's identity theory comes here, as does a past favourite of my own, the Union Theory.[10] This sort of thing is rightly said to be a dualism of properties, which you can take as a philosophical recommendation, but not enough of one.

Finally, immaterialism. Consciousness is a matter of properties and also a thing, one thing per person. Both are out of space. This is the vague idea of us all to start with, and the idea of Descartes, mentioned already as one end of the range or ranges of ideas of the subjectivity of consciousness. Is there a very great deal of philosophy that comes down to this sort of thing? Is it what non-materialists privately think they have to believe? Despite Wittgenstein's behaviourism, is it the implication of his piece of self-indulgent audacity that whatever thinking comes to, there is nothing happening in the brain that corresponds to it?[11] Certainly this immaterialism *is* in a good deal of elevated reflection by the philosophers of origination or Free Will.[12]

[9] 'Functionalism, Identity Theories, the Union Theory', *The Mind-Body Problem: A Guide to the Current Debate*, R. Warner and T. Szubka (eds.), (Oxford & Cambridge, MA: Blackwell, 1994).

[10] Davidson, 'Mental Events'; Honderich, *A Theory of Determinism: The Mind, Neuroscience, and Life-Hopes* (Oxford: Clarendon, 1988) or *Mind and Brain* (Oxford: Clarendon, 1999), both p. 71 ff.

[11] *Zettel*, trans. G. E. M. Anscombe and G. H. von Wright (Oxford, Blackwell, 1967), ss. 608–10.

[12] Robert Kane, (ed.), *Oxford Handbook of Free Will* (New York: Oxford University Press, 2001).

These six sorts of view, I propose, have recently exhausted the argued or contemplated possibilities. Consciousness could be material or strictly physical, maybe in a package not delivered yet or with ribbons. It could be abstract. It could be paired with the neural in single events. Or it could be traditionally mental.

3. Perceptual Consciousness as Existence

To these six sorts of view can be added one, which has now got some attention[13], about perceptual consciousness in particular.[14] It is that your being aware of this room consists in certain things existing in a certain sense. You being aware of this room, to put it into a mouthful, consists in there being a certain state of affairs—things outside your head occupying space and time, and being as coloured as things ever are and also propertied in other ways, and having a required or necessary condition in the unperceived physical world outside you and also such a condition in neural events in only your head. In virtue of this latter dependency on what is in your head and also where the head is, the state of affairs is different in what it contains from any other such state of affairs and also the states of affairs that are the perceived physical world and any part of the perceived physical world.

To repeat, what it is for you to be aware of this room, perceptually conscious, *is* for things to exist in this sense—spatio-temporally, with certain properties, with certain dependencies, and different from other such things. The awareness *is* the existing.

This view, Perceptual Consciousness as Existence, may have the unique recommendation of satisfying all the four criteria set out at the start for an adequate analysis of consciousness. Certainly a

[13] Rudiger Vaas, 'Consciousness and Its Place in Nature', *Journal of Consciousness Studies*, 9, 2, 2002.

[14] 'Consciousness as Existence,' in Anthony O'Hear, (ed.), *Current Issues in the Philosophy of Mind*, Royal Institute of Philosophy lectures for 1996–7 (Cambridge: Cambridge University Press), pp. 137–55; 'Consciousness as Existence Again,' in *Proceedings of the Twentieth World Congress of Philosophy*, Vol. 9, *Philosophy of Mind*, ed. B. Elevitch (Bowling Green: Philosophy Documentation Center, 1999), and also *Theoria*, No. 95, June 2000; The second paper corrects the first in certain important respects. See also 'Consciousness as Existence and the End of Intentionality', referred to in note 4. All the papers are on my website: http://www.ucl.ac.uk/~uctytho/

principal argument for the view is the extent to which the competing analyses do not satisfy the criteria.[15]

The three materialist views—functionalism on the first understanding is such a view[16]—clearly fail the subjectivity test. No coating can change the pill. Nothing will get us to agree that consciousness itself is cells. That consciousness is not cells is the most resilient proposition in the philosophy of mind, and has been since the 17th Century. Having seen off behaviourism, it will do the same with materialist functionalism. We can be as certain that a materialism of future science will fail for the same reason, leaving out the subject-matter on which we have a grip.

The fourth view, functionalism understood as being about abstract relations, fails the second test, about reality. No. 5, the dualistic identity theory, gives no contentful account of the property it assigns to the one thing that is identified by also having other properties. It doesn't get started. It doesn't come up for testing. The sixth view, Immaterialism, fails the second and fourth tests—reality and the input-output problem. None of the six views pays enough attention to the first criterion—in short, differences between the seeming and therefore maybe the actual natures of seeing, thinking and desiring.

Is Perceptual Consciousness as Existence the remaining arguable theory? How it gives us a clear and actual fact of subjectivity may be evident. According to this view, there actually are subjective worlds or states of affairs. There are worlds different from, if like or related to, physical or objective worlds. They are in a plain sense private and do not exist in the absence of a brain or the like—neither of which facts takes them seriously out of analogy with the perceived part of the physical world.[17] So subjectivity is rescued from mysterious and inapposite ideas and images, and of course a self or an elusive subjective aspect of each mental event.[18]

---

[15] That we need *something* new is the view of very many philosophers. See, for example, Thomas Nagel, 'Conceiving the Impossible and the Mind-Body Problem,' *Philosophy*, July, 1998.

[16] Argument for this, and also the objection that strict functionalism is incoherent, see my 'Functionalism, Identity Theories, The Union Theory,' op. cit.

[17] See in particular 'Consciousness as Existence', despite the mistakes in it.

[18] For an account in terms of a subjective aspect of each mental event, rather than a substance-subject or the like of mental events, see my *A Theory of Determinism: The Mind, Neuroscience and Life-Hopes*.

It is as evident that the view makes consciousness into a reality. It is *of the same sort* as the physical. Very roughly it makes awareness into a state of affairs akin to the state of affairs that is the perceived physical world. As for satisfying the first criterion, differential phenomenology, the view was prompted by it—prompted by the fact that what being aware seems to come to is indeed things somehow existing.

As for the input-output criterion, my world of perceptual consciousness consists in things in space. This state of affairs can be in plain causal connection with all other categories of things in space, in particular the things in the physical world. Certainly there can be cross-classification causation—causation between worlds of perceptual consciousness and the physical world.

4. Features of the View

This view of perceptual consciousness, rightly, makes it fundamental to reflective and affective consciousness. To say more of it, therefore, is also to speak of them. It can most easily be made clearer, perhaps, not by adding more formal content to the above somewhat formal statement of it, but by more informal means, the first one being a reminder having to do with heads.

The view does indeed take perceptual consciousness right outside of heads. What it is for you to be aware of the room is for an extra-cranial state of affairs to exist. This is not a certain familiar truth. It is not the truth that our ordinary concepts of seeing or touching, to the extent that there are ordinary concepts, bring in extra-cranial facts—that *seeing* by definition is different from hallucinating. That leaves it possible that the perceptual consciousness itself is in the head—cells, immaterial stuff, or whatever. That is not Perceptual Consciousness as Existence.

To say a word more about this radical externalizing of perceptual consciousness, contemplate the literal question 'Is your consciousness inside your head?' It is a question that we are all inclined at least to jib at.[19] Some of us want to say no, on account of what can be called folk immaterialism. Some of us want to say no on account of the fact just remarked on, that seeing etc. necessarily

---

[19] In my recent experience the fact has been illustrated in discussions with a couple of scientists, Susan Greenfield, author of *The Human Brain: A Guided Tour* and *The Private Life of the Brain*, and Roger Penrose, author of *The Emperor's New Mind* and *Shadows of the Mind*.

involve a thing seen or whatever. Is it possible to put aside both of these distractions and still want to say no—straight-off, so to speak? I think so. Conceivably Wittgenstein in one of his better moments did so, when he went on against thinking and feeling being 'a process in the head'.[20]

All this is bad news for the materialisms. My present point, though, is that it seems a virtue of our account of perceptual consciousness, whatever needs to be said of reflective and affective consciousness, that it saves us from further unhappiness, gives us a good reason for saying at least some consciousness is *not* stuff in our heads. It goes to the end of the path on which recent doctrines of externalism and anti-Individualism hesitate.[21] What the view leaves behind inside the head is only what is there for certain, which is a brain.

As a second informal reminder of the view, is it also worth remarking, as some have, that it makes consciousness part of ontology, not epistemology? Maybe the remark has some use. In it, what is the subject-matter of ontology taken to be? If that subject-matter includes existing states of affairs, and if the subject-matter of epistemology is taken to have to do with a mysterious mental relation of ours to those states of affairs, then the view in question does of course transfer perceptual consciousness from epistemology to ontology.

A third thing about the view is that it presupposes what some philosophers will hurry to call a Kantian premise. This is that there is a so-called noumenal reality to which we bring our own perceptual and neural machinery—our classificatory machinery. It is my own inclination to think of this reality-underneath as not being beyond or almost beyond our conceiving or classifying, but rather as being the unperceived but certainly theorized part of the physical world.

Of this world, the world of atoms, we make or construct the perceived physical world, that public world, and we also come to have exactly what you have been hearing of—worlds of perceptual consciousness. We make of the reality-underneath a lot of other worlds as well. So a somewhat familiar line of thought out of the history of philosophy is in Perceptual Consciousness as Existence. And,

---

[20] *Zettel*, s. 611.

[21] Honderich, 'The Union Theory and Anti-Individualism', in *Mental Causation*, John Heil and Alfred Mele (eds.), (Oxford: Oxford University Press, 1993).

incidentally, no real multiplying of worlds, no creative prodigality in the way of David Lewis.[22]

A fourth comparison has to do with the fact that philosophers of mind have hitherto been inclined to make out of the bottom world not only the perceived or public world outside of heads but also a mental world inside of heads, which latter world has then failed to measure up to good criteria for analyses of consciousness.

The present view having to do with existence constructs things differently. It is different in making out of the bottom world a generally perceived world outside of heads, a physical world having in it things of certain perceived properties and dependent on perceivers generally, and also worlds of perceptual consciousness, each to some extent different and having a different and unique dependency.

Fifthly, Perceptual Consciousness as Existence *is* separate from other views, and despite some misconceptions cannot be seen as or turned into any of them. It evidently is none of the listed materialisms—17th Century, futuristic or functionalist. It is also remote from functionalism when that doctrine is taken immaterialistically, as making consciousness into a matter of bare relations. Consciousness as Existence isn't the dualistic identity theory either. It is, by the way, less dualistic about mind and body than that theory. It does not assign unexplained properties of consciousness to the same events that also have other properties. That is, it does not leave properties of consciousness as possibly entirely unlike physical properties, but makes them akin to physical properties. Finally, the view is nothing like immaterialist.

One more informal characterization—which will lead us further down the agenda. Brentano regarded consciousness as consisting in *content* or *object* and something else. The second thing, which he referred to with commendable restraint in his talk of *direction*, also presupposed a self or inner point of view or what you will along these lines. There has since been some philosophical time given to the subject of content—the content of consciousness. One view takes the content of your present perceptual consciousness to be physical chairs and the like.

With this in mind it is possible to see the existential view of perceptual consciousness in a certain way. What it does is to reduce perceptual consciousness to something related to what others often more vaguely call its content or object. Those of sensitive philosophical dispositions, who react badly to talk of reduction, can as

---

[22] Lewis, David, *On the Plurality of Worlds* (Oxford: Blackwell, 1986).

well see the view as one that enlarges perceptual consciousness into a reality gestured at by others in talk of content or object.

Let us now press on. What of reflective and affective consciousness, thinking and the like and desiring and the like? Can these two other parts, sides or elements of consciousness be understood in a way that fits in with the nature of perceptual consciousness as we have it? For a start, can reflective and affective consciousness be identified with something like what others regard as only their content?

Certainly it will at least be embarrassing if the shortcomings of the six general views of consciousness are escaped in the case of perceptual consciousness and then have to be put up with to some extent in connection with reflective and affective consciousness. We really cannot put together what we have about perceptual consciousness with a materialist or an immaterialist view of thinking. Not only would we be falling into a kind of inconsistency, we would be back with the input-output problem or some other one. We cannot take up a merely functionalist view of our feeling, desiring and intending, not only because of inconsistency but also because such a view would have its own intrinsic shortcomings.

5. Reflective Consciousness, Possible Worlds, Concepts etc.

To start with reflective consciousness, thinking in a wide sense, you can try to bring it into a taxonomy.

(1) There are the sorts of thinking that enter into and are part of what we have been concerned with so far, perceptual consciousness. These reflective things implicit in perceptual consciousness include conceptualizing, mentioned already, and also attending.

(2) Reflective consciousness also includes memory—both the activity of remembering and the result of the activity.

(3) There is curiosity and inquiry. We ask questions, try to measure, seek causes and effects, experiment, guess, reason, seek to prove, and do philosophy, science and politics.

(4) Whether or not as a result of curiosity and inquiry, we suppose, judge and believe things to be the case. This is our thinking in a narrow sense—thinking that such-and-such in whatever way, thinking somehow that something has a property or relation.

(5) We imagine things, make up stories, create art.

(6) In sleep we dream.

Perceptual, Reflective and Affective Consciousness as Existence

That is a poor taxonomy, partly because much of a category or species may also fall into another one, but let us not try to do better. The thing aims us in the right direction.

It does remind us that reflective consciousness is not what perceptual consciousness seems to be—a somehow bounded and filled whole, what used to be called a perceptual field, and what it is indeed natural to call a world of perceptual consciousness. Reflective consciousness seems to consist, rather, in disparate activities, from conceptualizing in perceiving through believing a truth of arithmetic to dreaming. It has in it the different operations of our intelligent and intellectual existence.

Still, does the earlier account of perceptual consciousness in terms of an actual world tempt you to regard reflective consciousness in a related way? Are you tempted to the idea that thinking in the wide sense consists in their being possible worlds or anyway possible things, no doubt with a special dependency on one thinker's brain? It is the idea that to think something, in whatever way, is for a thing to exist in whatever way it is that possible things do exist. My theorizing with my eyes shut, say, consists in possible objects having possible properties.

Although some of us are capable of forgetting it, partly because the usage has helped out with some formal logic, the origin and clearest sense of our saying there are possible worlds is that our actual worlds, perceptual and physical, have a certain character or certain features. To say there is a possible world in which Jane Austen lived all her life in Bath is to say our actual worlds are such that it could have happened that she did. What that comes to, in brief, is that our actual worlds are such that our laws of nature and logic do not preclude her having lived her life in Bath. So with talk of possible things as against possible worlds. To talk of them is to talk of things not precluded by our laws of nature and logic.

So if we do not go in for the metaphysical prodigality of worlds mentioned earlier, the idea that our thinking in general is to be understood in terms of possible worlds and things is the idea that it is to be understood in terms of the natural constitution or operation of our worlds of perception and physical worlds, along with our conceptual schemes with respect to them. Whatever is to be said of how the idea fares with our adequacy-criteria, there is an immediate objection. It is plain that reflective consciousness goes far beyond this curious and limited subject-matter. In the relevant sense, for a start, and despite what was said of an intermingling of reflective and perceptual consciousness, I can think impossibilities. I can have thoughts that go beyond both kinds of limits on possibility.

Ted Honderich

The point that our thinking far outstrips possible worlds and things certainly persists, by the way, if you feel that what has just been said of them in terms of our laws is too deflationary. Possible worlds can be as real as mushrooms, popping up in ever-greater numbers every metaphysical spring, watered by modal logic. They remain, as their name reminds us, different from *impossible* worlds. But our thinking in general also has to do with impossible worlds.

Something very different from possible worlds and things may come to mind at this point. This is the idea that reflective consciousness consists in *concepts* and *propositions*, to which can be added *images*—images of the same order of reality or unreality.[23] It can be said for this idea that it does not defeat itself by putting a mistaken limit on the reach of our thinking. So in place of a view that may be conventional, that our thinking in the general sense has concepts and propositions *in it*, that it is something that *has* this content, should we consider the idea that what thinking in general comes to, all of what it comes to itself, *is* concepts and propositions?

In addition to the recommendation of no mistaken limits on thinking and, you may say, no superfluous addition to what others call the content of reflective consciousness, the idea may have other recommendations. Might it be carried forward in such a way as to satisfy the criteria of adequacy for accounts of consciousness having to do with differential phenomenology and subjectivity? Could be.

With respect to subjectivity, you can say that my reflective consciousness will be different from yours, and different from any set of concepts and propositions that has been ordered by us in a cooperative enterprise—the defining of a common language. The idea of concepts and propositions can also seem to have another virtue. Like its predecessor, about possible worlds and things, it allows us at least to wonder if being reflectively conscious is other than the fact of there being stuff literally in one's head.

But that is the end of the possible recommendations and virtues. The idea ordinarily understood shares a large flaw likely also had by its possible-worlds predecessor. If reflective consciousness is taken to consist in concepts, propositions and images, and these are *abstract objects*, not things or events taking up space and time, then there are the immediate results that reflective consciousness is not real in our required sense, and also is not itself in causal connection with the events of input and output. Abstract objects are not events,

[23] Hannay, Alastair, *Mental Images: A Defence* (London & New York: Allen & Unwin and Humanities Press, 1971).

not things in space and time. Whatever else is to be said of them, it seems they cannot be effects or causes. They have nothing to do causally with, say, locations of croquet balls.

You will agree, I hope, even if you do not share exactly my impulse about the real, that any view of any part of consciousness that denies its causal efficacy or functionality, makes it epiphenomenal, is intolerable? Will it not take more than a brave philosopher, indeed a philosopher of bravado, to defend epiphenomenalism? Will it not take such a philosopher to defend what has recently been correctly expressed as the view that 'remembering our childhood plays no part in the writing of our memoirs' and 'it is never pain that makes us wince, nor anger that makes us shout'. This is more than 'an affront to common sense'.[24]

So much for the bare idea, for a while, that my remembering the look of my father or thinking a sceptical thought about something is the inefficacious stuff of concepts, propositions and equally abstract images. Can we get to a better view by marrying something to it?

We can add to it for a start in that while my two pieces of thinking are not causes of my subsequent behaviour, the wholly neural processes that are associated with them are exactly such causes. They cause, for example, my subsequent speech-acts, the physical sentences that report my pieces of thinking. And further, to come to the essence of the strategy, we add in that a piece of thinking can be required or necessary for an associated neural process in something other than a causal or other nomic sense. So since the neural process is causally required for the later behaviour, that will give the right role to the pieces of thinking.

Or rather, this much being familiar enough, the real essence of this third strategy must be to try to conceive of a suitable relation of necessity between the abstract thinking and the neural process. It will be a long way from a causal or otherwise nomic relation, of course, given that the thinking is abstract. It can hardly be that the relation between a neural process and my thinking of the look of my father is *deductive*. It is not that a description of one entails a description of the other. Neuroscience is not an *a priori* discipline. Might the funny relation be a constitutive or part-whole relation? But hitherto those have been nomic or logical. Might it have the name of being a metaphysical relation? Easily said, but what is one of those?

[24] Keith Campbell and Nicholas J. J. Smith, 'Epiphenomenalism', *Routledge Encyclopedia of Philosophy*, Edward Craig (ed.), (London & New York: Routledge, 1998).

Ted Honderich

Being in bad trouble, and wanting to leave it behind, do you now stick to the idea of thinking being abstract concepts and propositions, but just give up on a funny relation that gives efficacy to consciousness? Contemplate epiphenomenalism after all, contemplate that remembering our childhood plays no part in the writing of our memoirs and that it is never pain that makes us wince nor anger that makes us shout? Maybe your mind turns to consolations. This epiphenomenalism of reflective consciousness being taken as abstract, you can say, goes perfectly well with *perceptual* consciousness having no tinge of epiphenomenalism to it. Worlds of perceptual consciousness are made up of things in space and time. So what you are swallowing is only a partial epiphenomenalism. Why shouldn't our conviction of the efficacy of the mental or mental causation be owed to and have to do with only part of the mental?

This hopeful idea does not register a larger problem. It is not just that we would need a new sort of relationship between thought and neural process for the purpose of escaping epiphenomenalism. We need such a relation actually to have such a view of reflective consciousness to consider. We need such a relation for this hopeful view we have been gesturing at. Its very essence is a relationship between what is abstract and what is physical. The problem for it at bottom is the input-output or mind-body problem. What is the relation it offers? Without at least the beginning of an answer to the question, we hardly have a view to consider.

That is not all. Making our thinking into concepts and propositions, with whatever funny relation to the brain, plainly runs up against another difficulty. I remarked that it might satisfy some of our adequacy-criteria, but there is the second criterion to think about. Consciousness is a reality, something physical or, as we said at the very beginning, of the sort of the physical. We achieved this with perceptual consciousness, but on reflection we are not achieving it with the idea on hand of reflective consciousness as concepts and propositions.

In these straits, let us not weaken and fall back into materialism about reflective consciousness, even a fancy kind—say functionalism or some related doctrine that in fact leaves out the fact of consciousness as we have a grip on it and in particular its subjectivity. All of that falls victim to our conviction that consciousness isn't cells, and hence to disproofs—say the excellent one articulated by Searle in terms of the Chinese Room in his bad old days before he found Free Will and a new and wonderful view of the mind.[25] Let

---

[25] John Searle, 'Consciousness, Free Action, and the Brain', *Journal of Consciousness Studies*, 'Mind the Gap' issue, 7 (10), 2000; Ted Honderich, 'Mind the Guff', *Journal of Consciousness Studies*, 8 (4), 2001.

us rather reflect on something new, or anyway something else, for the excellent reason that nothing on hand works.

6. Reflective Consciousness as Existence—Outer Representations

Let us start again, as in the case of perceptual consciousness, with the so-called phenomenology. As they say, what is reflective consciousness like? What is it now like, as they say, for you to remember the look of your father? That is, what is the seeming nature of your remembering the look of your father? The experience is a lot different from seeing him. To take another piece of reflective consciousness, what is the seeming nature of your consciously believing something, that the squirrel is going up the other side of the tree, or that some philosophy is up the spout? What about dreaming? It also has a seeming nature that is different from the seeming nature of daily life. So does picturing this room after you leave it, or otherwise imagining something.

Would that there were one answer to this question of differential phenomenology as persuasive as the answer that what it seems to be to be *perceptually* conscious is for a world somehow to exist. *Something* is a reality when I remember the look of my father, or believe something, or dream, or imagine. That reality sure isn't cells. But how *are* we to think of it? There is nothing to hand with which reflective consciousness can enlighteningly be compared, and by which it can be got into view—as perceptual consciousness could be compared with the perceived part of the physical world.

And to revert to our earlier reflections on possible worlds, there really is no phenomenological temptation to speak of reflective consciousness heuristically as a world. To talk of someone thinking with his eyes closed as being in a world of thought, maybe mathematics, is a poor metaphor at best. Thinking with your eyes shut isn't at all like being aware of this room. The closest thing to perceptual consciousness that can be found in reflective consciousness is dreaming, and for several reasons it is a good way off.

Still, it is not as if direct reflection on our thinking produces nothing. Something can be said of the phenomenon. It is that in all of our thinking, things *exist that may be true or may come to be true of other things*. In the case of me and my father, there is an image or the remains of one. In the case of me and the squirrel's going up the other side of the tree, there is a sentence of English or a part of one. Without asking about the ontological standing of the image and the sentence, we can make this our start of an account of thinking. We can take it that what we actually seem to know about reflective consciousness, as remarked above, is that it is a matter of representations.

These representations, it seems, even if they are more or less physical rather than abstract, cannot be adequately described just as effects of the things of which they may be true. That recent hope was futile. There are many more effects of my father than such signs of him.[26]

You make a better start on saying what a representation is by saying something about it itself being causal rather than the thing it represents being causal. It is that a representation is what shares some of the effects of what it represents. A representation can make you smile, or go into the next room, and so on. The picture of a tiger, or the image of a man or woman of a kind or doing something, or a symbol for fire, has some of the effects of what is represented. That is more or less what it comes to for a representation to stand for something else, isn't it?

Before we get into any philosophical deep water, say about relations between representations, and about systems of representations, remember we have a real grip on a certain kind of them. These are such instances of written or spoken words as those you are now reading—and the equally more or less physical images, photos, drawings, icons and what-not that fill and litter our lives.

I admit straightaway that we are not really sure how they have become representations, and have not quite worked out in general the related matter of what class of effects they share with what they represent. But we do in one clear sense know what they are: they are things that turn up in our worlds of *perceptual* consciousness. If your actual chair is in your world, so too is something else of the sort of the physical—the actual words or whatever that represent or are true of your chair.

So as to have a proposal clear quickly, here it is baldly. Reflective consciousness is partly a matter of certain representations—instances of representations, if you want. There are actual representations or signs in our worlds of perceptual consciousness. They are items like other items in these spatio-temporal states of affairs.

To go further with the proposal, what reflective consciousness more or less comes to in part *is* these actual representations. They are of course private in the way of all contents of perceptual worlds, and they have, so to speak, no unperceived existence, where the latter is a comment about their neural and otherwise bodily basis.

[26] 'Consciousness as Existence and the End of Intentionality', pp. 14–15.

Reflective consciousness so conceived, you will note, is no more than the sort of thing, or one sort of thing, that others take to be its content.

This proposal, to remember our adequacy-criteria, makes reflective consciousness different from perceptual consciousness. It also makes it a reality—what it consists in is of the sort of the physical, part of the reality of worlds of perceptual consciousness. Reflective consciousness so conceived, further, is as subjective as perceptual consciousness, as already indicated, and also something that causes and is caused by physical things—it passes the input-output test.

What about what can be contemplated for a while as almost another criterion of an adequate analysis of consciousness—the idea that consciousness is not in the head? Well, we do not have to say of reflective consciousness as so far conceived that it is inside our heads. The representations in question aren't.

Do you not rush into agreement with the given proposal about reflective consciousness? Is what delays you that question of how the actual representations become representations? I myself am not much concerned with this interesting and large matter. Our problem is the nature of consciousness, an analysis of consciousness, not an explanation of how it or any part of it comes about. No doubt the story has something to do with something like chimps making an involuntary sound while running away, and then coming to use the sound voluntarily and purposively to give advice about running away. The story will also have to do with the causes that are natural signs, so called, such as footprints in the sand. You will not expect me to do better at getting a great part of the evolution of a species into a sentence or two.

7. Circularity?

Are you delayed in your agreement with the given proposal because you object, as you might have with the existential analysis of *perceptual* consciousness, that the given analysis of reflective consciousness is no analysis but a case of something like circularity or *petitio principii*? That in fact we have set out to analyse thinking, and said it consists in part in some representations, but in fact ended up with the non-analysis that thinking is *thinking about* representations?

That is, you say a representation is only a representation if it is taken as such. For someone not in the know, the same item is no representation at all. So, to repeat, there is the embarrassment that we set out to say what it is to be in a way conscious, we come up with the answer that it is for certain representations to occur, but it transpires that the answer when explicit is such that our endeavour reduces to the circularity that to be conscious in a way is to be conscious of some representations. If this is not full circularity or *petitio principii*, it is no great advance.

It seems to me this is not the case—that the objection can be resisted. What it is for me to remember the look of my father, so to speak, is for my subjective representations to exist for a while, no more that that. They represent or symbolize away, so to speak, without my helping them by doing something else conscious. The label hereby put on the view, *Reflective Consciousness as Existence*, is in fact apposite. There is no more to this consciousness than the existing of the mentioned things.

That is not to deny a burden of what has just been asserted, however. Representations are representations only for those who are in some special way related to them. That is part of what it is for something to be a representation, but not necessarily something that gives rise to a circularity. What comes into view here is also a larger, more general consideration.

Our subject-matter has been and is consciousness. We all have a grip on it. Indeed in a sense we know what it is, know nothing better. You will not need much reminding that our subject-matter is not other nearby things. For example, it is not doing things without being conscious. There is a significant subject-matter there. If it can be called 'mental function' of a kind or whatever, and if it is spoken of in terms of some recent piece of neuroscience, say blindsight, it is as old as the hills, or anyway our relations to the hills. Philosophers noticed a good while ago that we walk without conscious planning, do some of our driving of cars while only aware of what is on the radio, and so on.

The main nearby subject-matter that is not ours in this inquiry, though, is not doing things without being conscious. It is the non-conscious side of conscious proceedings. There is a lot to thinking, you can say, that is not part of the conscious thinking. This subject matter of neuroscience, cognitive science and so on, is larger than that of doing things without being conscious.

A decent account of consciousness, and more particularly of consciousness as representations, does not have to transform the non-conscious side into a matter of consciousness, and will be absurd if it tries. Rather, to come to the main point, a decent account of consciousness will make use of the fact of non-conscious mental functioning where it is needed.

Perceptual, Reflective and Affective Consciousness as Existence

To revert to your objection, it was that it is futile to try to understand consciousness as being certain representations, since that must really be to understand it as a matter of being conscious of the representations. I don't think so. My line is that sometimes being conscious when that is thinking of your father may *be* the fact that something is representing him in a certain way—something in your world of perceptual consciousness is having certain effects. It would not have the effects in the absence of certain facts of non-consciousness, but that is nothing to the point. That something is a representation because of a lot of other things is not the proposition that it is a representation because someone is conscious of it as such.

8. Reflective Consciousness as Existence—Inner Representations

Will you say there are more representations than the actual ones in our worlds of perceptual consciousness? More representations that the ones on paper and in sounds and so on? And that they have to do with our thinking? Will you not give up the familiar idea that certain representations can be said in a way to be definitely *in the head*, making up a stream of reflection.

Certainly I grant it. Reflective consciousness is a matter of a second class of representations, inner rather than outer. They are states and events of ourselves and other forms of life of which we know and maybe other things. These representations—things sharing some effects with what they are said to represent—stand in a relation to the contributing organism that is analogous to that relation of perception, so to speak, in which the contributing organism stands to its world of *perceptual* consciousness.

These representations, then, items in an actual language of thought, have an existence different from but related to that of the contents of the physical world itself—the perceived part of the physical world. These inner representations, as you will anticipate, have a subjective character as clearly as do things, including the other representations, in worlds of perceptual consciousness.

To take this line, of course, is to give up in this sector on the idea that consciousness is not in the head. To take this line accepts the truth that generality can be pursued at too great a cost, an overriding of recalcitrant facts. An analysis of consciousness may have a recommendation on account of satisfying some idea *for the most part*. While an adequate analysis of consciousness has to avoid saying that consciousness is always stuff *inside heads*, we can have a little in there. This ecumenical spirit might also be engaged in with other objections.

Instead let me conclude quickly about reflective consciousness, or rather repeat, that it consists in representations in our outer worlds of perceptual consciousness and also representations in our heads acceptable to a tolerant physicalism.

As a result, to repeat some of what was said earlier, we have an account of reflective consciousness that makes it satisfactorily different from perceptual consciousness. The representations in question also have reality. They are subjective as well, as just remarked. How I contribute to my cranial ones, the counterpart of my perceptual apparatus with perceptual consciousness—that question is for friends in the laboratories. To say that my representations are subjective is also to say they are not exactly your representations, or of course the agreed representations of our physical and objective worlds. Further, they are private in something like the way of things in perceptual worlds and they have, so to speak, no uncontemplated existence—which facts to not subtract them from an actual world. To remember the last of our adequacy-criteria, the representations in question pass the input-output test too.

9. Affective Consciousness as Existence

To come now to affective consciousness, or desiring in a general sense, which has more in it than speaking of affect has sometimes conveyed, here too we can contemplate an informal taxonomy.

(1) Evidently *particular* desires and wants of very many kinds, and, quite as important, satisfactions and frustrations of them, are at least part of affective consciousness. The desires and wants range from inclinations and hankerings, through wants and appetites, to cravings and lusts, to irresistible compulsions, which is but one one sorting-out of them. They seem to be separable in general into attractions and repulsions.

(2) Affective consciousness includes a wide range of sensations, feelings, emotions and attitudes, different in their subjects or objects and also a good deal else. They include pain, pleasure, hunger, satiety, hope, fear, courage, pride, shame, happiness, anger, sadness, love, loyalty, respect, wonder, depression, calm and so on.

(3) This consciousness also includes what is somehow separable from all this, which is valuing. Almost all things can have some

value for us. They are good or bad for me or you from the point of view of self-interest. They are right or wrong morally. They are legal or not, rational or not, beautiful, expensive, preferable, tolerable and so on. Other persons as well as things have these values.

(4) We have intentions of two kinds, the forward-looking or inactive kind, such as the intention today to travel by train tomorrow, and the active kind of intentions, these being involves in the actual initiation and carrying forward of actions. Active intentions are close to what have traditionally been regarded as willings, volitions and the like, but they need to be understood, less traditionally, as being a considerable part of what can be called our consciousness of or in acting.[27]

A little reflection on this attempt at taxonomy brings out its shortcomings. Very clearly, at least many of the particular desires and wants in the first category enter into the sensations, feelings, emotions and attitudes in the second category, and vice versa. So with the sensations etc. and the valuing. Pride cannot be taken in what is worthless, of no value, and to think one has done right is to respect oneself for a while. Also, all three sorts of affective consciousness are involved in the fourth, the intentions. To intend to do something, tomorrow or now, is to want something, feel about it, and put some value on it.

To speak differently but as truly, there is the fundamental fact that the first category's particular desires and wants and their satisfactions and frustrations are more or less pervasive in and are much of the stuff of the following three categories of affective consciousness. Some of the sensations, feelings and so on of the second category, say hunger, are close to being desires themselves. All of the sensations, feelings and so on include desires. Think of fear or hope.

So with the third and fourth categories. Think of what is good for America or right for all of us, or of intending to do this rather than that. These at least have desire or want as a component. Evidently forward-looking intentions can be regarded as complexes of a desire for what is said to be intended together with beliefs of several kinds, and active intentions as such complexes with the addition of an executive element, something that can have the name of being a command to one's body.

As in the case of reflective consciousness, then, all I claim for the taxonomy is that it aims us in the right direction.

[27] *A Theory of Determinism*, pp. 216–31.

Ted Honderich

Here is one of three quick proposals about affective conscious-ness—it has to do in the first instance and most clearly with the first category of particular desires and wants. The proposal is that what it is to desire a thing is for the thing to have properties that it has independently of the desirer. For reasons just remarked on, the pervasiveness of desires in affective consciousness, this is also part of what it is to have feelings about something, value something, and intend something.

The proposal goes against what philosophers have sometimes seemed to drift into or anyway towards, the attitude that someone's desiring something is just a fact about that person. To this a salu-tary response is that the thing has to be *desirable*. That is, it has to have some property, whatever mistakes are made about it, in virtue of which the person desires it—whatever desiring comes to. The thing has to be bigger, more highly paid, quiet or whatever, or of course dirty, dangerous, ignorant, fatal or whatever. This is no matter of projecting value onto a world, gilding a world, and so on,[28] but of value being in part in the world.

Here we also encounter a common inclination and also some faded philosophy, to the effect that things have not only natural but also non-natural properties, and these are what is in question with valuing and the like. There is the non-natural property of goodness. The existence of such a thing was supposed to be proved by the proposition that it is an open question whether any natural proper-ty is the or a property of moral goodness. It would not be such if there was a definitional or conceptual connection between the two items.[29]

This is not the time for a return to all that. Let me say simply that nothing can obscure the fact that I want to meet someone because of their smile, reputation or what-not, and that I may take a policy as right because it distributes goods to those in greater need or, very differently, in favour of my already well-fed nation. That we do not agree about what is desirable or right, and hence that certain defin-itions are not written into language, has no tendency whatever to show that the properties in virtue of which we have feelings about things—hope for them, are shamed by them or whatever—are not ordinary properties of them.

So, a part of what it is somehow to desire something is for it to have certain actual properties. That is to say, to come to a crux, that

[28] Cf. Simon Blackburn, *Essays in Quasi-Realism* (Oxford: Oxford University Press, 1993).

[29] G. E. Moore, *Principia Ethica* (Cambridge: Cambridge University Press, revised edition ed. Thomas Baldwin, 1993).

part of what it is for you to desire something is for things in your world of perceptual consciousness, or as we can add, for things as represented in your reflective consciousness, to have certain properties. It follows that what it is for you to desire something is a fact or reality, and subjective in a clear sense, of course, and that it involves no barrier to the causal connections of input and output.

That cannot be the end of the story of affective consciousness, however. We need a further proposal, since the first has nothing in it about differential phenomenology, the different nature of affective as against perceptual and reflective consciousness, desiring in general as against seeing and thinking. To take the first category of affective consciousness, there is a difference that asserts itself between wanting and just seeing something. To turn to the second category, there is a difference between having the pain of being burned and seeing a match burning. Similar remarks are to be made about valuing and intending. All of desiring is different from seeing and thinking.

The difference has often been taken as having to do with our behaviour and our bodies. A ludicrous view here, reduced to useful parody, was the radical behaviourism that made my wanting to get a book for my son no more than my movements in ordering it from Amazon.com. Not my *actions*, note, since the ordinary idea of an action imports mental content excluded from radical behaviourism's idea of wanting something.

But if this is to be put aside, it is clear we must not put aside everything about behaviour and bodies in attempting an analysis of affective consciousness. Indeed it is impossible to do so with pain and the rest of what are rightly referred to as *bodily* sensations— some of the items in the second category of facts of affective consciousness. These, to come to a point, can perhaps or presumably be treated somehow along the lines of reflective consciousness. To have a headache is for something *in my body* in a way to exist.

As with bodily sensations, so, in ways and degrees, with the rest of what is in the second category of affective consciousness. We can give some place to the existence of inner bodily items with feelings, emotions and attitudes. In fact a bodily component in fear, courage, shame, even respect and wonder, has been a reasonable assumption before now. A related account can be given of the particular desires and wants of the first category. So with the two kinds of intentions. With respect to active intentions, those involved in the actual initiation and carrying forward of actions, there is what we ordinarily call direct awareness of items of bodily movement. Something similar if weaker can be said in connection with valuing.

A third part of an analysis of affective consciousness, separable from what has just been said, has to do with behaviour or action in another way. Again to take simple cases from the second species of affective consciousness, fear and courage involve thinking of whole actions, say fleeing and attacking. To be afraid is partly a matter of the existence of representations of actions. So affective consciousness takes into itself some reflective consciousness. Similar remarks can be made about particular desires and wants, values, and of course intentions.

The conclusion about affective consciousness, then, is that it is to be understood as consisting in (1) a side of perceptual consciousness, this having to do with actual properties of things and people, and in (2) states or events in our bodies, and in (3) reflective consciousness having to do with actions. This view of affective consciousness thus inherits the recommendations of its components with respect to the adequacy-criteria with which we started. It makes affective consciousness into kinds of existence of things.

10. A Doubt and a Certainty

The view in sum, Consciousness as Existence, is that what it is to be conscious in any of the three ways is *for certain things in a way to exist*, different things in each case. Consciousness is its content—what others have called its content with at least the implication that there is more to it.

Of what worth is the view? Well, the stuff on perceptual consciousness seems to me an enlightening reorganization of thinking on the subject, a conceptual revision that serves truth better—the truth of the four criteria of consciousness. Anyway it seems to have this recommendation on a clear day, in the morning. The stuff on reflective and affective consciousness is not much more than preliminary sketches. My doubt about it includes some about the possibility of concealed circularity.

The certainty is that although Consciousness as Existence may not be true, or a good reorganization of our thinking, it has the use of illustrating how much change is needed in the plodding industry of our current philosophy of mind. A lot of it is only philosophy of mind so-called. It has or aspires to strengths other than those of philosophy, more or less scientific strengths. It is not good at logic in a large sense. While the essential science goes on, we need to get back to that—logic about the mind.

The Domain of Folk Psychology

JOSÉ LUIS BERMÚDEZ

I

My topic in this paper is social understanding. By this I mean the cognitive skills underlying social behaviour and social coordination. Normal, encultured, non-autistic and non-brain-damaged human beings are capable of an impressive degree of social coordination. We navigate the social world with a level of skill and dexterity fully comparable to that which we manifest in navigating the physical world. In neither sphere, one might think, would it be a trivial matter to identify the various competences which underly this impressive level of performance. Nonetheless, at least as far as interpersonal interactions are concerned, philosophers show a rare degree of unanimity. What grounds our success in these interactions is supposed to be our common mastery of (more or less similar versions of) folk psychology.

Most philosophers would, I think, be inclined to agree on something like the following minimal characterization of folk psychology.

> Human beings are social creatures. And they are reflective creatures. As such they continually engage in a host of cognitive practices that help them get along in their social world. In particular, they attempt to understand, explain and predict their own and others' psychological states and overt behaviour; and they do so by making use of an array of ordinary psychological notions concerning various internal mental states, both occurrent and dispositional. Let us then consider folk psychology to consist, *at a minimum*, of (a) a set of attributive, explanatory and predictive practices, and (b) a set of notions or concepts used in those practices. (Von Eckhardt, 1994,)

No philosopher has, as far as I know, denied that this set of attributive, explanatory and predictive practices exists, nor that these practices implicate a network of psychological concepts. In the following I shall use the expression 'folk psychology' in what I take to the standard way—namely, as picking out certain practices of ascribing propositional attitudes (and other mental states) to other agents and explaining/predicting their behaviour on the basis of those attributions.

25

José Luis Bermúdez

The few challenges that have been levelled at folk psychology have been directed at its explanatory adequacy. Paul Churchland and other eliminative materialists have suggested that folk psychology will eventually be replaced by a theory capable of dealing with complexities that folk psychology cannot tackle—a theory that will be derived from neuroscience rather than from commonsense psychological concepts. They do not doubt, however, that folk psychology is currently our dominant tool for interpersonal cognition. The issue they contest is the security of its dominance. There is also considerable debate about the particular way in which folk psychology should be understood. The idea, popular among both philosophers and psychologists, that folk psychology is essentially theory-like has come under pressure from the suggestion that folk psychological understanding is essentially grounded in empathetic simulation rather than upon applying principles about how different types of mental state might interact and manifest themselves in behaviour. But participants in this debate still see it as a debate about how to understand folk psychology—that is to say about how we actually go about attributing attitudes and employing those attributions to explain and predict behaviour.[1]

Strikingly, the centrality of folk psychology in explaining what makes social interactions possible has rarely been challenged. It is taken for granted by almost everyone that we accommodate ourselves to the behaviour of our fellow human beings by attributing to them beliefs and desires (or other propositional attitudes), assuming that they will act in a way that is more or less rational given those beliefs and desires, and then working out the course of action which that rationality assumption appears to dictate. Of course, everyone will agree that we don't *consciously* go about doing this, but it is usual to think that, in the vast majority of cases, this practice of attribution, explanation and prediction proceeds tacitly. The analogy with linguistic understanding is suggestive at this point.[2] Gricean accounts of linguistic meaning and understanding propose that the process of understanding an interlocutor involves making complex assessments of his conversational intentions. To the objection that we have no awareness of doing any such thing (except in non-standard cases of irony and so forth) proponents of such accounts main-

---

[1] See, for example, the introduction to Davies and Stone, 1995a.

[2] In fact, it is not really an analogy, since neo-Gricean accounts of linguistic understanding reflect precisely the hegemony of folk psychological categories in social interaction and understanding that this paper is questioning.

tain that our attributions reflect the tacit mastery and application of a theory of conversational implicature.

There can be no doubt, of course, but that we do engage in folk psychological explanation, sometimes working forwards from what we know about someone's beliefs and desires to what we think they will do, and sometimes working backwards from their behaviour and general knowledge of how their minds work to their particular motivations for acting in a certain way. The question is whether this provides a model for social understanding in general. Granted that we sometimes do make reflective and explicit use of the concepts of folk psychology in making sense of the behaviour of others, should we conclude that our *unreflective* social understanding involves an implicit application of the concepts of folk psychology in the interests of explanation and prediction? Should we conclude that all our social understanding involves deploying the concepts and explanatory/predictive practices of folk psychology?

With these questions in mind, let me distinguish two conceptions of the domain of folk psychology—or, more accurately, the two ends of a spectrum of conceptions of the domain of folk psychology. At one end lies the narrow construal of the domain of folk psychology. According to the narrow construal, the domain of folk psychology should not be presumed to extend further than those occasions on which we explicitly and consciously deploy the concepts of folk psychology in the services of explanation and/or prediction. At the other end of the spectrum lies the broad construal, which makes all social understanding a matter of the attribution of mental states and the deployment of those attributed states to explain and predict behaviour.

There are several reasons why the dominant conception in contemporary philosophy of mind of the domain of folk psychology is broad rather than narrow. The first is that the philosophy of mind tends to operate with a clearcut distinction between two ways of understanding behaviour. We can either understand behaviour in intentional terms, as rationalized by propositional attitudes, or in non-intentional terms. The standard examples in philosophy of mind textbooks (and indeed in philosophy of action textbooks) of behaviours not to be understood in intentional terms are those that are either reflex or not properly attributable to the agent. It is standard to distinguish, for example, between an arm-raising that is intentional, comprehensible as issuing from a particular nexus of beliefs and desires, and one that is the result of a reflex response, or of someone else lifting my arm for me. It seems pretty clear that social understanding does not involve understanding the behaviour of others in either of these latter two ways. So, if the choice really is a stark one between behaviour being unintentional in one of these senses, on the one hand, and its being intentional in the sense of being rationalized by propositional attitudes on the other, then it is easy to see why unreflective social understanding should be thought to involve the tacit application of folk psychology.

Secondly, a folk psychological construal of social understanding goes hand in hand with the dominant understanding of the 'springs of action'—not surprisingly since in many cases the way that we understand an action is intimately related to how we take that action to have come about.[3] Many philosophers assume that we act in virtue of our beliefs and desires and understand the 'in virtue of' to be causal in nature. The way in which this view is developed usually leaves no room for 'thinking behaviour' that is not causally generated by beliefs and desires. To the extent, then, that the activities of social coordination are thinking activities, the folk psychological construal seems to follow immediately.

At a more general level, and this is an idea that can be traced at least as far back as Kant's kingdom of ends, lies the background thought that it is a mark of the distinctiveness of persons that we treat them in a fundamentally different manner from the way that we treat non-persons. The idea that we have this distinctive way of treating persons is bound up with the idea that there is a distinctive mode of explanation appropriate to the behaviour of persons and not appropriate to other parts of the animate world, namely, personal-level intentional explanation that treats agents as more or less rational beings striving to satisfy their desires and aspirations in the light of the information they possess about the world. So, one might think, it is an integral part of what it is to treat persons as persons that we should strive to explain their behaviour in terms of the broadly normative concepts of folk psychology.[4]

However, I can see little evidence to support the tacit assumption that belief-desire psychology is even universally applicable, let alone universally applied. There is a range of reasons for thinking that the application of folk psychology is a relatively circumscribed part of

[3] I mention this as a separate point because of the influential minority of philosophers who deny this reciprocal relation between the terms in which we understand action and how we take those actions to have been caused. The type of instrumentalism canvassed by Daniel Dennett falls into this category.

[4] For further discussion of the distinction between personal and subpersonal explanation see Bermúdez, 2000 and the other essays in Bermúdez and Elton, 2000.

our social and cognitive life and the burden of this paper will be that our conception of the domain of folk psychology should be far closer to the narrow end of the spectrum than to the broad end. In section II, I will discuss how the issue between the narrow and broad construal of the domain of folk psychology relates to the debate between theory-theory and simulationist conceptions of folk psychology. Both the simulationist and theory-theory camps can be understood in either broad or narrow terms—although, as it happens, they are almost invariably understood in broad terms. In section III, I will present some general considerations counting against the broad construal. Section IV will explore concrete examples of how different types of social interaction might involve non-folk-psychological forms of social understanding.

II

The issue between narrow and broad construals of the domain of folk psychology is orthogonal to the debate about whether folk psychology should be understood in terms of the application of a theory or in terms of empathetic simulation (see the papers collected in Davies and Stone, 1995a and 1995b and in Carruthers and Smith, 1997). According to proponents of the so-called theory-theory, folk psychological understanding involves the application of a tacitly known network of principles connecting mental states to each other and to behaviour. Simulationists, on the other hand, think that we explain and predict the behaviour of other agents by projecting ourselves into the situation of the person whose behaviour is to be explained/predicted and then using our own mind as a model of theirs. This involves running our own decision-making processes off-line taking as inputs the mental states that it seems appropriate for the other person to have in that situation. Both the simulation theory and the theory-theory maintain that social understanding proceeds essentially by the attribution of beliefs and desires. The issues separating the theory-theorist and the simulationist are (a) how we arrive at the attributions of beliefs and desires and (b) how we get from those attributions to explanations/predictions. The following passage from Gregory Currie makes clear both the differences between the two positions and the ground they share.

> Simulation theorists say that our access to the thoughts of others is not through the application of a primitive but effective theory, as advocates of the 'theory-theory' of folk psychology suppose,

but through a kind of internal, largely spontaneous, re-enactment that allows us to imagine ourselves in some rough approximation to the situation of another. In so imagining, we tend to acquire, in imagination, the beliefs and desires an agent would most likely have in that situation, and those imaginary beliefs and desires have consequences in the shape of further pretend beliefs and desires as well as pretend decisions that mimic the beliefs, desires and decisions that follow in the real case. (Currie 1995, p. 158)

Both parties to the debate think that we arrive at predictions and explanations by moving from beliefs and desires, either through theoretical principles that link particular complexes of beliefs and desires to particular behaviours or through working out what one would oneself do in that situation with those beliefs and desires.

It is true that simulationists often write as if simulations proceed simply by 'putting oneself into the perspective of another'. Here is another, more ambiguous passage from Gregory Currie

[The simulation view] says that I understand the minds of others by imaginatively projecting myself into their situations and using my own mind as a model of their's. Running my own mental state 'off-line', I am able to *simulate* the mental process of another, and thereby to learn, for example, what decision he will make. (Ibid., p. 242)

The ambiguity concerns whether the 'situation' into which I project myself includes some specification of what the other person believes, desires, hopes and so forth, or whether I simply adopt their perceptual perspective on the world and start simulating from there. It seems clear, however, that we cannot simulate someone, except in the most straightforward of cases, simply by adopting their perceptual perspective on the world. That would give us a fairly accurate way of determining how they are likely to be perceiving the world, but in order to work out how they might act on the basis of what they perceive we need to know how those perceptions are likely to feed into their propositional attitudes more widely understood. And nor, of course, can we work out what people are likely to believe simply by adopting their perceptual perspective—we need to attribute some attitudes to get started on the process of simulating the attitudes that someone might acquire in a given situation.

The debate between mainstream simulationists and theory-theorists is in an important sense orthogonal to the question of whether we should construe folk psychology in narrow or broad terms. The question of the domain of folk psychology is the

question of whether we should make sense of our unreflective practices of social coordination in terms of the tacit application of the
explanatory and predictive practices of explicit folk psychology.
One's answer to this should not be affected by how one understands
the explanatory and predictive practices of explicit folk psychology.
The simulation theory is perfectly compatible with a broad construal of folk psychology. On such a view social coordination would
be underpinned by constant off-line simulations of the mental
states and processes of other participants, not to mention simulations of their simulations of oneself. But the simulation theory can
equally be interpreted in narrow terms, as applying only to the
relatively infrequent occasions when we make an explicit effort to
make sense out of someone's behaviour. The same holds of the
theory-theory. There is nothing about the theory-theory which
demands that it be applied broadly rather than narrowly.

III

There are some very general reasons for being inclined towards a
narrow rather than a broad conception of folk psychology. Some
stem from considerations of cognitive architecture and the structure
of the mind. Others stem from considerations of computational
complexity. Both sets of reasons are ultimately suggestive rather
than conclusive. The real argument, if it can be called that, will
come from providing concrete examples of how areas of social
understanding can be modelled in non-folk psychological terms.
The general reasons will occupy us in this section and the concrete
examples in section IV.

The computational argument is straightforward. It is motivated
by the thought that the vast majority of our social interactions
involve almost instantaneous adjustments to the behaviour of
others, whereas folk psychological explanation is a complicated and
protracted business, whether it is understood according to the
simulation theory or the theory-theory. It is no easy matter to
attribute beliefs and desires and then to work either backwards from
those beliefs and desires to an explanation or forwards to a
prediction. The point is perhaps easiest to see with respect to the
theory-theory. To apply folk psychological explanation is to sub-
sume observable behaviour and utterances under general principles
linking observable behaviour to mental states, mental states to other
mental states and mental states to behaviour. As many authors have
stressed, the application of these principles requires identifying,

31

among a range of possible principles that might apply, the ones that are the most salient in a given situation. It requires identifying whether the appropriate background conditions hold, or whether there are countervailing factors in play. It requires thinking through the implications of the principles one does choose to apply in order to extrapolate their explanatory/predictive consequences. It would be an overreaction to suggest that the need to do all these things makes folk psychological generalizations essentially useless. But it certainly makes them rather unwieldy. And it is no surprise that the paradigms of folk psychological explanations given by theory-theorists tend to be complicated inferences of the sort either found in the final chapters of detective novels (e.g. Lewis, 1972) or in dramatic and self-questioning soliloquies (e.g. Fodor, 1987). These are indeed striking cognitive achievements, but it seems odd to take them as paradigms of interpersonal cognition. Do our everyday cognitive interactions with people really involve deducing hypotheses from general principles, drawing out the deductive consequences (more accurately: the *relevant* deductive consequences) of those general principles and then putting those hypotheses before the tribunal of experience? If that is what is required then it is a wonder that such a thing as social coordination exists.

The practical difficulties here are obscured by the narrow range of examples that tend to be considered. Folk psychological explanation is usually considered by philosophers to be a one-on-one activity. This is exactly what one would expect given that the paradigms are the detective drawing together the strands of the case, or the puzzled lover trying to decode the behaviour of her paramour. But social understanding is rarely as circumscribed as this. In many examples of social coordination there is a range of people involved and the behaviour of any one of them is inextricably linked with the behaviour of the others. Suppose that the social understanding involved in such examples of social coordination is modelled folk psychologically. This would require each participant to make predictions about the likely behaviour of other participants, based on an assessment of what those participants want to achieve and what they believe about their environment. For each participant, of course, the most relevant part of the environment will be the other participants. So, my prediction of what another participant will do depends upon my beliefs about what they believe the other participants will do. The other participant's beliefs about what the other participants will do are in turn dependent upon what they believe the other participants believe. And so on.

It is clear that there will be many layers in the ensuing regress, and that the process of coming to a stable set of beliefs that will allow one to participate effectively in the coordinated activity will be lengthy and computationally demanding. Of course, none of this shows that there are any objections in principle to modelling coordinative social understanding in folk psychological terms. Any such claim would be absurd, not least because we have a well worked out mathematical theory that allows us to model social understanding in what are essentially folk psychological terms (or at least a regimentation of them). Game theory is a theory of social coordination and strategic interaction employing analogues of the folk psychological notions of belief and desires (in the guise of probability and utility assignments). What thinking about computational tractability should do, however, is at least to begin to cast doubt upon whether this could be a correct account of the form of social understanding in the vast majority of situations.

It is important to distinguish this point from another charge levelled at the theory-theory. Simulation theorists have sometimes suggested that issues of computational tractability work in favour of the simulation theory. Jane Heal, for example, has argued that theory-theorists run into difficulties analogous to the frame problem in computer science (Heal, 1996). The frame problem is essentially the problem of determining which, among the myriad aspects and deductive consequences of a principle or of a belief, are relevant in a given situation (Dennett, 1987). Any psychological theory incorporating a satisfactory response to the frame problem will of necessity incorporate a theory of relevance, specifying why certain psychological factors will be deemed relevant in particular situations but not in others, how changing the parameters of a situation can radically alter those aspects of it relevant to decision-making and how what is taken to be relevant can vary systematically with determinate aspects of the psychology of the individual. It is, according to Heal, a weighty consideration against the theory-theory that any such, presumably tacitly known, theory of relevance would be far more complex than any other postulated tacit theory to explain, for example, our grasp of grammar or of so-called naïve physics.

This worry is well grounded (although one might wonder whether a simulation theorist can avoid postulating at some level a tacitly known theory of relevance governing both our on-line decision-making processes and our off-line simulations). But it is orthogonal to the computational worry I am raising. That computational worry would still be there even if we granted the theory-theorist the legitimacy of postulating a tacitly known theory of relevance. The worry about relevance is a worry about how it is even possible to tailor the generality of folk psychological principles to the particularity of specific situations. The computational worry, on the other hand, is about the combinatorial explosion that will occur when the situation in question involves several individuals who are potentially collaborating. Even if we can fix the parameters of relevance in a way that will permit folk psychological principles to come into play, the key problem comes from the fact that the application of folk psychological explanation to a multi-agent inter-action will require a computationally intractable set of multiply embedded higher-order beliefs about beliefs.

The worry about combinatorial explosion is not confined to the theory-theory. Let us suppose that the simulation theory can get by without having to assume a tacitly known theory of relevance, so that a simulation simply involves using one's own mind as a model of the minds of the other participants in the interaction. One would still need to plug into the decision-making processes an appropriate set of inputs for all the other participants and then run simultane-ous simulations for all of them. This is multiply problematic. There is, first of all, a straightforward question about how many simula-tions it is actually possible to run simultaneously. Since the practi-cal details of how the process of simulation might work have not really been explored, there is little concrete to say about this. *Prima facie*, however, one might think that there will be some difficulties with the idea of multiple simultaneous simulations, given that a simulation is supposed to work by running one's own decision-mak-ing process off-line and those processes are presumably designed to give an output for a single set of inputs. But there is a more serious problem. The simultaneous simulations will not be independent of each other. Suppose that the interaction contains three participants, A, B and C, in addition to me. In order to simulate B properly I will need to have views about what A and C will do—without that infor-mation I will not have any sense of what initial beliefs it would be reasonable to attribute to B. But, by parity of reasoning, this infor-mation about what A and C will do will depend upon each of them having information about what the other participants will do. It is very difficult to see how the notion of simulation can be stretched to accommodate, not just simultaneous simulations, but simultaneous simulations that are interdependent. So, the simulation theory, no less than the theory-theory, is bound to confront problems of computational tractability if it adopts a broad construal of the domain of folk psychology.

Let us turn now to the second general reason for scepticism about the broad interpretation of the domain of folk psychology. Here I will be painting with very broad strokes of the brush indeed. Folk psychological reasoning is a paradigm of metarerepresentational thinking, where metarepresentational thinking involves thinking about thoughts—taking thoughts as the objects of thought, attributing them to other subjects, evaluating their inferential connections with other thoughts, and so on. It has been suggested that metarepresentational thinking is in some sense language-dependent (Dennett, 1996, Bermúdez, 2003). One might argue, for example, that thoughts must be vehiced in a way that is consciously and reflectively accessible if they are to feature in metarepresentational thinking, and that the only possible vehicles are linguistic. I have developed this line of thought in more detail elsewhere (Bermúdez, 2003, Ch. 8). If the thesis of language-dependence is correct then it seems highly likely, on the basis of our best current theories of cognitive archaeology, that many of the cognitive skills involved in social coordination emerged long before the capacity for metarepresentational thinking, and hence long before folk psychological explanation was even possible.[5] Early hominids appear to have been capable of an impressive range of types of collective behaviour, involving the social transmission of knowledge (e.g. knowledge of the natural world); the tracking of social relations within social groups; complex forms of social coordination (in hunting and migratory behaviour) and technical training in tool manufacture (Mithen, 1996). All these forms of social coordination require high degrees of social understanding. *Ex hypothesis* this social understanding could not have involved the concepts and explanatory/predictive strategies of folk psychology.

Of course, this does not allow us to draw any immediate inferences about the current state of our social cognition—perhaps the metarepresentational abilities that emerged with language acquisition (or at any rate relatively late in cognitive evolution) simply wrote over their primitive precursors, in the way that some developmental psychologists think that the earliest conceptions of the physical world acquired in infancy are completely superseded by the 'naïve physics' emerging later in development (Gopnik and Meltzoff, 1997). That would doubtless be the position of those who adopt what I have termed the broad construal of the domain of folk psychology. But much of what we know about the evolution of cognition suggests that this is unlikely to have happened. Evolution works by tinkering, grafting new structures onto already existing

[5] In fact, this suggestion is independently plausible even without the thesis of language-dependence.

ones, changing the function of structures that are already there. All the evidence is that our cognitive architecture is a palimpsest of superimposed structures of varying phylogenetic pedigree.

Moreover, the points about computational tractability made earlier in this section suggest good reasons for thinking that these primitive structures have not only persisted but in fact continue to play an important role in our social lives. It is not, I have suggested, feasible to think that all or even most of our social interactions can be modelled in folk psychological terms. It is natural to think, therefore, that much of our current social cognition may well reflect a residue of skills and abilities that long preceded the emergence of metarepresentation and folk psychology. There is little to be gained, however, from pursuing this line of thought without providing concrete examples of the form that these non-folk-psychological skills and abilities might take. We will turn to that task in the next section.

IV

In thinking about how social understanding might be modelled in non-folk psychological terms a good place to start is with emotion perception. The form and level of one's participation in social interactions is frequently a function of one's assessment of the emotional states of other participants. This is most clear when the interaction is a competitive one—a zero-sum game for example (taking a game in the technical sense as a strategic interaction among players). It may be to my advantage, for example, to press ahead to take advantage of another participant's dilatoriness—or to retreat and retrench when I notice the aggressiveness of one of the competitors. But something similar holds for cooperative interactions. My own commitment to a shared project is likely to be at least partly determined by my sense of the extent to which my partners value the shared goal. And the exact form of my participation in the shared activity will be tailored to how I read my partners' varying and changing levels of enthusiasm. I need to be sensitive to whether and when my partners are bullish, bearish, frustrated or enthusiastic. Without this we will not be able to work together effectively.

There are three points to make about the various types of emotion perception implicated in social interactions. The first is the most obvious. The type of emotional sensitivity at play in social interactions is highly diachronic. Social interactions are extended processes in which the relevant affective valences are constantly changing. Successfully negotiating such interactions is not in any sense a matter of identifying relatively long-term dispositional states or character traits. The affective indices are in constant flux. Think, for example, of the emotional dynamics of a team game or a committee meeting. This makes folk psychological attributions, whether derived through a process of simulation or through the application of a theory, particularly inapposite. The processes by which folk psychological attributions are reached are too unwieldy to permit of rapid real-time monitoring and revision. The second point is that in many social interactions the actual content of the relevant affective and emotional states will be apparent from the context. Participants need to be sensitive not to what is represented but rather to the fine details of the attitudes taken to what can be presumed to be shared representational contents. The third point is the least obvious, but perhaps the most important. What matters in social interactions and coordinated activities is that the participants succeed in acting with due sensitivity to the affective and emotional states of other participants. There is no need for those affective and emotional states to be explicitly identified and attributed. These forms of social understanding do not require forming judgments about the emotional states of the other participants.

It has been known for some time that emotion perception is highly dependent upon cues operating far below the threshold of conscious awareness. Emotional states can be transmitted directly from person to person, something which plays an important role in many types of social interaction, particularly those involving collective behaviour. We have a reasonably worked out understanding of how this transmission of emotional states can take place. The role of facial expression in the communication and detection of emotion has been systematically studied since Charles Darwin's pioneering study (Darwin, 1872). Recent neuroscientific research, based on the study of brain-damaged patients and on lesion studies in animals has postulated the existence of neural circuits dedicated to the production and understanding of expressive behaviour, the so-called limbic system.

It is important, however, to separate out two possible claims that might be made. The simple claim that emotion perception is frequently subliminal and a matter of pattern recognition should be uncontroversial, and in itself does not count against what I have been terming the broad conception of folk psychology. Directly perceived emotional states can easily serve as inputs to the processes of simulation, or as the raw material to which the generalizations of theoretical folk psychology are applied. The more interesting, and potentially controversial, suggestion is that we frequently act upon the perception of emotional and affective states without explicitly identifying them. The idea here is that we regulate our own behaviour as a function of our sensitivity to the emotional and affective states of those with whom we are interacting without at any point making explicit the identifications on which our behaviour rests. The understanding of emotional expression feeds directly into behaviour. Sensitivity to emotional states feeds directly into action without any attribution of emotional states.

This second suggestion certainly is incompatible with the broad construal of the domain of folk psychology, for the essence of the broad construal is that social understanding requires categorizing the behaviour of others in the concepts of folk psychology, in order to bring to bear either the mechanics of simulation or the appropriate tacitly known theory. It seems to me that this second suggestion is a better characterization of what is going on in very many cases of social interaction and coordination. The case for the broad construal of folk psychology is correspondingly weakened.

It might be wondered, however, just how significant this conclusion actually is. The types of social understanding that we have been considering are all highly circumscribed in at least the following sense. The issue is often not what other participants will do but how they will do it, since we may well know that other participants are constrained to act within narrowly prescribed limits. These are often not situations in which issues of explanation and prediction arise in the sort of ways for which one might think that folk psychological forms of social understanding would be required. Moreover, the fact that many social interactions involve an element of 'affect attunement' that is achieved without recourse to folk psychology hardly shows that no element of those interactions is controlled folk psychologically. Even someone sympathetic to the general line that many basic forms of social interaction fall outside the domain of folk psychology might pose the question of whether the type of deflationary account I have been offering really counts against the broad construal of the domain of folk psychology.

There are two different issues to be distinguished here. The first has to do with the nature of those interpersonal situations that are *not* circumscribed by shared goals or a relatively small number of clearly defined possible outcomes. We might ask whether these are always situations in which we can only act effectively by actively explaining and/or predicting the behaviour of other participants in terms of what they believe and desire. I shall suggest that in fact there are many situations in which one can act effectively without having any beliefs about the propositional attitude of others.

Nonetheless, it seems clear that there will always be situations in which we do need to predict and explain the behaviour of other people. The second question to be addressed, therefore, is how we generally proceed in those situations. Do we exploit the mechanisms of folk psychology, whether construed in simulationist or in theoretical terms? Or can we explain and predict what is going to happen without exploiting those mechanisms?

Let us start with the question of what happens in interpersonal situations that are *not* circumscribed by shared goals or a relatively small number of clearly defined possible outcomes. Those favouring the broad construal of the domain of folk psychology will suggest that, as soon as we move beyond highly circumscribed collaborative enterprises such as games or mending an aeroplane, we enter a realm of interpersonal interaction that can only be successfully negotiated by fitting the behaviour of other participants into the conceptual framework of folk psychology. In fact, however, it is far from clear that this is the case. The well-studied game-theoretical problem of how to behave in an indefinitely iterated prisoner's dilemma is a case in point, and one that has plausibly been argued to have wide application.

A prisoner's dilemma is any strategic interaction in which the dominant strategy for each player leads inevitably to an outcome in which each player is worse off than he could otherwise have been. A dominant strategy is one that is more advantageous than the other possible strategies, irrespective of what the other players do. In the standard example from which the problem derives its name, the two players are prisoners being separately interrogated by a police chief who is convinced of their guilt, but as yet lacks conclusive evidence. He proposes to each of them that they implicate the other, and explains the possible consequences. If each prisoner implicates the other then they will both end up with a sentence of 5 years in prison. If neither implicates the other, then they will each be convicted of a lesser offence and both end up with a sentence of 2 years in prison. If either prisoner implicates the other without being implicated himself, however, then he will go free while the other receives 10 years in prison. The dominant strategy for each player is to implicate the other. Since we are dealing with rational players who know each other to be rational, it follows that each will implicate the other, resulting in both spending 5 years in prison—even though had they both kept quiet they would have ended up with just 2 years apiece.

Although some authors have tried to argue otherwise (e.g. Gauthier, 1986), it is hard to see how it can be anything but rational to follow the dominant strategy in a *one-off* strategic interaction obeying the logic of the prisoner's dilemma. But what about social interactions that have the same logic but are repeated? Repeated interactions create the possibility of one player rewarding another for not having implicated him (or whatever the relevant non-cooperative activity might be). Surely this will change what is a rational to do. In fact, however, it only does so in a limited range of situations. The well-known backwards induction argument suggests that the rational course of action where each player is rational, knows the other player to be rational and is certain in advance how many strategic interactions there will be is to defect on the first play. It is only when it is not known how many plays there will be and/or the rationality of the other participant is not known that scope opens up for cooperative play. And this is where we rejoin the question of the domain of folk psychology. Suppose that we find ourselves, as we frequently do, in social situations that have the structure of an indefinitely repeated prisoner's dilemma. The issue may simply be how hard one pulls one's weight in the department.[6] It will be to my advantage to cut the examination meeting, provided that my colleagues do my work for me. But how will that affect their behaviour when we next need to wine and dine a visiting speaker? Will I find myself dining tête-à-tête and footing the bill on my own? Before I decide whether or not to cut the examination meeting I had better think about that possibility, and all the other possibilities when some or all of us applying dominance reasoning will lead to a suboptimal outcome. But how do I do this?

It is natural to think that I will need to make a complex set of predictions about what my colleagues will do, based on my assessment of their preference orderings and their beliefs about the probability of each of us defecting as opposed to cooperating, and then factor in my own beliefs about how what will happen in future depends upon whether or not I come to the examining meeting—and so on. This, of course, would be an application of the general explanatory framework of folk psychology (again on the simplification that utilities and probability assignments are regimentations of desires and beliefs). The broad construal of the domain of folk psychology is committed to saying that this is the way decision-making proceeds in strategic situations of these kinds—simply because these strategic situations depend upon social understanding and, according to the broad construal, all social understanding more complex

---

[6] This is not, strictly speaking, a prisoner's dilemma, since it involves more than two players. The multi-person equivalent of the prisoner's dilemma is usually known as the tragedy of the commons.

than simple sensitivity to the emotional and effective states of others has to be a matter of folk psychological explanation and prediction.

Even if we can make sense of the idea that strategic interaction involves these kinds of complicated multi-layered predictions involving expectations about the expectations that other people are expected to have, one might wonder whether there is a simpler way of determining how to behave in that sort of situation. And in fact game theorists have directed considerable attention at the idea that social interactions taking the form of indefinitely repeated prisoner's dilemmas might best be modelled through simple heuristic strategies in which, to put it crudely, one bases one's plays not on how one expects others to behave but rather on how they have behaved in the past. The best known of these heuristic strategies is TIT-FOR-TAT, which is composed of the following two rules:

A. Always cooperate in the first round
B. In any subsequent round do what your opponent did in the previous round

The TIT-FOR-TAT strategy is very simple to apply, and does not involve any complicated folk psychological attributions or explanations/predictions. All that is required is an understanding of the two basic options available to each player, and an ability to recognize which one of those strategies has been applied by other players in a given case. The very simplicity of the strategy explains why theorists have found it such a potentially powerful explanatory tool in explaining such phenomena as the evolutionary emergence of altruistic behaviour (see Axelrod, 1984 for an accessible introduction and Maynard Smith, 1982 and Skyrms, 1996 for more detailed discussion).

For our purposes, the lesson to be learnt from this example is not that we should model extended social interactions in terms of TIT-FOR-TAT. TIT-FOR-TAT has only a limited applicability to practical decision-making, simply because, in a situation in which two players are each playing TIT-FOR-TAT, a single defection will rule out the possibility of any further cooperation. This is clearly undesirable, particularly given the possibility in any moderately complicated social interaction that what appears to be a defection is not really a defection (suppose, for example, that my colleague misses the examination meeting because her car broke down). So any plausible version of the TIT-FOR-TAT strategy will have to build in some mechanisms for following apparent defections with cooperation, in order both to identify where external factors have influenced the situation and to allow players the possibility of building bridges back towards cooperation even after genuine defection.

The important point is that strategies such as TIT-FOR-TAT do not involve any exploitation of the categories of folk psychology. They can be followed without attributing of folk psychological states to those with whom one is interacting. In fact, a stronger conclusion is warranted. Such strategies do not involve any processes of explanation or prediction at all. It is clear that no prediction is required, given that what I do in any particular situation is determined by how I interpret what the other player did in the previous encounter. It may seem that this introduction of the notion of interpretation allows that folk psychological notions of explanation can get a grip, but this would be a mistake. In order to apply TIT-FOR-TAT, or some descendant thereof, all I need to do is to work out whether the behaviour of another player should best be characterized as a cooperation or a defection—and indeed to work out which previous behaviours are relevant to the ongoing situation. This will often be achievable without going into the details of why that player behaved as they did. Of course, sometimes it will be necessary to explore issues of motivation before an action can be characterized as a defection or a cooperation—and sometimes it will be very important to do this, given that identifying an action as a defection is no light matter. But much of the time one might well get by perfectly well without going deeply at all into why another agent behaved as they did.

From a game-theoretical point of view, therefore, there is nothing mysterious about the idea that one can act effectively in complicated social interactions without bringing to bear the explanatory and predictive apparatus of folk psychology. Within game theory, construed as a normative theory of rational behaviour, it can make perfectly good sense to adopt strategies that are, in an important sense, folk psychologically 'blind'. The real question is with the extent to which the normative theory applies descriptively. How frequently do we employ heuristically simple strategies in social interactions, taking our cue from very simple understandings of what other people have done—rather than from complicated attributions of folk psychological states? The general considerations canvassed in the previous section seem to suggest that it's likely that we do. At the very least this brief excursion into game theory gives us a way of interpreting in non-folk-psychological terms a large class of social interactions that are *not* circumscribed by shared goals or a relatively small number of clearly defined possible outcomes.

Let us take stock. A case has been made for the following claims

(I) The form and level of one's participation in many social interactions is often a function of one's assessment of the emotional states of other participants in a way that feeds directly into action without any attribution of emotional states. This frequently occurs in social interactions circumscribed by shared goals or a relatively small number of clearly defined possible outcomes. Many such activities are controlled without anything that looks like a folk psychological attribution at all.

(II) We can participate effectively in social interactions that are not so circumscribed without making use of the predictive and explanatory apparatus of folk psychology.

Let us turn now to the second of the two questions identified earlier. Let us consider social interactions that do not fall under either (I) or (II). *Ex hypothesi* these social interactions require explaining and predicting the behaviour of others. Have we now arrived within the domain of folk psychology? As matters are generally understood by philosophers we must have arrived there, simply because it is pleonastic that explanation and prediction proceed in folk psychological terms.

There is an important class of social interactions, however, in which it is true both that they involve predicting and/or explaining the actions of other participants and that the relevant predictions and explanations do not proceed via the attribution of folk psychological states. These are situations involving stereotypical routines and behaviour patterns. Let us start with two very simple examples. Whenever one goes into a shop or a restaurant, for example, it is obvious that the situation can only be effectively negotiated because one has certain beliefs about why people are doing what they are doing and about how they will continue to behave. I can't effectively order dinner without interpreting the behaviour of the person who approaches me with a pad in his hand, or buy some meat for dinner without interpreting the person standing behind the counter. But do I need to attribute folk psychological states to these people in order to interpret them? Must these beliefs about what people are doing involve second-order beliefs about their psychological states? Surely not. Ordering meals in restaurants and buying meat in butcher's shops are such routine situations that all one needs to do is to identify the person approaching the table as a waiter, or the person standing behind the counter as a butcher. That is all the interpretation required. These are both cases in which simply identifying social roles provides enough leverage on the situation to allow one to predict the behaviour of other participants and to understand why they are behaving as they are. There is no need to make any folk psychological attributions. There is no need to think about what the waiter might desire or the butcher believe—any more than they need to think about what I believe or desire. The point is not that the routine is cognitively transparent—that it is easy to work out what the other participants are thinking. Rather, it is that we don't need to have any thoughts about what is going on in their minds at all. The social interaction takes care of itself once the social roles have been identified (and I've decided what I want to eat).

The basic lesson to be drawn from highly stereotypical social interactions such as these is that explanation and prediction *need not* require the attribution of folk psychological states. It would be too strong even to say that identifying someone as a waiter is identifying him as someone with a typical set of desires and beliefs about how best to achieve those desires. Identifying someone as a waiter is not a matter of understanding them in folk psychological terms at all. It is understanding him as a person who typically behaves in certain ways within a network of social practices that typically unfold in certain ways. The point is that this is a case in which our understanding of individuals and their behaviour is parasitic on our understanding of the social practices in which their behaviour takes place. Nor, of course, is this understanding of social practices a matter of mastery of a primitive theory. We learn through experience that certain social cues are correlated with certain behaviour patterns on the part of others and certain expectations from those same individuals as to how we ourselves should behave. Sometimes we have these correlations pointed out to us explicitly—more often we pick them up by monitoring the reactions of others when we fail to conform properly to the 'script' for the situation.

One of the interesting characteristics of this type of social understanding is that it involves a type of reasoning clearly different from the way in which folk psychological reasoning is understood according to either the theory-theory or the simulation theory. For proponents of the theory-theory, social understanding involves what is essentially subsumptive reasoning. Folk psychology is a matter of subsuming patterns of behaviour under generalizations and deducing the relevant consequences. For proponents of the simulation theory, in contrast, folk psychological reasoning is a matter of running one's own decision-making processes off-line and feeding into them appropriate propositional attitude inputs for the person one is interpreting. For those types of social understanding that involve exploiting one's knowledge of social routines and stereotypes, however, the principal modes of reasoning are similarity-based and analogy-based. Social understanding becomes a matter of matching perceived social situations to prototypical social situations and working by analogy from partial similarities. We do not store general principles about how social situations work, but rather have a general template for particular types of situation with parameters that can be adjusted to allow for differences in detail across the members of a particular social category.

Some researchers in computer science defeated by the practical difficulties of trying to provide rule- and logic-based models of common-sense reasoning—difficulties associated with the 'frame problem' discussed earlier—have moved towards what are known as *frame-based* forms of knowledge representation. Here is Minsky's original articulation of the notion of a frame:

> Here is the essence of the theory: when one encounters a new situation (or makes a substantial change in one's view of the present problem) one selects from memory a structure called a *frame*. This is a remembered framework to be adapted to fit reality by changing details as necessary.
>
> A *frame* is a data structure for representing a stereotyped situation, like being in a certain kind of living room, or going to a child's birthday party. Attached to each frame are several kinds of information. Some of this information is about how to use the frame. Some is about what one can expect to happen next. Some is about what to do if those expectations are not confirmed.
>
> We can think of a frame as a network of nodes and relations. The top levels of a frame are fixed, and represent things that are always true about the supposed situation. The lower levels may have *terminals*—slots that must be filled by specific instances or data. Each terminal can specify conditions its assignments must meet. (The assignments themselves are usually smaller sub-frames.) Simple conditions are specified by *markers* that might require a terminal assignment to be a person, an object of sufficient value, or a pointer to a sub-frame of a certain type. More complex conditions can specify relations among the things assigned to several terminals. (Minsky, 1974, pp. 111–12)

The frame-based approach is not, of course, confined to the representation of social situations and interpersonal configurations. Frames can have patterns of behaviour built into them. They provide a concrete example of the form that a routine-based approach to social understanding and social coordination might take.

45

Once again, we should separate out different possible claims here. Conceding that much of our social understanding may be frame-based rather than rule-based is not automatically to provide a further narrowing of the domain of folk psychology. It may be that the parameters in the frame that need to be set (what Minsky calls the terminals or slots) include specifications of the mental states of the other parties in the interaction. However, the claim I am putting forward, albeit tentatively, is that this will not be the case (or at least will not be the case for many of our frame-based social interactions). The parameters associated with the other participants are set by specifications of roles and behaviour, rather than by specifications of beliefs and desires.

The frame-based approach has obvious applicability to scenarios such as that in the restaurant. But it is natural to ask how much of our everyday social interaction can be modelled in this way? How much of our social understanding is a function of our mastery of social roles, frames and routines? My inclination here would be to say: rather more than we think. It would be odd, given the element of repetition in all our social lives, if we had to start *ab initio* each time we participate in a repeated social interaction—if we operated with general principles that need to be tailored to meet the demands of specific situations, with all the difficulties of relevance that such tailoring involves. Again, it is hard to see what could count as a knock-down argument in this area, but the considerations of computational tractability canvassed in the previous section, together with the observation that many of our social interactions involve a considerable amount of high-speed, real-time adjustment to the behaviour of others suggests that the routine-based approach to social understanding should be taken very seriously.

Ex hypothesi, however, the understanding of social roles and routines associated with frame-based reasoning is restricted to familiar social situations. What happens when we find ourselves in unfamiliar social situations? What happens when none of our frames can be brought to bear; when we have no obvious contextual cues which will allow us to get a handle on the likely behaviour patterns of the other people with whom we are engaging; when the interaction is open-ended and the potential pay-offs and trade-offs too unclear for it to count as an instance of a prisoner's dilemma-type strategic interaction? It is natural to think that here we have arrived at the proper domain of folk psychology. One might think that social understanding is a complex tool for negotiating the social world. The social world is often transparent, easily comprehensible in terms of frames, social roles and social routines. Other agents can be predicted in terms of their participation in those routines and roles, while their emotional and affective states can simply be read off from their facial expression and the 'tenor' of their behaviour. When the social world is in this way 'ready-to-hand', to borrow from Heidegger's characterization of the practical understanding of tools, we have no use for the reflective apparatus of folk psychology. We do not need to bring to bear the machinery of folk psychological attribution to navigate through the social world, to accommodate ourselves to the needs and requirements of other people and to succeed in coordinated activities. But sometimes the social world becomes opaque. We find ourselves in social interactions where it is not obvious what is going on; that cannot easily be assimilated to prototypical social situations; where we cannot work out what to do simply on the basis of previous interactions with the other participants. And it is at this point that we find ourselves in need of the type of metarepresentational thinking characteristic of folk psychology—not as a mainstay of our social understanding, but rather as the last resort to which we turn when all the standard mechanisms of social understanding and interpersonal accommodation break down.

Early formulations of the notion of folk psychology stressed the idea that folk psychology is an explanatory theory. This is very much to the fore, for example, in Sellars's influential mythical account of how folk psychology might have emerged (Sellars, 1956). For Sellars, the attribution of propositional attitudes is a process akin to the postulation of unobservables in science. We attribute folk psychological states as a way of trying to make sense of what is going on in the 'black box' of other people's minds. Beliefs and desires are explanatory posits put forward to make sense of observable behaviour in a manner analogous to the way in which, say, subatomic particles are postulated to make sense of observable effects. Of course, on one way of taking it, this way of looking at folk psychology is closely aligned with the theory-theory. The theory-theory is a natural consequence of this way of understanding folk psychology if we stress the idea that the explanatory posits of folk psychology are given their content by the principles and laws in which they feature. But there is a broader issue here that applies equally to the simulationist understanding of folk psychology. It is a natural corollary of Sellars's understanding of folk psychology that we need only embark upon the process of folk psychological attribution when other people are inscrutable—when it is not possible to read off what they will do and why they are doing it from the social context and from observable behaviour. But it is a philosophical myth that all our social interactions fall into this category.

José Luis Bermúdez

References

Axelrod, R. 1984. *The Evolution of Cooperation* (Harmondsworth: Penguin).

Bermúdez, J. L. 2000. 'A Difference Without A Distinction', *Philosophical Explorations* 2, 63–82.

Bermúdez, J. L. 2003. *Thinking Without Words* (New York: Oxford University Press).

Bermúdez, J. L. and Elton, M. 2000. *Personal and Subpersonal: Essays on Psychological Explanation.* Special issue of *Philosophical Explorations* (January 2000).

Carruthers, P. M. and Smith, P. K. 1997. *Theories of Theories of Mind* (Cambridge: Cambridge University Press).

Currie, G. 1995. 'Imagination and Simulation' in Davies and Stone (eds) 1995b.

Darwin, C. 1872. *The Expression of the Emotions in Man and Animals* (London: Murray).

Davies, M. and Stone, T. 1995a. *Folk Psychology* (Oxford: Basil Blackwell).

Davies, M. and Stone, T. 1995b. *Mental Simulation* (Oxford: Basil Blackwell).

Dennett, D. 1969. *Content and Consciousness* (London: Routledge Kegan Paul).

Dennett, D. 1987. 'Cognitive Wheels: The Frame Problem of AI', in *Minds, Machines, and Evolution*, C. Hookway (ed.) (Cambridge: Cambridge University Press).

Dennett, D. 1996. *Kinds of Minds* (New York: Basic Books).

von Eckhardt, B. 1994. 'Folk Psychology and Scientific Psychology', in S. Guttenplan (ed.) *A Companion to the Philosophy of Mind* (Oxford: Blackwell).

Fodor, J. A. 1987. *Psychosemantics* (Cambridge MA: MIT Press).

Gauthier, D. 1986. *Morals by Agreement* (Oxford: Oxford University Press).

Gopnik, A. and Meltzoff, A. 1997. *Thoughts, Theories and Things* (Cambridge MA: MIT Press).

Heal, J. 1996. 'Simulation, Theory and Content', in Carruthers and Smith 1996.

Lewis, D. 1972. 'Psychophysical and Theoretical Identifications', *Australasian Journal of Philosophy* 50, 249–58.

Minsky, M. 1974/1997. 'A Framework for Representing Knowledge' in *Mind Design II*, J. Haugeland (ed.) (Cambridge MA: MIT Press).

Mithen, 1996. *The Prehistory of the Mind* (London: Thames and Hudson).

Sellars, R. W. 1956/1997. *Empiricism and the Philosophy of Mind* (Cambridge MA: MIT Press).

Skyrms, B. 1996. *The Evolution of the Social Contract* (Cambridge: Cambridge University Press).

Smith, Maynard 1982. *Evolution and the Theory of Games* (Cambridge: Cambridge University Press).

Minds, Persons and the Unthinkable

D. Z. PHILLIPS

In a series of lectures on minds and persons, I am going to take advantage of the occasion to ask what kind of person should one be if one has a philosophical mind. I ask the question because it is itself a philosophically contentious issue. Indeed, I shall be offering answers in a climate which is generally hostile to them. I want to raise the issue in three contexts: first, in relation to questions which have been treated epistemologically, but which I think belong to logic; second in relation to miracles; and third in relation to moral convictions. I shall spend most of my time on the first context.

I

What kind of a person has a philosophical mind? There is an extremely influential answer to this question which needs examining. To have a philosophical mind, it is said, is to be prepared to think what, for other people is unthinkable, to question what they would not dream of questioning. It may be thought that, in this respect, the philosopher is exercising a more general intellectual virtue. Refusal to question creates mental complacency about our present practices, and negligence about making explicit the rational justifications of those practices which possess them.

It has been suggested that a good example of philosophical complacency can be found in Wittgenstein's *On Certainty*. Writing in 1951, he said that it made no sense for a person to doubt whether he had been on the moon, because the issue simply did not arise. It was unthinkable to say that anyone had been on the moon. Too much of what we knew stood in the way of such a thought. But, as we know, things changed, and men did land on the moon. This goes to show, it is said, that what is unthinkable is independent of what we are prepared to doubt at any given time. Progress depends on having the mind of an epistemic entrepreneur.

But suppose I say that even now, for me, a doubt whether I have been on the moon does not arise. If my geography and memory are hazy, I may doubt whether I was in India or Pakistan five years ago. But can I doubt whether I have been on the moon? It may be said of course I can, if the context is right. Perhaps I was one of the

D. Z. Phillips

astronauts who landed on the moon. A walk on the moon was planned after celebrating the landing and having some sleep. But I have smuggled alcohol on board and celebrate too well. When I am fully aware of my surroundings again, we are homeward bound. I say to my colleagues, 'I have only vague recollections, but, surely, after all this, you saw to it that I walked on the moon, however briefly. You didn't leave me out of that did you?' They assure me that they did not. But, in later years, I have doubts, and from time to time say, 'I doubt whether I walked on the moon'.

Even with this story, however, the doubt cannot arise for the vast majority of people. But, for the philosophical mind, all this shows is that the doubt *does* not arise, not that it *cannot* arise. The epistemic stay-at-home says, 'The doubt is unthinkable'. The person with the philosophical mind says, 'That's just what *you* think. Come fly with me in the face of that, and one day we'll fly to the moon. Yesterday's unthinkable facts are tomorrow's achievements.'

The conclusions drawn from examples such as these, by the person said to have a philosophical mind, is that our certainties are not timeless or static. In thinking otherwise, it is said, we have been too influenced by mathematics. The equation '2 + 2 = 5' is said to be 'unthinkable', and this is said to depend on the inherent meanings of the symbols '2', '+' and '='. Given their meanings, the next symbol we write after '2 + 2 =' *must* be '4'. But it is pointed out that these symbols have no inherent meaning. To think otherwise is to have what Wittgenstein called 'a magical conception of symbols'. They have their sense in arithmetic. Outside that context, they need have no more significance than wallpaper patterns. Moreover, in an alternative arithmetic, one may be allowed to say, '2 + 2 = 5'. As Rush Rhees has argued, there is no point in saying that the alternative arithmetic contradicts the meanings of the symbols, since it is not the symbols that determine the meaning of the arithmetical practice, but the arithmetical practice which determines the meaning of the symbols. Arithmetic does not spring from the symbols like shoots from a bulb.[1]

It might well be thought that the conclusion which *should* be drawn from the argument, is that the availability of an alternative arithmetic does not show that '2 + 2 = 5' is thinkable within the arithmetic we use. Seeing that it is ruled out is involved in learning

[1] See 'On Continuity' in *Discussions of Wittgenstein* (London: Routledge and Kegan Paul, 1970). Rhees is not defending the notion of 'the philosophical mind' I am propounding. His sympathies are with the comments I make in the next paragraph.

50

how to count. When we learn, we learn what is ruled out. Or better: that such-and-such is ruled out is a condition of learning anything.

To have a philosophical mind, according to the conception I am elucidating, is to come to a very different conclusion. It is to see that *nothing* can be ruled out as unthinkable, even in mathematics. It may be that, as a matter of fact, we find certain things unthinkable, but that is a contingent fact, and, as we have seen, times can change. Who would have thought that human beings would fly? It was unthinkable, but they did. The 'unthinkable' became thinkable. We can now fly from London to New York in three hours. How about an hour? Is that unthinkable? But what if someone talks of getting from Los Angeles to Swansea in two minutes? We can't do anything with this talk, of course, especially if he speaks of being beamed up from Los Angeles. But although one might say that is too big for a development, such as reducing a flight from six hours to three, is it 'unthinkable'? Not for a person with a philosophical mind. He argues that because of the fluidity of our practical circumstances, we should never say that anything is unthinkable. All we should say is that certain matters are ruled out for the moment.

What hangs on whether we accept this view of the mind of a philosopher is connected with fundamental issues in the subject. We need to recognize, it is argued, that what is unthinkable for us is, nevertheless, *logically* possible. That being so, it is said, we are faced with the task of showing *why* we follow the practices we actually do, rather than others which, we admit, are logically possible. To simply say that they are 'unthinkable' is to avoid this justificatory task.

A person with a philosophical mind may attempt this justificatory task in a positive or a negative way. The positive way is the attempt to find some indubitable propositions on which our practices are based. The trouble is that when these propositions are produced, sceptical philosophers produce circumstances in which they can be doubted. In *On Certainty*, for example, Wittgenstein discussed one's certainty that one is seeing a tree, when sitting near it in one's garden. But he is not saying that, 'That is not a tree', could not be true, despite one's thinking that one was seeing a tree. There is nothing unthinkable about this. We can think of countless examples where this would be so. Wittgenstein is saying that in *certain circumstances*, the ones I have described, doubt is unthinkable. But this will not satisfy the philosophic mind. It wants to ask questions about those circumstances. Why give them the final word? Similarly, with the rather different proposition, 'The earth has existed for a long time', Wittgenstein argues that it is not the basis of our practices, but is held fast by them. So, once again, we are thrown back on the practices for which the philosophic mind wants a further justification.[2]

The justificatory task may also be attempted in a negative way. Here, no attempt is made to show that our practices are based on indubitable propositions. Instead, we are offered a kind of practical rationality. The philosophical mind, in this context, is one which tells us not to regard our practices as guilty, until they are proved to be innocent, but, rather, to regard them as innocent, until they are proved guilty. We have found our practices are reliable, and so have no good reason to distrust them. But this does not mean that we *know* that our practices correspond to 'how things are', since, it is logically possible that this is not so. We *believe* that our practices do so, but it is not unthinkable that they do not. The philosophical mind, on this view, is free of the hubris of reason and knowledge. We take our practices on trust, but the trust is a rational trust. It is not unthinkable that the most outrageous proposition is true; it is simply that we have no good reason to think so. So although the justification is in the negative mode, it still responds, as did the positive response, to the call for justification.

In both the positive and negative responses, we see a characteristic said to be essential to the philosophical mind, namely, its readiness to question everything. It may be thought to be the hallmark of the intellectual life to do so. Yet, we need to examine, 'as philosophers, the assumption that to have the mind of a philosopher is to think that it always makes sense to ask questions, and that it always makes sense to say that they have answers.'[3]

II

I am not asking whether it is tactful, wise, or practical, to ask questions in all circumstances, but whether it is intelligible to do so. In saying that the readiness to do so is a feature of a philosophical mind, are we giving an intelligible account of it? I suggest not for the following reason: *the grasping of any concept depends on certain*

---

[2] For further discussion see Rush Rhees, *Wittgenstein's On Certainty*, D. Z. Phillips (ed.) (Basil Blackwell 2003).

[3] See Rush Rhees, 'Unanswerable Questions', *Proceedings of the Aristotelian Society*, Supp. Vol. XL (1966), a symposium with Renford Bambrough. A discussion of the response to scepticism in these terms was the basis of my *Introducing Philosophy* (Oxford: Blackwell, 1996), where I try to show how this issue applies to every branch of philosophy.

questions not being asked. If this claim can be established, there will need to be a radical reappraisal of what it is to have the mind of a philosopher.[4]

If I say, 'My headache has gone now', I don't ask, 'Where has it gone to?'. If I say, 'I have put the book in the drawer', I don't ask how I know it is still there a second later. These questions simply do not arise. If someone tried to ask them, it would show a failure of understanding of what has been said. So the sign that the questions are not asked is not a sign of obscurantism, but a grammatical claim about our use of certain concepts. Which questions we do not ask depends on which concepts we are talking about.[5]

Other examples could be multiplied. When we teach children to count, the question of why we call our reiterated calculations 'going on in the same way' does not arise. When a surgeon having dissected only a few skulls, says that all skulls contain a brain, the question of why what he says is obvious does not arise.

The point I am urging needs to be stated with great care. The *wrong* way to state the point would be this: we refrain from asking certain questions *because* such-and-such is a headache, a book, a calculation, or inductive inference. The *right* way to state the point is to say that part of what we *mean* by a headache, a book, a calculation, or an inductive inference, is shown in the fact that certain questions are not asked. So the point being made concerns concept formation. That this is so can be brought out by considering the inadequacy of three philosophical responses to what has been said, each thought to epitomize the rationality of the philosophical mind.[6]

The first response says that in not asking the questions I have mentioned, we are showing that we are adopting a philosophical

[4] In attempting to do so, I shall draw on a discussion of this topic at the 1992 Claremont Conference on the Philosophy of Religion surrounding a paper by Peter Winch on that occasion called, 'Asking Too Many Questions', published in *Philosophy and the Grammar of Religious Belief*, Timothy Tessin and Mario von der Ruhr (eds.) (Basingstoke: Macmillan and St. Martin's Press, 1995).

[5] This paragraph repeats, more or less, one found in 'Voices in Discussion' in *Philosophy and the Grammar of Religious Belief*.

[6] I was stimulated to think further about such responses by papers read at a Research Colloquium in October 1997 (now published as *Identity and Change in the Christian Tradition*, Marcel Sarot and Gijsbert van den Brink (eds.) (Frankfurt: Peter Lang, 1999)) and by informal discussions of my introduction to the Plenary Session of the Colloquium, especially a discussion with Peter Helm. The first version of this paper was written in 1997.

principle, namely, the principle of credulity. This does not grasp the conceptual point being made. For example, it assumes that we grasp the concept of a book, and then exercise the principle of credulity in taking for granted that it does not disappear when put in a drawer. The point being made, by contrast, is that our understanding of what a book is *already* involves not asking such questions. Credulity is too refined a notion to account for the primitive concept-formation I am taking about. Credulity is parasitic on our understanding of what a book is. Without that, there is nothing to be credulous about in other circumstances. The philosophic mind being advocated makes ordinary credulity incredulous.

The second response says that we reject the conception of the philosophical mind I am discussing, only because we assume that all its questions must be asked all at once. Of course, on that assumption, there would be no firm ground beneath our feet to make our questions intelligible. But this does not mean, it is argued, that any individual question is unintelligible. We are asked to compare this with standing on the planks of a boat. If one took up all the planks at the same time, the boat would sink. But every plank, nevertheless, is open to inspection in its turn.

Again, this response does not appreciate that we are talking about concept-formation. It treats the not asking of certain questions as a matter of pragmatic unfeasibility. We have the plank, but postpone asking certain questions about it. The parallel suggestion is: we have the concept, but we postpone asking certain questions of it. But the point is that, in that case, we neither have the plank nor the concept. We do not first have either of them, and then decide whether or not to ask certain questions of them. The point is that being a plank or this concept is itself dependent on certain questions not being asked.

The third response states that the reason why a person with a philosophical mind cannot rule out the questions I have in mind, is because they are logical possibilities, well-formed sentences, which make perfectly good sense. Consider the following example. I put my pen on a table. I do not raise the question of whether it is there a few seconds later. Of course, someone may take it away, or the building may collapse, but these are not the circumstances we have in mind. We are referring to the normal expectation that when I put my pen on the table I expect it to remain there. Suppose I turn away for a few moments and then pick up my pen again. Does it make sense to say that, in the meantime, my pen has been to Australia and come back again? It was put to me that this makes perfectly good sense. In order to say this, I was told, we do not have to believe this has happened, but its sense cannot be denied. I, on the other hand, argued that the person wanting to attribute sense to the supposition cannot mean what he wants to mean. I said that we can't do anything with the suggestion. If a person advanced the suggestion, I'd think that the person had not understood what I said when I told him that I had put my pen on the table a few seconds earlier.

In response to this argument, I was told that I sounded like Carnap, like someone still in the grip of the verificationist principle, as was Wittgenstein in his attack on metaphysics. I am asked to show *why* I choose to say that my pen has remained on the table, rather than say that it has been to and come back from Australia. I am told that since I do not know how to verify those propositions one way or another, I assume, prematurely, that there is no issue to be addressed. But there is: the issue is, why choose to say that my pen has remained on the desk, rather than embrace one of the logical alternatives? Answers could be given, it is suggested, in terms of the positive or negative modes of justification we have already discussed.

Again, this response misses the concept formation involved. According to the response, a person with a philosophical mind knows what a pen is, and then considers two possibilities: whether it stayed on the desk, or whether it had been to and come back from Australia. But my conceptual point is that part of our understanding of what a pen is, involves not raising these questions. That option is not a pragmatic one, but part of our understanding of pens and our dealings with them. I do not *rule out* the so-called logical possibilities. They are not considered. And if we are asked whether our eyes are closed to them, we should reply—yes, they are closed. That they are closed makes them the concepts they are. It shows their place in our common understanding, which the philosophical mind I am attacking fails to recognize; and this common understanding includes a grasp of questions which do and do not arise.

Does this mean that after putting my pen down on a table it could not be in Australia? Not at all. I may have been interviewing a student who was leaving thereafter for Australia. He picks up my pen by mistake. A few days later I exclaim, 'I know where my pen is. It's in Australia!' Such a story does not undermine, but underlines our common understanding. If nothing were ruled out in our common understanding, nothing would be relevant to it either.

As I write this paper, it would be absurd to say, 'I know that there is no hippopotamus in my room'. Where does my confidence come from? Not from the result of having checked, and found no hippopotamus, but from the fact that the question does not arise. In the same way, I do not expect the words in a book to disappear or change their order, not because I have red millions of words and found this not to be the case. This supposition as to my conduct makes me sound as weird as the person who asks me, in the first place, how I know that the words won't disappear.[7] My confidence comes from the authority of our common understanding. This is what the philosophical mind misses when it says that the propositions, 'I know that there is no hippopotamus in my room' or 'I know that words in books do not disappear and reassemble in a different order', are true, but simply not worth saying. That is to argue as though the truth-values of propositions considered abstractly, determine our common understanding, whereas it is our common understanding which determines what we do or do not consider. Or better: that our eyes are closed to certain doubts or conjectures, for example, conjecturing or doubting whether there is a hippopotamus in my room, or whether words on a page disappear, is what constitutes our common understanding. It is my familiar life with my room and books which makes the questions of the philosophical mind a denial of our human world.

I read Raimond Gaita's essay, 'Forms of the Unthinkable' three years after I wrote the original version of this paper. I think he would find my conclusions congenial. For example, he says that Descartes' resolve to doubt everything is not an exemplar of an intelligence purified of the dross of human existence, seeking the truth however strange it may turn out to be.' Rather, it is a false semblance 'of a radical, critical intelligence'.[8]

Gaita's view is that there can be no serious version of Descartes' doubts. He does not mean that they should not be discussed. It is through discussing them, including our temptations to indulge in them, that we learn in philosophy; learn, for example, the way what is taken to be a philosophically desirable mind, can put out of our minds, the importance of our common understanding and our human world. Gaita holds that the person said to possess what I have called a philosophical mind, cannot seriously mean what he wants to say. This is why he is different from the mad person, who *does* seriously believe these things.[9] Nevertheless, it is important to place the circumstances the philosophical mind asks us to consider, in the context of what our common understanding would have us

[7] I owe this example to Stanley Cavell, *The Claim of Reason* (Oxford: Oxford University Press, 1979).

[8] Raimond Gaita, *A Common Humanity* (Melbourne, Australia: Text Publishing, 1999), 172.

[9] Ibid., 174.

say of them. According to the philosophical mind I have been attacking, my most familiar surroundings may turn out to be other than I take them to be. That is a logical possibility. Should it occur, then, on this philosophical view, I should have to say that what I took for granted is false, and that what I thought was unthinkable is true. But let us imagine such an upheaval. Suppose, for example, that someone could convince me that I am not in the sun-lounge of my home writing this paper, but am still at a conference centre at Soesterberg surrounded by an anxious looking staff. This would mean that I did not travel last week in a taxi to Amsterdam with friends, that I did not fly to Cardiff with K.L.M., was not driven home to Swansea by my wife, am not now sitting in my house, am not watching a blazing sun go down as I write these words, and so on, and so on. If I could be brought to admit half this, in some sense, to realize that something is radically wrong, I would not be in the position of one whose false beliefs needed correction, but of someone whose world is falling apart, who is having difficulty in handling any distinction between truth and falsity. As Wittgenstein says in *On Certainty*, I'd be losing all my yardsticks. I would not be a person with a philosophical mind, revising my opinions, but a person going out of his mind. What I would need is not correction, but treatment.

III

If we take seriously the notion of our common understanding, we can add countless examples to saying that when I put a pen on a table, the question of whether it goes somewhere between the glances I give it simply does not arise. What about these? If a man loses a leg, the question of whether he can grow another one simply does not arise. If a man dies, the question of whether he'll be around next week simply does not arise. If I'd like a glass of wine, hoping that a glass of water will turn into it simply does not happen. If a bush is burning, the question of it not being consumed is simply ruled out. Aren't all these examples of the same exercise of the common understanding we discussed in the last section?

What, then, are we to say of miracles? Most of the examples I have just mentioned are well known Biblical miracles. Do you believe in them? What sort of question is that? Can it be settled by an appeal to a common understanding? I don't think so. Nevertheless, a large number of philosophers whom, I suspect, regard a belief in miracles as mindless credulity, ignore our common understanding in the account they give of this mindlessness. In this, they are influenced by Hume.

D. Z. Phillips

Some philosophers tell us that we can never believe that a miracle has occurred, because the probabilities are always against it, namely, the uniformity of experience which stands against it. But the evidence is not uniform, since we have the evidence of those who have witnessed miracles. We are told that this evidence is credulous, but when we ask why, the reply is, because they believe in miracles. This whole response is circular and question begging. An appeal to majority opinion cannot yield the previous notion of the common understanding which expressed agreement. Here, the minority are simply ruled out by fiat.

But there is more to Hume's argument than that. The appeal to the uniformity of experience is linked to his belief in the uniformity of laws of nature, a uniformity which is based on the constant conjunctions of the events we call causes and effects. Critics have pointed out that constant conjunctions must be of significance to yield laws, and this significance comes from acquaintance with the workings of the phenomena being investigated, but this is a matter I do not want to pursue further.

For our present purposes, I want to show that the appeal to constant conjunction robs us of our common understanding. Do we need to reflect on the constant conjunction of the stumps of lost legs and the non-growth of new legs, on dead people and the constant conjunction of their non-reappearance among us, on water and the constant conjunction of its not turning into wine, on fire and the constant conjunction of its consuming of what it burns, to come to the conclusion that what we are being asked to contemplate is simply ruled out? To keep checking would be as weird as peering at thousands of words to check that they do not disappear. Once we are acquainted with the most elementary knowledge of lost legs, death, water and fire, the suppositions put to us are simply ruled out as impossible. And, it is said, that this is so is part of our common understanding.[10]

But what of people who did or still do believe in miracles? It will not do to say that in Biblical times people lacked scientific concepts and hence were credulous about miracles, since they obviously had a sense of what is possible and impossible which comes from a common understanding we share with them. What is more, even with our scientific concepts, there are people who believe in miracles. A pathologist may believe that Jesus raised Lazarus from the dead. Does this mean that he must be mindless, lacking a

---

[10] These arguments are found in R. W. Beardsmore, 'Hume and the Miraculous' in *Religion and Hume's Legacy*, D. Z. Phillips and Timothy Tessin (eds.) (Basingstoke: Macmillan and St. Martin's Press, 1999).

common understanding? I don't see why. Perhaps he was the pathologist who was once being pressed by an over-zealous barrister who asked him why he was sure that a certain person was dead. The pathologist replied, 'Because I had his brain in a jar'. The barrister persisted, 'But don't you admit that it is logically possible that he may still be alive?' The pathologist replied, 'Of course I admit it. He may be around somewhere without a brain practising law'.

But having a common understanding does not preclude us from saying that, now and again, inexplicable events occur. These are sometimes said to be violations of laws of nature. But laws simply systematize certain phenomena. If a phenomenon doesn't fit in, sometimes, it turns out not to be a deviation from the law, or, more rarely, leads to a modification of the law. But some events may remain inexplicable. Is one mindless to believe that they happened?[11]

The problem is that some philosophers think that this conclusion can only be avoided if we bring miracles within the context of causal operations. They tell us that God caused them. I share an unease at this suggestion.[12] We can use certain proxy words for 'cause' such as 'hit', 'cut', 'magnetized', 'burned', 'spilt', and so on. The problem is that 'God' is not one of these. To say 'God did it' promises an explanation without providing one. Ironically, the philosophical cum theological mind, wanting to show that science cannot explain everything, testifies to the influence of that same science by turning God into a super-scientist.[13]

It is important to keep the character of the event as inexplicable. Thus if I say that my pen has simply vanished after being placed on the table, it is important to recognize that 'The pen has vanished' is not the description of an event awaiting explanation as 'The pen was stolen' would be, nor is it an explanation of what has happened to the pen as 'The pen disintegrated' would be. 'The pen has vanished' is simply an expression of bewilderment at what has

---

[11] See R. F. Holland, 'The Miraculous' in *Against Empiricism* (Oxford: Blackwell, 1980); 'Lusus Naturae' in *Wittgenstein: Attention to Particulars: Essays in Honour of Rush Rhees*, D. Z. Phillips and Peter Winch (eds.) (London: Macmillan, 1989); and 'Naturalism and Preternatural Change' in *Values and Understanding: Essays for Peter Winch*, Raimond Gaita (ed.) (London: Routledge, 1990). See also D. Z. Phillips, 'Miracles and Open-Door Epistemology', *Scottish Journal of Religious Studies* (1993).

[12] See Beardsmore, op. cit., 142–3.

[13] The importance of emphasising this point was brought home to me by a discussion of a version of this paper at a Philosophy Research Colloquium at Swansea in November 1997.

happened.[14] Shouldn't 'Jesus raised Lazarus from the dead' be regarded in the same way? The phrase provides neither a description nor explanation of what has happened as 'Jesus resuscitated Lazarus' would. It is an expression of awe faced by an inexplicable event. One philosopher responds to Lazarus by saying 'I always think of him as mostly silent, unable to understand what had happened to him: unable to understand what is meant, why it had happened to *him*, and what he was supposed to conclude from it. Something like that would be too much for a human being.'[15]

Some people will find it unthinkable that miracles ever happened. They can make nothing of the claim. This is different from the philosophical claim that miracles cannot happen. Others may say, 'If they happened, they happened', and even wonder at the fact that they did. Perhaps they even think that this teaches humility to those who think everything is explicable. Nevertheless, they are still reacting to them as inexplicable *natural* events, not as miracles.[16]

So this brings us back to the question of the relation of our common understanding to the acknowledgement of the miraculous. Why is there more than an accidental tension between them? Is it not because that common understanding, no doubt influenced by science and technology, but also by our varied practical ends and the means of achieving them, is suffused with the naturalness of our explanatory questions? Moses was rebuked for wanting to explore why the bush burned without being consumed. He is told to recognize that he is on holy ground and to hear God's voice in it. It is so much harder now to obey that restriction, not to press for an explanation. This is why so many philosophers of religion, as we have noted, turn the miraculous into an explanatory category. What has weakened in the culture, and is perhaps lost for many, is the connection between miracles and revelation for people in the bible. Obviously, the miracles, as religious phenomena, were extremely important to them in what they revealed of God. It is that

---

[14] For a detailed discussion of these points see Peter Winch, 'Ceasing to Exist' in *Trying to Make Sense* (Oxford: Blackwell, 1987). See also D. Z. Phillips, 'Waiting for the Vanishing Shed', in *Wittgenstein and Religion*, Basingstoke: Macmillan 1993.

[15] Rush Rhees, 'Miracles' in Rush Rhees, *On Religion and Philosophy*, D. Z. Phillips, assisted by Mario von der Ruhr (eds.) (Cambridge: Cambridge University Press, 1998), 326.

[16] See Rhees, ibid.

revelatory link that is weak in our culture.[17] As Lessing put it, we lack the spirit and the power.[18]

This is not to say that there are no impressive examples of acknowledgement of the miraculous in our time. One philosopher witnessed a discussion surrounding the claim that a statue of the Virgin Mary in a church was seen to weep. As usual, there were the customary reactions. On one side, were those who tried to explain it away as a natural phenomenon: trickery, condensation, and so on. On the other side, were those who argued that God had caused the statue to weep by methods only known to himself. The philosopher wondered how any of this was religiously connected with the Holy Mother, and was equally disgusted by both sides in the dispute. But there was also a woman involved in the discussion whose attitude was quite different. For her, questions of explanations simply did not arise. All she said was, 'Why shouldn't the Holy Mother weep for the sins of the world'.[19]

No doubt some will say that the woman is simple-minded; that she may be naïvely taken in by tricks and coincidences. Perhaps. But the blindness is not on one side only. One may say to someone who always seeks explanations, suspects trickery, and so on, 'You'll never see the Virgin weep'.

I hope this discussion shows why an appeal to a common understanding cannot resolve the issue of whether or not we should believe in miracles, if only because, in our culture, that belief is not common. The philosopher cannot show, in any a priori way, whether one is or is not out of one's mind in believing in miracles. In another sense, however, if the philosopher wants to do conceptual justice to the world in all its variety, he must strive to see what it might be like to believe in miracles. In this sense, he must have the possibility of belief in him. This does not mean the possibility of believing, but of seeing how it would be to think like that. This task will be enormously difficult if what is taken to constitute the philosophical mind is formed by those elements in our common understanding which make acknowledging the concept of the miraculous problematic. Our present philosophical situation is problematic precisely because the kind of mind one is thought to need, has been affected in precisely this way in the majority of philosophers who defend or attack the concept of the miraculous.

[17] Rhees and Winch emphasize this point.

[18] See 'On the Proof of the Spirit and of Power' in Gotthold Ephraim Lessing, *Theological Writings*, Henry Chadwick (ed.) (London: Adam and Charles Black, 1956).

[19] See Winch, 'Asking Too Many Questions'.

IV

In this penultimate section of the paper, I want to discuss the issue of what kind of person a philosopher needs to be to account for the notion of the unthinkable in morality. In teaching students, and in discussions with colleagues, one often comes across the view that nothing is unthinkable in this context. This often comes about as the result of a certain kind of relativism. An example may help to bring out how this confusion comes about.

Think of a small community, remote and ignorant of life elsewhere. Within it, not repaying a debt is unthinkable. There are no conceptions of excuses, or of waiving the repayment of debts. Sooner or later debts are simply paid by oneself, one's family, or one's descendants. Now think of their ignorance being overcome. They come to learn of other communities where unpaid debts are common, are sometimes incurred with impunity, and are sometimes waived. In the community 'unthinkable' simply meant 'not thought of by anyone'. They assumed this practice was universal. Their newly acquired knowledge shows that this assumption was false. They then have to admit that what they thought was unthinkable was, in fact, thinkable.

Students often transfer this thought to ethics. One may give an example of what someone regards as unthinkable, only to find that someone else does not so regard it. How, then, is it asked, can one continue to call it 'unthinkable' in face of that fact? Relativism is correct: to speak of 'unthinkability' is to give an absolute status to one's own opinion.

This conclusion confuses the logical space occupied by the notion of 'unthinkability' in ethics. It is itself a term which marks a moral limit in one's thinking, it is itself an expression of one's recognition of the evil that is being done. For example, someone may think it is unthinkable that he should put a friend out of business in order to expand his own. If he hears of someone who does this he is disgusted. But this information does not lead him to say that what is 'unthinkable' has become 'thinkable', but, rather, that the person has done something unthinkable. The philosopher who asks what kind of person can deny that what he thought was unthinkable is thinkable after all, faced by such an example, is a philosopher who is confused about what a person who says that putting one's friend out of business is saying when he says that is unthinkable. To say 'He treats her in unthinkable ways' is not to deny the facts about how he treats her, but to express one's moral reaction to them.

It is clear from these examples that what is held to be morally unthinkable need not refer to something unusual. After all, friends betray each other often enough, and people treat others in despicable ways. These actions are not news. We are capable of doing unthinkable things to each other. When we realize this we may feel guilty, and seek to make restitution, but, sometimes, it may be too late for that, if not too late for penance. The friend put out of business may have committed suicide.

Sometimes, however, the 'unthinkable' is news, the 'unheard of' in human behaviour. Even here, this does not imply universal agreement. Gaita, in a successful effort to stir students out of a contrived intellectualized scepticism about evil, tells them of a man in London in the early nineties, who, brandishing a knife, threatened to mutilate a baby being wheeled by her young mother, unless he was given money. The mother gave him her purse and jewellery. He slashed the baby's face and ran off. The baby died in hospital, and its mother was admitted to a psychiatric hospital. I hope I am speaking to people who regard what was done as an unthinkable evil, but I realize that within certain gang codes or moralities, this need not be the case.[20] Gaita, after all, calls our attention to the astounding way philosophers discuss, as a live option for them, Peter Singer's view that one would not wrong one's three-week old child by killing it if it got in the way of one taking up a job one really wanted.[21] The idea that argument might lead one to this conclusion, ignores the fact that 'That's unthinkable!' is itself a moral response which refuses to go wherever such arguments want to take us.

Gaita recognizes that what is unthinkable varies in different cultures. When there are changes in notions of the unthinkable, people will differ in whether they think the change is for good or ill. Gaita says that, in our own, it is 'unthinkable that we should eat our dead or can them for pet food in order to reduce the slaughter of animals.'[22] But what of eating our dead to save ourselves? Now and again we hear of people who, in order to survive after an aeroplane crash, or some other disaster, eat the flesh of the dead victims around them, including, sometimes, their own parents or relatives. I remember Rush Rhees saying, at the Philosophy Society at Swansea, that he did not want to judge these people, but that he hoped, in the same circumstances, that he would not act in the same way. If he did, he would regard himself as having done something

[20] Gaita, op cit., 177.
[21] Ibid., 182–3.
[22] Ibid., 181.

unthinkable. Perhaps the survivors of the plane crash did too, in which case, Rhees' reaction shows how we can say 'They did the unthinkable' without that being a condemnation. Indeed, it can be an expression of compassion for their involvement in the terrible.

What Rhees could not understand were those who, having eaten the flesh of the dead, including, sometimes, that of their parents or relatives, then wanted to write books about the matter, give newspaper interviews, appear on television chat shows, become celebrities. Rhees regarded their readiness, even eagerness, to do so, as despicable and unthinkable too—a further degrading of the dead. Connected with this was his own fear that such behaviour would help to erode our sense of what had been done as 'unthinkable'. It would be made familiar. We ought to be silent about such matters. Indeed, he added, his own raising of the example for purposes of philosophical discussion might well contribute to this evasion. One begins to discuss questions which, on one's view, should not arise, and, soon, they come to be regarded as options in philosophical discussions alongside Singer's example of killing a three-week old child for the sake of convenience. One risks the erosion of the very concept one is hoping to elucidate. This is a further illustration of the complex relation between philosophical contemplation and personal moral appropriation.

V

As I said at the outset, in a series of lectures on minds and persons given by philosophers, I have taken advantage of the occasion to ask what kind of person one should be if one has a philosophical mind.

A theme which links the three contexts discussed in this paper had to do with the claim that to grasp any concept is to grasp what cannot be asked with respect to it. In the first context, I challenged the view of the philosopher as someone who stands outside all our modes of thinking and provides rational justifications of them. I argued, by contrast, the philosophical urgency of pointing out the importance of questions which do not arise, an importance which indicates what goes deep in our ways of thinking and makes them the ways of thinking that they are.

In the second context, I discussed belief in miracles as involving not asking certain questions which make natural explanations paramount. In a culture in which such questions are paramount, the acknowledgement of miracles becomes problematic, all the more so when they are discussed by philosophers in precisely the language which erodes the sense of the miraculous. The philosophical task is to do conceptual justice to that sense, not to decide whether or not there are miracles; a task which does not depend on whether or not a philosopher personally believes in miracles.

In the third context, I discussed notions of 'the unthinkable' in morality. Here, too, we saw the importance of questions which are not asked. It is important to recognize that these are not the same for everyone. The great moral distances between people may be seen in what they do or do not regard as unthinkable. Someone who sees a person who, out of sheer malice, is prepared to lie in order to ruin a person's career, may regard him as having done something unthinkable, and be astonished at the inability of the person himself to see his conduct in that way. There is even a darker side to 'the unthinkable', a flirtation or even fascination with it, an experimenting with going 'too far'. In such cases, the ordinary terms of disapproval seem inadequate, and talk of monstrous evil seems more appropriate. For those fascinated by the extremities of evil, there can be no surprises. There may be moralities with no conception of 'the unthinkable' in these latter contexts, in which case, of course, there will be no conception of the monstrous in them.

What I hope this discussion has shown, however, is the confusion in the notion of philosophical argument as that which, free of all values, leads us to the moral values we should adopt. Rather, the philosophical task is to do conceptual justice to the mixed scene in which the notion of the morally unthinkable enters in different ways.

There are further questions to be explored which I shall not pursue now. These have to do with issues concerning whether certain personal commitments or certain extreme fascinations, in a person, are compatible with the contemplative task I have ascribed to philosophy. Writing from within extremities can often throw new light on the ordinary. I do not deny that. Nevertheless, that is not the same as the contemplative task in philosophy which I have made central in this paper, a contemplation which is central to the attention demanded of us if we want to do conceptual justice to the world around us. But what is often taken to be a prerequisite of a philosophical mind is, as I hope to have shown, one of the major barriers to philosophical contemplation.

Moderately Massive Modularity

PETER CARRUTHERS

This paper will sketch a model of the human mind according to which the mind's structure is massively, but by no means wholly, modular. Modularity views in general will be motivated, elucidated, and defended, before the thesis of moderately massive modularity is explained and elaborated.

1. Modular models of mind

Many cognitive scientists and some philosophers now accept that the human mind is *modular*, in some sense and to some degree. There is much disagreement, however, concerning what a mental module actually *is*, and concerning the *extent* of the mind's modularity. Let us consider the latter controversy first.

1.1 How much modularity?

Here the existing literature contains a spectrum of opposed modularist positions. At one extreme is a sort of minimal *peripheral-systems modularity*, proposed and defended by Fodor (1983, 2000). This holds that there are a variety of modular input and output systems for cognition, including vision, audition, face-recognition, language-processing, and various motor-control systems. But on this view *central* cognition—the arena in which concepts are deployed, beliefs are formed, inferences drawn, and decisions made—is decidedly *non*-modular. Then at the other extreme is the hypothesis of *massive modularity* proposed and defended by evolutionary psychologists (Cosmides and Tooby, 1992, 1994; Tooby and Cosmides, 1992; Sperber, 1994, 1996; Pinker, 1997). This holds that the mind consists *almost entirely* of modular systems. On this view there is probably no such thing as 'general learning' at all, and all—or almost all—of the processes which generate beliefs, desires and decisions are modular in nature. Then in between these two poles there are a variety of positions which allow the existence of *central* or *conceptual modules* as well as peripheral input and output modules, but which claim that the mind also contains some significant non-modular systems or processes (Carey,

1985; Carey and Spelke, 1994; Spelke, 1994; Smith and Tsimpli, 1996; Carruthers, 1998, forthcoming a, b; Hauser and Carey, 1998; Hermer-Vazquez *et al.*, 1999; Cosmides and Tooby, 2001).

The position to be sketched and defended here is variety of this latter sort of 'moderate modularity'. But although moderate, it is pitched towards the massively modular end of the spectrum. For the main non-modular central processing arena postulated on this view is itself held to be constructed from the resources of a number of different modules, both central and peripheral. More specifically, it will be held that it is the natural-language module which serves to integrate the outputs of the various central–conceptual modules, and which subserves conscious belief-formation and decision-making. On this conception, then, the degree of modularity exhibited by the human mind is, not massive, but moderately massive.

1.2   What is modularity?

As for the different conceptions of what modularity *is*, here there are two cross-cutting spectra of opinion, to be introduced shortly. According to Fodor's classic (1983) account, however—which was designed to apply only to modular input and output systems, it should be noted—modules are domain-specific innately-specified processing systems, with their own proprietary transducers, and delivering 'shallow' (non-conceptual) outputs (e.g., in the case of the visual system, delivering a $2^1/_2$-D sketch; Marr, 1983). Modules are held to be mandatory in their operation, swift in their processing, isolated from and inaccessible to the rest of cognition, associated with particular neural structures, liable to specific and characteristic patterns of breakdown, and to develop according to a paced and distinctively-arranged sequence of growth.

Those who now believe in central–conceptual modules are, of course, required to modify this account somewhat. They can no longer believe that all modules have proprietary transducers, deliver shallow outputs, or that modules are wholly isolated from the rest of cognition. This is because central modules are supposed to be capable of taking conceptual inputs (that is, to be capable of operating upon beliefs), as well as to generate conceptual outputs (issuing in beliefs or desires, for example). But it can still be maintained that modules are innately-channelled processing systems, which are mandatory, fast, liable to specific patterns of breakdown, and follow distinctive patterns of growth in development. It can also still be held that central modules operate using their own distinctive processing algorithms, which are inaccessible to, and perhaps largely unalterable by, the remainder of cognition.

Can anything remain of the *encapsulation*/isolation of modules, however, once we switch our attention to central-conceptual modules? For this is the feature which many regard as the very essence, or core, of any worthwhile notion of modularity (Currie and Sterelny, 1999; Fodor, 2000). One option here is to claim that central modules can be *domain-specific* (or partially encapsulated), having access only to those beliefs which involve their own proprietary concepts. This option can seem well-motivated since (as we shall see in section 2 below) one of the main arguments for central modularity derives from the domain-specific character of much of human child-development.

Encapsulation of modules was never really about limitations on module *input*, however (that was rather supposed to be handled by them having proprietary transducers, in Fodor's 1983 account). Rather, encapsulation relates to the *processing data-base* of the modular system in question (Sperber, 2002). A radically un-encapsulated system would be one which could access any or all of the agent's beliefs in the course of processing its input. In contrast, a fully encapsulated module would be one which had no processing data-base at all—it would be one that was unable to draw on any of the agent's beliefs in performing its computations. Thus understood, encapsulation is fully consistent with central-process modularity. But this notion, too, admits of degrees. Just as a system can be more or less domain-specific in its input-conditions, so it might be capable of drawing on a more or less limited content-specific data-base in processing that input.

So much for points of agreement, *modulo* the disagreements on which kinds of module exist. One spectrum of *dis*agreement about the nature of modules concerns the extent of their innateness. At one extreme are those who think that modules are mostly fixed at birth or shortly thereafter, needing only the right sorts of support (e.g. increases in short-term memory capacity) in order to manifest themselves in thought and behaviour (Fodor, 1983, 1992; Leslie, 1994; Spelke, 1994). At the other extreme are those who think that the extent of innate specification of modules may be fairly minimal—perhaps amounting only to an initial attention-bias—but that human cognition becomes *modularized* over the course of normal experience and learning (Karmiloff-Smith, 1992). (On this sort of view, there may be no real difference between a child's knowledge of language and a grand-master's knowledge of chess in respect of modular status.) And then in between these poles, there are those who think that conceptual modules may be more or less strongly *innately channelled*, following a distinctive developmental sequence which is more or less reliably buffered against environmental variation and perturbation (Baron-Cohen, 1995, 1999; Botterill and Carruthers, 1999).

The other spectrum of disagreement about the nature of modules concerns the extent to which modules should be thought of as information *processors*, on the one hand, or as *organized bodies of information*, on the other. Classically, most modularists have adopted the former option (Fodor, 1983; Cosmides and Tooby, 1992; Sperber, 1996; Pinker, 1997)—although Chomsky, for example, often writes as if the language system were a body of *beliefs about* language, rather than a set of processing algorithms (1988).[1] But more recently Samuels (1998, 2000) has developed what he calls the 'library model' of the mind, according to which modules consist of largely-innate stored bodies of domain-specific information, whereas the processing of this information is done using general-purpose algorithms. Intermediate between these two poles, one can think of a module as consisting *both* of a set of domain-specific processing algorithms *and* of a domain-specific body of information, some of which may be learned and some of which may be innate (Fodor, 2000).

I shall not enter into these disputes concerning the nature of modules in any detail here. But since I think that the case for innate channelling of modules is powerful (Botterill and Carruthers, 1999), I shall here adopt a conception of modules which is closer to the nativist end of the spectrum. I shall also assume that modules will contain distinctive processors, at least, even if they also contain domain-specific bodies of information. This is because one of the main arguments supporting central–conceptual modularity seems to require such a conception. This is the broadly-methodological argument from the possibility of computational psychology, which goes roughly as follows. The mind is realized in processes which are computational, operating by means of algorithms defined over sentences or sentence-like structures. But computational processes need to be *local*—in the sense of having a restricted access to background knowledge in executing their algorithms—if they are to be tractable, avoiding a 'computational explosion'. And the only known way of realizing this, is to make such processes modular in

---

[1] One source of ambiguity here, however, is that any processor can be said to embody information *implicitly*. For example, a processing system which takes you from *Fa* as input to *Ga* as output can be said to embody the belief that *All Fs are Gs*, implicit in its mode of operation.

nature. So if computational psychology is to be possible at all, we should expect the mind to contain a range of modular processing systems.[2]

2. The case for massive modularity

There is a raft of different arguments, of varying strengths, supporting some form of (or some aspects of) a massively modular conception of the mind. I shall sketch just some of these here, without providing much in the way of elaboration or justification. This is by way of motivating the project of this paper, which is to defend a thesis of moderately massive modularity against the critics of massive modularity.

One argument for massive modularity has already been mentioned, based on the assumption that the mind is computationally realized. For if the mind is so realized, then it is very hard to see how its basic structure could be other than modular. Of course, this argument is only as strong as the assumption on which it is based. But computationalism still seems to a great many cognitive scientists to be the only game in town, despite the recent rise in popularity of distributed-connectionist approaches.[3]

A second set of arguments is broadly developmental. Young children display precocious abilities in a number of conceptual domains, especially naïve physics and naïve psychology (and also, on some views, naïve biology—Atran, 2002). They begin to display competence in these domains very early in infancy, and the development of their understanding of them is extremely fast. This provides the basis for a 'poverty of stimulus' argument paralleling the argument Chomsky has famously deployed in support of the innateness of linguistic knowledge. (For a comprehensive review

[2] See Cosmides and Tooby, 1992. Of course it is possible to reverse this argument, as does Fodor, 2000—arguing that since the mind *isn't* massively modular, no one really has any idea how to make progress with computational psychology; see section 4 below.

[3] As is familiar, it is possible to run a traditional 'symbol-crunching' programme on a connectionist machine; and anyone attracted by massive modularity will think that the computational processes in the mind are massively *parallel* in nature. So the relevant contrast is just whether those computations operate on structured localist states (as classical AI would have it), or whether they are distributed across changes in the weights and activity levels in a whole network (as more radical forms of connectionism maintain).

and assessment of this argument, see Laurence and Margolis, 2001.) The problem is to explain how children manage to know so much, so fast, and on such a meagre evidential basis. In response to this problem, many in the cognitive sciences have concluded that this cannot be explained without postulating a rich endowment of innate domain-specific information and/or of innate processing algorithms (Carruthers, 1992; Leslie, 1994; Spelke, 1994; Baron-Cohen, 1995).

Related arguments derive from psychopathology; either developmental, or resulting from disease and/or brain-injury in adults. As is now well known, autism is a developmental condition in which children show selective impairment in the domain of naïve psychology—they have difficulty in understanding and attributing mental states to both themselves and other people, but can be of otherwise normal intelligence (Baron-Cohen, 1995). Conversely, children with Williams' syndrome are socially and linguistically precocious, but have severe difficulties in the domain of practical problem-solving (implicating both spatial reasoning and naïve physics; Karmiloff-Smith *et al.*, 1995; Mervis *et al.*, 1999). Moreover, some stroke-victims have been found to display a selective impairment of their deployment of concepts for living kinds, suggesting that some sort of localized naïve biology system has been damaged (Atran, 2002; Sartori and Job, 1988; Job and Surian, 1998).

A different set of arguments for massive modularity has been put forward by proponents of evolutionary psychology. They maintain that biological systems in general evolve by 'bolting on' specialized components to already-existing systems in response to specific evolutionary pressures; and they argue that for this and a variety of other reasons, the anti-modular 'general-purpose computer' model of the mind cannot be correct, because no such computer could evolve. They have then gone on to postulate a number of different modular components which our minds should contain, reasoning from the evolutionary pressures which we can be confident our ancestors faced—including (in addition to those already mentioned above) a module for reasoning about social contracts, especially detecting cheaters and free-riders; and a module for assessing and reasoning about risks and dangers. These postulates have then been tested experimentally, with a good deal of success—showing that people perform much better on reasoning-tasks within these domains than they perform on structurally-isomorphic tasks outside of them, for example (Cosmides and Tooby, 1992; Fiddick *et al.*, 2000).

A word of caution about the way in which evolutionary

psychology is sometimes presented, however: evolutionary psychologists often write as if the mind should contain a suite of elegantly engineered processing machines (modules). But there is no reason to think that this should be so. On the contrary, evolution of any new mechanism has to start from what is antecedently available, and often a new adaptation will arise by co-opting, linking together, and utilizing systems which already exist for other functions. (This process is often called 'exaptation'.) On this model, we might expect a module to be 'kludgy' rather than elegant in its internal organization. Thus, for example, Nichols and Stich (forthcoming) argue that the mind-reading system is a highly complex combination of specially-selected components, adaptations of independently-existing domain-specific processes, and some general-purpose (non-domain-specific) functions. Given the loose way in which I understand the notion of a module, the heart of this system can still count as modular in nature; but it is decidedly *not* an 'elegantly engineered machine'.

3. Some misunderstandings of evolutionary psychology

The recent movement known as evolutionary psychology is the successor to a more long-standing programme of work in sociobiology, which came to prominence in the 1970s and 80s. Many philosophers have been critical of sociobiology for its seeming-commitment to genetic determinism, flying in the face of the known flexibility and malleability of human behaviour, and of the immense cultural diversity shown in human behaviours and social practices (Kitcher, 1985; O'Hear, 1997; Dupré, 2001). Sociobiologists had a reply to some of these criticisms, in fact, since it is not specific types of behaviour but only behavioural *tendencies* which have been selected for, on their account. And which behavioural tendencies are actually expressed on any given occasion can be a highly context-sensitive—and hence flexible—matter.

The charge of genetic determinism is even less applicable to evolutionary psychology. For what such a psychology postulates, in effect, is a set of innate belief and desire generating mechanisms. How those beliefs and desires then issue in behaviour (if at all) is a matter of the agent's practical reasoning, or practical judgment, in the circumstances. And this can be just as flexible, context-sensitive, and unpredictable-in-detail as you like. Thus, there may be a 'mind-reading' module charged with generating beliefs about other people's mental states. These beliefs are then available to subserve an indefinitely wide variety of plans and projects, depending on the agent's goals. And there may be a 'social status' module charged with generating desires for things which are likely to enhance the status of oneself and one's kin in the particular cultural and social circumstances in which agents find themselves. *How* these desires issue in action will depend on those agents' beliefs; *whether* these desires issue in action will depend upon those agents' other desires, together with their beliefs. There is no question of genetic determinism here.

Philosophers are also apt to have an overly-narrow conception of the operations of natural selection, as being wholly or primarily *survival based*. Many of us have a picture of natural selection as 'red in tooth and claw', 'survival of the fittest', and so on. And of course that is part—an important part—of the story. But survival is no good to you, in evolutionary terms, if you don't generate any off-spring, or if your off-spring don't live long enough to mate, or for other reasons aren't successful in generating off-spring in turn. In the human species, just as in other species, we should expect that sexual selection will have been an important force in our evolution, shaping our natures to some significant degree (Miller, 2000). In the animal world generally, sexual selection has always been recognized by evolutionary biologists as an important factor in evolution, and perhaps as the main engine driving speciation events. There is no reason to think that the human animal should have been any different.

In fact Miller (2000) makes out a powerful case that many of the behaviours and behavioural tendencies which we think of as distinctively human—story-telling, jokes, music, dancing, sporting competition, and so on—are products of sexual selection, functioning as sexual displays of one sort or another (like the peacock's tail). And as Miller (1998, 2000) also argues, when you have a species, such as our own, who are accomplished mind-readers, then sexual selection has the power to reach deep into the human mind, helping to shape its structure and functioning. Emotional dispositions such as kindness, generosity, and sympathy, for example, may be direct products of sexual selection. Consistently with this, it appears to be the case that members of both sexes, in all cultures, rate kindness very highly amongst the desired characteristics of a potential mate (Buss, 1989).

In addition to what one might call 'survival-selection' and sexual selection, there is also *group* selection, for whose significance in human evolution a compelling case can be made out (Sober and Wilson, 1999). As selection began to operate on the group, rather than just on individuals and their kin, one might expect to see the appearance of a number of adaptations designed to enhance group cohesion and collective action. In particular, one might expect to see the emergence of an evolved mechanism for identifying, memorizing and reasoning about social norms, together with a powerful motivation to comply with such norms. And with norms and norm-based motivation added to the human phenotype, the stage would be set for much that is distinctive of human cultures.

To see how some of this might pan out, consider an example which might seem especially problematic from the perspective of a survival-based evolved psychology. Consider Socrates committing suicide when convicted of treason (O'Hear, 1997), or a kamikaze pilot plunging his aircraft into the deck of a battle-cruiser. How can such behaviours be adaptive? Well no one actually claims that they are, of course; rather, they are the product of psychological mechanisms which are normally adaptive, operating in quite specific local conditions. An evolved mechanism charged with identifying and internalizing important social norms may be generally adaptive; as might be one whose purpose is to generate desires for things which will enhance social status. If we put these mechanisms into a social context in which there is a norm requiring sacrifices for the community good, for example, and in which the greatest status is accorded to those who make the greatest sacrifices, then it is easy to see how a suicide can sometimes be the result.

4. Philosophers against central–conceptual modules

The idea of central-process modularity hasn't, as yet, enjoyed wide popularity amongst philosophers. In part this may reflect some of the misunderstandings documented in section 3 above, and in part it may result from an intuitive resistance to beliefs in innate cognitive structures or innate information, within an intellectual culture still dominated by blank-slate empiricism in the humanities and social sciences. But a number of philosophers have presented arguments against central-process modularity, generally grounded in the claim that central cognition is in one way or another *holistic* in nature. I shall consider two sets of arguments here, due to Fodor (1983, 2000) and Currie and Sterelny (1999).

4.1 Fodor

Fodor (1983, 2000) famously argues that all and only input (and output) processes will be modular in nature (although language-processing is construed as both an input *and* an output process for these purposes). And only such processes will be amenable to explanation from the perspective of computational psychology. This is because such processes are *local,* in the sense that they only need to consider a restricted range of inputs, and can only be influenced in a limited way (if at all) by background knowledge. In contrast, central processes are said to be holistic, or non-local. What you believe on one issue can depend upon what you think about some seemingly-disparate subject. (As Fodor remarked in his 1983 book, 'in principle, our botany constrains our astronomy, if only we could think of ways to make them connect.') Indeed, at the limit, what you believe on one issue is said to depend upon everything else that you believe. And no one has the least idea how this kind of holistic process could be modelled computationally.[4]

The holistic character of central cognition therefore forms the major premise in a two-pronged argument. On the one hand it is used to support the pessimistic view that computational psychology is unlikely to make progress in understanding central cognitive processes in the foreseeable future. And on the other hand it is used in support of the claim that central cognition is a-modular in nature.

For the most part we are just invited to believe in the holism of the mental on the strength of Fodor's say-so, however. The closest we get to an argument for it, are some examples from the history of science of cases where the acceptance or rejection of a theory has turned crucially on evidence or beliefs from apparently disparate domains. But science is, in fact, a bad model for the cognitive processes of ordinary thinkers, for a number of different reasons (I shall mention two).

One point is that science is, and always has been, a social enterprise, requiring substantial external support. (Fodor actually mentions this objection in his recent book—which must have been put

---

[4] As an illustration of the supposed holism of belief, consider an episode from the history of science. Shortly after the publication of *The Origin of Species* a leading physicist, Sir William Thompson, pointed out that Darwin just couldn't assume the long time-scale required for gradual evolution from small differences between individual organisms, because the rate of cooling of the sun meant that the Earth would have been too hot for life to survive at such early dates. Now we realize that the Victorian physicists had too high a value for the rate at which the sun is cooling down because they were unaware of radioactive effects. But at the time this was taken as a serious problem for Darwinian theory—and rightly so, in the scientific context of the day. (Thanks to George Botterill for this example.)

to him by one of his pre-publication readers—but responds in a way which completely misses the point.)[5] Scientists do not and never have worked alone, but constantly engage in discussion, co-operation and mutual criticism with peers. If there is one thing which we have learned over the last thirty years of historically-oriented studies of science, it is that the positivist–empiricist image of the lone investigator, gathering all data and constructing and testing hypotheses by him- or her-self, is a highly misleading abstraction.

Scientists such as Galileo and Newton engaged in extensive correspondence and discussion with other investigators over the years when they were developing their theories; and scientists in the 20th century, of course, have generally worked as members of research teams. Moreover, scientists cannot operate without the external prop of the written word (including written records of data, annotated diagrams and graphs, written calculations, written accounts of reasoning, and so on). In contrast, ordinary thinking takes place within the head of an individual thinker, with little external support, and within the relatively short time-frames characteristic of individual cognition.

These facts about science and scientific activity can explain how seemingly disparate ideas can be brought to bear on one another in the course of scientific enquiry, without us having to suppose that something similar can take place routinely within the cognition of a single individual. What many different thinkers working collectively over the course of a lifetime can achieve—conducting painstaking searches of different aspects of the data and bringing to bear their different theories, heuristics and reasoning strategies—is a poor model for what individuals can achieve on their own in the space of a few seconds or minutes. There is certainly nothing here to suggest that ordinary belief-formation routinely requires some sort of survey of the totality of the subject's beliefs (which really would be computationally intractable, and certainly couldn't be modular).

Another reason why scientific cognition is not a good model for cognition in general, is that much scientific reasoning is both conscious and verbal in character, being supported by natural language

---

[5] Fodor (2000), pp. 52–3. Fodor wrongly assumes that 'science is social' is intended to mean 'scientific cognition is individualistic cognition which has been *socially constructed*'; for he responds that it is implausible that the structure of human cognition might have changed radically in the past few hundred years. But the point is rather that the (fixed, innate) architecture of individual cognition needs. to be externally supported and enriched in various ways in order for science to become possible—through social exchange of ideas and arguments, through the use of written records, and so on.

representations (whether internal or external). And it may well be possible to explain how linguistically formulated thought can be partially holistic in nature without having to suppose that central cognitive processes in general are holistic, as we shall see in section 5 below. Indeed, it may well be possible to provide a *moderately massively modular* account of natural-language-mediated cognition which explains the partly-holistic character of such conscious thinking in modular terms, as we shall see.

In short, then, the holism of science fails to establish the holism of central cognition in general. So we need to look elsewhere if we are to find arguments against central-process modularity.

4.2 Currie and Sterelny

Fodor's argument from the holism of the mental seems to require that information from many different domains is routinely and ubiquitously brought together in cognition. Yet, as we have seen, he fails to provide evidence for his major premise. For Currie and Sterelny (1999), in contrast, the mere fact that information from disparate domains *can* be brought together in the solution to a problem shows that central cognitive processes aren't modular in nature. The focus of their argument is actually the alleged modularity of mind-reading or 'theory of mind'; but it is plain that their conclusion is intended to generalize—if mind-reading can be shown to be a-modular, then it is very doubtful whether *any* central modules exist. For the purposes of this paper I shall accept this implication, treating mind-reading as a crucial test-case.

Currie and Sterelny's argument is premised on the fact that information of any kind can be relevant in the interpretation of someone's behaviour—such as underpinning a judgment that the person is lying. They write (1999):

> If Max's confederate says he drew money from their London bank today there are all sorts of reasons Max might suspect him: because it is a public holiday there; because there was a total blackout of the city; because the confederate was spotted in New York at lunch time. Just where are the bits of information to which we are systematically blind in making our social judgments? The whole genre of the detective story depends on our interest and skill in bringing improbable bits of far-away information to bear on the question of someone's credibility. To suggest that we don't have that skill defies belief.

This is an unfortunate example to have taken, since the skill in question is arguably not (or not largely) a mind-reading one. And insofar as it *is* a mind-reading skill, it is not one which requires the mind-reading system to be radically holistic and un-encapsulated. Let me elaborate.

Roughly speaking, to lie is to assert that P while believing that *not-P.* So evidence of lying is evidence that the person is speaking contrary to their belief—in the case of Max's confederate it is evidence that, although he *says* that he drew money from the London account today, he actually believes that he didn't. Now the folk-psychological principle, 'If someone didn't do something, then they believe that they didn't do that thing' is surely pretty robust, at least for actions which are salient and recent (like travelling to, and drawing money from, a bank on the day in question). So almost all of the onus in demonstrating that the confederate is lying will fall onto showing that he didn't in fact do what he said he did. And this isn't anything to do with mind-reading per se. Evidence that he was somewhere else at the time, or evidence that physical constraints of one sort or another would have prevented the action (e.g. the bank was closed), will (in the circumstances) provide sufficient evidence of duplicity. Granted, many different kinds of information can be relevant to the question of what actually happened, and what the confederate actually did or didn't do. But this doesn't in itself count against the modularity of mind-reading.

All that the example really shows is that the mind-reading faculty may need to work in conjunction with other elements of cognition in providing us with a solution to a problem.[6] In fact most of the burden in detective-work is placed on physical enquiries of one sort or another—investigating foot-prints, finger-prints, closed banks, whether the suspect was somewhere else at the time, and so forth—rather than on mind-reading. The contribution of the latter to the example in question is limited to (a) assisting in the interpretation of the original utterance (Does the confederate mean what he says? Is he joking or teasing?); (b) providing us with the concept of a lie, and perhaps a disposition to be on the lookout for lies; and (c) providing us with the principle that people generally know whether they have or haven't performed a salient action in the recent past.

Currie and Sterelny may concede that it isn't supposed to be the work of the mind-reading faculty to figure out whether or not

[6] See Nichols and Stich (forthcoming) who develop an admirably detailed account of our mind-reading capacities which involves a complex array of both domain-specific and domain-general mechanisms and processes, including the operations of a domain-general planning system and a domain-general suppositional system, or 'possible worlds box'.

someone actually did something. But they would still think that examples of this sort show that mind-reading isn't an *encapsulated* process, and so cannot be modular. Following Fodor (1983), they take the essence of modularity to be given by encapsulation—a modular process is one which can draw on only a limited range of information, and which cannot be influenced by our other beliefs. But recall the distinction we drew in section 1.2 above (following Sperber, 2002) between limitations on the *input* of a system, on the one hand, and limitations on its *processing data-base,* on the other. Encapsulation is only really about the latter. So, fully-consistently with the encapsulation of the mind-reading module, it may be that such a module can take any content as *input*, but that it cannot, in the course of processing that input, draw on anything other than the contents of its own proprietary domain-specific memory store.

So here is what might happen in a case like that described above. The confederate's utterance is perceived and processed to generate a semantic interpretation. Max then wonders whether the utterance is a lie. The mind-reading system uses the input provided by the confederate's utterance together with its grasp of the nature of lying to generate a specific principle, 'His statement that he withdrew money from our London account today is a lie, if he *believes* that he *didn't* withdraw the money'. The mind-reading system then deploys one of its many generalizations, 'If someone didn't do something salient recently, then he believes that he didn't do that thing' to generate a more-specific principle, namely, 'If he *didn't* withdraw the money from our London account today, then he *believes* that he didn't withdraw the money today'. In making these inferences few if any background beliefs need to be accessed. The mind-reading system then generates a question for other central-cognitive systems (whether modular or a-modular) to answer, namely, 'Did he *actually* withdraw money from our London account today, or not?', and one of those systems comes up with the answer, 'No, because the banks were closed'. The content, 'He didn't withdraw our money today' is then received as input by the mind-reading system, enabling it to draw the inference, 'My confederate is lying'.

All of the above is fully consistent with the mind-reading system being a largely-encapsulated module. That system can operate by deploying its own distinctive algorithms (not shared by other central-process modules nor by general learning), and these algorithms may be isolated from the remainder of the agent's beliefs. And most importantly, the processing in question might only be capable of accessing a small sub-set of the agent's beliefs, contained in a domain-specific mind-reading memory store. So the mind-reading system can be an encapsulated one, to some significant degree, and its processing can be computationally tractable as a consequence.

Of course, such back-and-forth processing has to be orchestrated somehow. And more specifically, if the mind-reading module can take any sort of content as input, then something has to *select* those inputs. But this needn't be inconsistent with the modularity of mind-reading, even if it does raise a problem for the thesis of massive modularity. One way for us to go, here, would be to postulate some sort of a-modular executive system, charged with determining appropriate questions and answers, and shuffling them around the other (modular) systems. This might conflict with massive modularity, but it doesn't conflict with the modularity of mind-reading, or with any moderate form of modularity thesis. But we surely don't *have* to go this way, in fact. We might equally appeal to various processing-principles of *salience* and *relevance* to create a kind of 'virtual executive' (Sperber, 2002). So the account just sketched above is fully consistent even with a thesis of massive modularity, I think.

Let me now make a related criticism of Currie and Sterelny to that developed above. For they take, as the target of their attack, the thesis that social belief-fixation is cognitively impenetrable. And they take this to mean that *all* of the post-perceptual processes which eventuate in social belief should constitute one encapsulated system.[7] But this is absurd. No defender of the modularity of mind-

---

[7] Similarly, Nichols and Stich (forthcoming) argue against modularist accounts of mind-reading on the same grounds. They assert that mind-reading cannot be encapsulated, since all of a mind-reader's background beliefs can be involved in predicting what another will do, through the process of *default attribution* (i.e. 'assume that others believe what you believe, *ceteris paribus*'). And they assume that modularists are committed to the view that *all* of the post-perceptual processes which eventuate in mental-state attribution form one encapsulated system. But, firstly, what modularists are committed to here is only that the mind-reading system can only access a domain-specific data-base, not that it is encapsulated from all belief. And secondly, a modularist can very well accept that the mind-reading module needs. to work in conjunction with other aspects of cognition—both modular and non-modular—in doing its work. The architecture sketched by Nichols and Stich is actually a very plausible one—involving the use of a suppositional reasoning system (a 'possible worlds box') with access to all background beliefs, as well as an action-planning system, a variety of inferential systems for updating beliefs, and so on. But a modularist can maintain that at the heart of the workings of this complex architecture is a modular mind-reading system, which provides the core concepts and principles required for mind-reading.

reading believes this. What such people believe is that *one of* the systems which is engaged in the processes eventuating in social belief is an encapsulated mind-reading system (where the 'encapsulation' of this system is to be understood as explained somewhat along the lines of the paragraphs above).

There is yet another way in which Currie and Sterelny actually set up a straw man for their attack, as well. This is that they take the thesis of the modularity of mind-reading to be the claim that the process which serves to fix social *belief* is modular. And they point out, in contrast, that social appearances (which might plausibly be delivered by some sort of modular system, they concede) can always be over-ridden by our judgments made in the light of any number of different kinds of background information.

At the outset of this line of thought, however, is a mistaken conception of what central-process modularity is, in general. They take it to be the view that there are modules which serve to fix belief. One way in which this is wrong, of course, is that many modularists believe in the existence of central-process modules which serve to generate desires or emotions. The best way of explaining what a 'central' process is, for these purposes, is not that it is one which eventuates in belief, but rather that it is one which operates upon *conceptual* contents or conceptualized states. And there may well be central modules which issue *neither* in beliefs *nor* in desires or emotions, but which rather deliver conceptualized states which can feed into the further processes which issue in full-blown propositional attitudes (e.g. beliefs and desires).

More importantly for our purposes, Currie and Sterelny tacitly assume that belief is a *unitary* kind of state. A good number of writers have, in contrast, explored the idea that belief may admit of at least two distinct kinds—one of which is non-conscious and which is both formed and influences behaviour automatically, the other of which is conscious and results from explicit *judgment* or *making up of mind* (Dennett, 1978, 1991; Cohen, 1993; Evans and Over, 1996; Frankish, 1998a, 1998b, forthcoming). It may then be that some conceptual modules routinely generate the automatic kind of belief, below the level of conscious awareness. Consistently with this, when we give explicit conscious consideration to the same topic, we may reach a judgment which is at odds with the deliverances of one or more conceptual modules. And it is no news at all that in our conscious thinking all different types of information, from whatever domains, can be integrated and united. (How such a thing is possible from a modularist perspective will form the topic of section 5 below.)

There is also a weaker way to save the hypothesis that (some) conceptual modules function to fix belief, which need not require us to distinguish between different kinds of belief. For one might merely claim that these conceptual modules will issue in belief *by default,* in the absence of explicit consideration. So the mind-reading module will routinely generate beliefs about other people's mental states, for example, *unless* we consciously ask ourselves what mental states *should* be attributed to them, and engage in explicit weighing of evidence and so forth. The fact that these latter processes can over-ride the output of the mind-reading module doesn't show that central modules don't function as fixers of belief.

4.3 A consciousness-based intuition

I conclude, then, that where philosophers have argued explicitly against central-process (or conceptual) modularity, they have rejected the idea on inadequate grounds. Either, like Fodor, they have just assumed, without argument, that central processes are a-modular and holistic. Or, like Currie and Sterelny, they have imposed inappropriate constraints on what a central-process module would have to be like. But it may be that underlying such arguments is a deeper intuition, grounded in our conscious awareness of our own thoughts. For we know that we can, in our conscious thinking, freely link together concepts and beliefs from widely disparate domains. I can be thinking about new academic course structures one moment and about horses the next, and then wonder what process of association led me to entertain such a sequence—in effect then combining both topics into a single thought. How is such a thing possible if any strong form of central-process modularity is true?

It is very important to note that this argument isn't really an objection to the idea of central-process modularity as such, however. For the existence of belief-generating and desire-generating conceptual modules is perfectly consistent with there being some sort of holistic central arena in which all such thoughts—irrespective of their origin—can be freely inter-mingled and assessed. So all of the less extreme, more moderate, versions of the thesis of central-process modularity are left untouched by the argument. The argument only really starts to bite against *massively* modular conceptions of the mind. For these accounts would seem to fly in the face of what is manifest to ordinary introspective consciousness.

The challenge for massive modularity, then, is to show how such a domain-general 'central arena' can be built from the resources of a suite of domain-specific conceptual modules. This is the challenge which I shall take up in the next section, providing just enough of a sketch of such an architecture to answer the possibility-challenge. (For further elaboration, see Carruthers, forthcoming a, b.) The result will be, of course, not a full-blown massively modular conception of the mind—since the existence of domain-general conscious thought will be granted—but still a *moderately* massively modular conception.

5. The moderately massively modular mind

The thesis which I want to sketch, here, maintains that it is the natural-language module which serves as the medium of inter-modular integration and conscious thinking. Note, for these purposes, that the language-faculty is, uniquely, *both* an input (comprehension) *and* an output (speech-production) system. And note, too, that just about everybody agrees that the language faculty is a module— even Fodor (1983), who regards it as an archetypal input (and output) module.

On any version of central-process modularity, the language module looks likely to be one of the down-stream consumer systems capable of receiving inputs from each of the central modules, in such a way that it can transform the outputs of those modules into spoken (or signed) language. Since we are supposing that the various central modules deliver conceptualized thoughts as output, the initial encoding process into natural language can be exactly as classical accounts of speech-production suppose (e.g. Levelt, 1989), at least in respect of the outputs of any single central module. That is, the process will begin with a thought-to-be-expressed, provided by some central module—e.g. MAXI WILL LOOK IN THE KITCHEN[8]—and the resources of the language faculty are then harnessed to select appropriate lexical items, syntactic structures, and phonological clothing to express that thought, before issuing the appropriate commands to the motor-control systems which drive the required movements of the mouth and larynx—in this case, in such a way as to utter the words, 'Maxi will look in the kitchen'.

Similarly, on any version of central-process modularity, the language module will surely be one of the up-stream input systems capable of feeding into the various central modules for domain-specific or specialized processing of various sorts. So what someone tells you about Maxi's goals, for example, can be one of the inputs

[8] I follow the usual convention of designating structured propositional thoughts, when expressed in some form of Mentalese, by means of capitalized sentences.

to the mind-reading module. What sort of interface would be required in order for this to happen? One plausible proposal is that it is effected by means of *mental models*—that is, analog, quasi-perceptual, cognitive representations. So the role of the comprehension sub-system of the language faculty would be to build a mental model of the sentence being heard (or read), with that model then being fed as input to the central-process conceptual modules. For notice, first, that there is considerable evidence of the role of mental models in discourse comprehension (Harris, 2000, for a review). And note, second, that the central-process modules would in any case need to have been set up to receive perceptual input (i.e. the outputs of the perceptual input-modules), in such a way that one can, for example, draw inferences from *seeing* what someone is doing, or from *hearing* the sounds which they are making. So the use of mental models to provide the interface between the comprehension sub-system of the language faculty and the central-process modules would have been a natural way to go.

The language faculty is ideally placed, therefore, to link together a set of central-process conceptual modules. But if it is to play the role of *integrating* the outputs of those central-process modules, rather than just receiving those outputs on a piecemeal one-to-one basis, then more needs to be said, plainly. Given that the language faculty is already capable of encoding propositional representations provided by central-process modules, the problem reduces to that of explaining how different natural language sentences concerning some of the same subject-matters can be integrated into a single such sentence. It is at this point that it seems appropriate to appeal to the abstract and recursive character of natural language syntax. Suppose that the geometric system has generated the sentence, 'The object is in the corner with the long wall to the left', and that the object–property system has generated the sentence, 'The object is in the corner near the red wall'.[9] And suppose, too, that the common reference of 'the object' is secured by some sort of indexical marking to the contents of short-term memory. Then it is easy to see how the recursive character of language can be exploited to generate a single sentence,

---

[9] This example is drawn from Hermer-Vazquez *et al.* (1999), who provide evidence that such contents cannot be integrated in rats and young children when they become spatially disoriented, and that it is actually language which enables those contents to be integrated in older children and adults. For example, the capacity to solve tasks using both forms of information is severely disrupted when adults are required to 'shadow' speech through a set of headphones (thus tying up the resources of the language faculty), but not when they are required to shadow a complex rhythm.

such as, 'The object is in the corner with the long wall to the left near the red wall'. And then we will have a single representation combining the outputs of two (or more) central-process modules.

That the language faculty is capable of integrating the outputs from the central modules for purposes of public communication is one thing; that it serves as the medium for non-domain-specific thinking might seem to be quite another. But this is where it matters that the language faculty is *both* and input *and* an output module. For a sentence which has been initially formulated by the output sub-system can be displayed in auditory or motor imagination—in 'inner speech'—and can therefore be taken as input by the comprehension sub-system, thereby being made available to the central process modules once again. And on most views of consciousness, some (at least) of these imagined natural language sentences will be conscious, either by virtue of their quasi-perceptual status (Dretske, 1995; Tye, 1995, 2000), or by virtue of their relationship to the mind-reading faculty, which is capable of higher-order thought (Armstrong, 1968; Rosenthal, 1986, 1993; Carruthers, 1996, 2000; Lycan, 1996). One can therefore imagine cycles of conscious language-involving processing, harnessing the resources of both the language faculty and the central-process domain-specific modules.

There is more to our conscious thinking than this, of course. We also have the capacity to generate new suppositions (e.g, 'Suppose that the object has been moved'), which cannot be the output of any module or set of modules. And we then have the capacity to evaluate those suppositions, judging their plausibility in relation to our other beliefs. It is arguable, however, that these additional capacities might require only minimal adjustments to the basic modular architecture sketched above—but I shall not attempt to show this here (Carruthers, 2002, forthcoming a, b). The important point for present purposes is that we have been able to sketch the beginnings of an architecture which might enable us to build non-domain-specific conscious thinking out of modular components, by harnessing the resources of the language faculty, together with its unique position as both an input and an output system for central cognition.

6. Conclusion

I have explained what central-process modularity is, or might be; and I have sketched some of the arguments supporting some sort of massively modular model of the mind. The explicit arguments against such a model which have been propounded by philosophers have been shown to be unsound. And a sort of *Ur*-argument grounded in introspection of our conscious thoughts has been responded to by sketching how such thoughts might result from the operations of a set of central–conceptual modules together with a modular language faculty. Since very little has been firmly established, this is not a lot to have achieved in one paper, I confess; but then who ever thought that the architecture of the mind could be conquered in a day?

References

Armstrong, D. 1968. *A Materialist Theory of the Mind*. Routledge.

Atran, S. 2002. 'Modular and cultural factors in biological understanding', In P. Carruthers, S. Stich and M. Siegal (eds.), *The Cognitive Basis of Science*. Cambridge University Press.

Baron-Cohen, S. 1995. *Mindblindness*. MIT Press.

Baron-Cohen, S. 1999. 'Does the study of autism justify minimalist innate modularity?' *Learning and Individual Differences*, 10.

Botterill G. and Carruthers, P. 1999. *The Philosophy of Psychology*. Cambridge University Press.

Buss, D. 1989. 'Sex differences in human mate preferences: Evolutionary hypotheses tested in 37 cultures', *Behavioral and Brain Sciences*, 12.

Carey, S. 1985. *Conceptual Change in Childhood*. MIT Press.

Carey, S. and Spelke, E. 1994. 'Domain-specific knowledge and conceptual change', In L. Hirshfeld and S. Gelman (eds.), *Mapping the Mind*. Cambridge University Press.

Carruthers, P. 1992. *Human Knowledge and Human Nature*. Oxford University Press.

Carruthers, P. 1996. *Language, Thought and Consciousness*. Cambridge University Press.

Carruthers, P. 1998. 'Thinking in language?: evolution and a modularist possibility', In Carruthers and J. Boucher (eds.), *Language and Thought*. Cambridge University Press.

Carruthers, P. 2000. *Phenomenal Consciousness: a naturalist theory*. Cambridge University Press.

Carruthers, P. 2002. 'The roots of scientific reasoning: infancy, modularity, and the art of tracking', In P. Carruthers, S. Stich and M. Siegal (eds.), *The Cognitive Basis of Science*. Cambridge University Press.

Carruthers, P. forthcoming a. 'Is the mind a system of modules shaped by natural selection?' In C. Hitchcock (ed.), *Great Debates in Philosophy: Philosophy of Science*. Oxford: Blackwell.

Carruthers, P. forthcoming b. 'Distinctively human thinking: modular precursors and components', In P. Carruthers, S. Laurence and S. Stich (eds.), *The Structure of the Innate Mind*.

Chomsky, N. 1988. *Language and Problems of Knowledge*. MIT Press.

Cohen, L. 1993. *An Essay on belief and Acceptance*. Oxford University Press.

Cosmides, L. and Tooby, J. 1992. 'Cognitive adaptations for social exchange', In J. Barkow, L. Cosmides and J. Tooby (eds.), *The Adapted Mind*. Oxford University Press.

Cosmides, L. and Tooby, J. 1994. 'Origins of domain specificity: the volution of functional organization', In L. Hirschfeld and S. Gelman (eds.), *Mapping the Mind*. Cambridge University Press.

Cosmides, L. and Tooby, J. 2001. 'Unraveling the enigma of human intelligence', In R. Sternberg and J. Kaufman (eds.), *The Evolution of Intelligence*. Laurence Erlbaum.

Currie, G. and Sterelny, K. 1999. 'How to think about the modularity of mind-reading', *Philosophical Quarterly*, 49.

Dennett, D. 1978. 'How to change your mind', In his *Brainstorms*. Harvester Press.

Dennett, D. 1991. *Consciousness Explained*. Penguin Press.

Dretske, F. 1995. *Naturalizing the Mind*. MIT Press.

Dupré, J. 2001. *Human Nature and the Limits of Science*. Oxford University Press.

Evans, J. and Over, D. 1996. *Rationality and Reasoning*. Psychology Press.

Fiddick L., Cosmides, L. and Tooby, J. 2000. 'No interpretation without representation; the role of domain-specific representations and inferences in the Wason selection task', *Cognition*, 77.

Fodor, J. 1983. *The Modularity of Mind*. MIT Press.

Fodor, J. 1992. 'A theory of the child's theory of mind', *Cognition*, 44.

Fodor, J. 2000. *The Mind doesn't Work that way*. MIT Press.

Frankish, K. 1998a. Natural language and virtual belief. In P. Carruthers and J. Boucher (eds.), *Language and Thought*. Cambridge University Press.

Frankish, K. 1998b. 'A matter of opinion', *Philosophical Psychology*, 11.

Frankish, K. forthcoming. *Mind and Supermind*. Cambridge University Press.

Harris, P. 2000. *The Work of the Imagination*. Blackwell.

Hauser, M. and Carey, S. 1998. 'Building a cognitive creature from a set of primitives', In D. Cummins and C. Allen (eds.), *The Evolution of Mind*. Oxford University Press.

Hermer-Vasquez L., Spelke, E., and Katsnelson, A. 199). 'Source of flexibility in human cognition: Dual-task studies of space and language', *Cognitive Psychology*, 39.

Job, R. and Surian, L. 1998. 'A neurocognitive mechanism for folk biology?', *Behavioral and Brain sciences*, 21.

Karmiloff-Smith, A. 1992. *Beyond Modularity*. MIT Press

Karmiloff-Smith, A., Klima, E., Bellugi, U., Grant, J., and Baron-Cohen, S. 1995. 'Is there a social module? Language, face processing and theory of mind in individuals with Williams syndrome', *Journal of Cognitive Neuroscience*, 72.

Kitcher, P. 1985. *Vaulting Ambition: sociobiology and the quest for human nature*. MIT Press.

Laurence, S. and Margolis, E. 2001. 'The poverty of the stimulus argument', *British Journal for the Philosophy of Science*, 52.

Leslie, A. 1994. 'ToMM, ToBY and Agency: Core architecture and domain specificity', In L. Hirschfeld and S. Gelman (eds.), *Mapping the Mind*. Cambridge University Press.

Levelt, W. 1989. *Speaking*. MIT Press.

Lycan, W. 1996. *Consciousness and Experience*. MIT Press.

Marr, D. 1983. *Vision*. Freeman.

Mervis, C., Morris, C., Bertrand, J. and Robinson, B. 1999. 'Williams syndrome: findings from an integrated program of research', In H. Tager-Flusberg (ed.), *Neurodevelopmental Disorders*. MIT Press.

Miller, G. 1998. 'Protean primates: the evolution of adaptive unpredictability in competition and courtship', In A. Whiten and R. Byrne (eds.), *Machiavellian Intelligence II*. Cambridge University Press.

Miller, G. 2000. *The Mating Mind*. Heinemann.

Nichols, S. and Stich, S. forthcoming. *Mindreading*. Oxford University Press.

O'Hear, A. 1997. *Beyond Evolution*. Oxford University Press.

Pinker, S. 1997. *How the Mind Works*. Penguin Press.

Rosenthal, D. 1986. 'Two concepts of consciousness', *Philosophical Studies*, 49.

Rosenthal, D. 1993. 'Thinking that one thinks', In M. Davies and G. Humphreys (eds.), *Consciousness*. Blackwell.

Samuels, R. 1998. 'Evolutionary psychology and the massive modularity hypothesis', *British Journal for the Philosophy of Science*, 49.

Samuels, R. 2000. 'Massively modular minds: evolutionary psychology and cognitive architecture', In P. Carruthers and A. Chamberlain (eds.), *Evolution and the Human Mind*. Cambridge University Press.

Sartori, G. and Job, R. 1988. 'The oyster with four legs: a neuro-psychological study on the interaction of semantic and visual information', *Cognitive Neuropsychology*, 5.

Smith, N. and Tsimpli, I. 1996. *The Mind of a Savant*. Blackwell.

Sober, E. and Wilson, D. 1999. *Unto Others: the evolution and psychology of unselfish behavior*. Harvard University Press.

Spelke, E. 1994. 'Initial knowledge: six suggestions', *Cognition*, 50.

Sperber, D. 1994. 'The modularity of thought and the epidemiology of representations', In L. Hirschfeld and S. Gelman (eds.), *Mapping the Mind*. Cambridge University Press.

Sperber, D. 1996. *Explaining Culture*. Blackwell.

Sperber, D. 2002. 'In defense of massive modularity', In I. Dupoux (ed.), *Language, Brain and Cognition Development*. MIT Press.

Tooby, J. and Cosmides, L. 1992. 'The psychological foundations of culture', In J. Barkow, L. Cosmides and J. Tooby (eds.), *The Adapted Mind*. Oxford University Press.

Tye, M. 1995. *Ten Problems of Consciousness*. MIT Press.

Tye, M. 2000. *Consciousness, Color and Content*. MIT Press.

Warrington, E. and Shallice, T. 1984. 'Category specific impairments', *Brain*, 107.

A Theory of Phenomenal Concepts

MICHAEL TYE

1. There is widespread agreement that consciousness must be a physical phenomenon, even if it is one that we do not yet understand and perhaps may never do so fully. There is also widespread agreement that the way to defend physicalism about consciousness against a variety of well known objections is by appeal to phenomenal concepts (Loar, 1990; Lycan, 1996; Papineau, 1993; Sturgeon, 1994; Tye, 1995, 2000; Perry, 2001). There is, alas, no agreement on the nature of phenomenal concepts.

2. Concepts are mental representations of worldly entities—things, events, states, properties etc. They are exercised whenever we undergo cognitive mental states. One cannot notice something, recognize it, make a judgment about it without conceptualizing it in some way, without bringing it under a concept. A child who is unable to count may see four pieces of candy but he/she cannot notice that four pieces are present. A dog may hear a Beethoven symphony, but it cannot recognize the sounds as being a Beethoven symphony.

3. Phenomenal concepts are the concepts we exercise when (but not only when) we notice or become aware of the phenomenal character of our experiences and feelings via introspection. Our experiences have phenomenal character whether or not we attend to them, but when we notice how an experience feels, what it is like, in doing so we are bringing it beneath a phenomenal concept. Without phenomenal concepts, we would be 'blind' to our phenomenal feels (Dretske, 1995; Tye, 1995), just as the child who cannot count is 'blind' to the fact that there are four pieces of candy in front of her.

4. Physicalists about consciousness typically agree with the following claims:

a) Absent qualia are conceivable. We can conceive of physical duplicates, one of whom has experiences while the other has no experiences at all. Such duplicates may be metaphysically impossible, but they are conceivable (just as it is conceivable that I am not Michael Tye even though, given the actual facts, it is metaphysically impossible).

b) Frank Jackson's Mary (1982)—the colour scientist imprisoned since birth in a black and white room and possessed of all the physical information about colour and colour vision—doesn't know what it is like to experience red, green, etc while she remains in the room. When she is freed and she starts to undergo colour experiences, she makes some important discoveries.

c) Presented with the full physical story about pain (or any other experience), we can still intelligibly ask, 'Why do those physical states feel like that? Why do they feel any way at all?'

5. The natural way for the physicalist to explain (a) is to say that phenomenal concepts are not physical concepts[1]. Since phenomenal concepts are different from physical concepts, we can conceive of absent qualia. There is no contradiction or incoherence in the thought that a given organism meets whatever are the relevant physical conditions for consciousness and yet feels nothing—any more than there is a contradiction or incoherence in the thought that I am not Michael Tye, or that water is not H_2O, or that now is not 2:15pm.

6. The natural way for the physicalist to explain (b) is to say that Mary in her room does not possess the phenomenal colour experience concepts the rest of us possess. She acquires these concepts as she notices the colours of flowers, trees, houses, etc and as she attends to her colour experiences in doing so. Once the new concepts are acquired, Mary can come to think new thoughts, and thereby she is able to make new discoveries. I shall return to this point later.

This line of reply to the Mary example requires again that phenomenal concepts not be physical concepts. For if they were, Mary would possess them in her room, given her complete knowledge of all the physical facts.

There is a further conclusion to be drawn here. Phenomenal concepts are not demonstrative concepts utilizing physical sortals. To appreciate this, suppose that Mortimer is undergoing an experience of red and that Mary is viewing the physical state in Mortimer with which this phenomenal experience is identical through a cerebroscope suitably attached to her black and white room. She conceives

[1] This is not to say, of course, that phenomenal concepts do not refer to physical entities. The concept THIS is not a physical concept, nor is the concept I, but it does not follow that these concepts pick out nonphysical items.

of the state she sees as that F state, where 'F' is a physical predictate expressing the appropriate physical property. Patently, when she leaves her room and attentively experiences red, she still makes a significant discovery.

7. The intelligibility of the question in (c) requires again that phenomenal concepts not be physical concepts. It also requires that there be no physical concepts that are a priori co-referential with any phenomenal concepts. To see this, suppose that 'pain*' below is used purely phenomenally for a state whose essence is the specific, unpleasant phenomenal character of pain and that 'F' is a physical predicate. Now consider the following argument form:

   (i)   Pain* is the F
  (ii) Physical state so-and-so is present
 (iii) Physical state so-and-so is the F

Therefore,

 (iv) Pain* is present.

(ii) and (iii) are straightforwardly empirical, physical claims. Thus, if (i) is an a priori truth knowable by anyone who possesses the phenomenal concept PAIN*, then since (iv) is a priori deducible from (i)–(iii), there will be an explanation for why physical state so-and-so feels the way pain* does that is available without further empirical investigation to anyone who has that concept and who also has the requisite physical information. And this will be the case, note, even if (i) is not a *necessary* a priori truth.

8. For the physicalist, then, any satisfactory account of phenomenal concepts must allow that, although phenomenal concepts refer to physical properties, (a) they are not physical concepts, (b) they are not demonstrative concepts utilizing physical sortals, and (c) they have no a priori associated co-referential physical concepts. (c) entails that phenomenal concepts are not concepts that designate their referents rigidly but whose reference is fixed by an a priori associated physical description.

9. Corresponding points can be made with respect to phenomenal concepts and the view that consciousness is a functional phenomenon that is realized physically. For ease of exposition, I shall not consider this view separately.

10. Having said what phenomenal concepts are not, what positive alternatives remain open? One possibility is that phenomenal con-

Michael Tye

cepts are concepts having explicitly non-physical definitions. A second possibility is that phenomenal concepts are primitive rigid concepts whose reference is fixed by an explicitly nonphysical description. A third alternative is that phenomenal concepts are indexical concepts utilizing explicitly nonphysical sortals. All three of these alternatives entails that physicalism about consciousness is false.

Another alternative is that phenomenal concepts are concepts having phenomenal definitions. This sets off a vicious regress and so gives us no satisfactory account of how phenomenal concepts operate. The same is true if we say that phenomenal concepts are primitive rigid concepts whose reference is fixed by a phenomenal description. For how do the concepts expressed in the phenomenal description refer? Given that phenomenal concepts have their reference fixed by a phenomenal description, the answer must be by further associated phenomenal descriptions; and so on without end.

A further alternative is to hold that phenomenal concepts are demonstrative concepts utilizing phenomenal sortals. Prima facie, this proposal sets off a similar regress. But the threat of such a regress is staved off by a recent proposal by Ned Block (APA presentation, 2001[2]) that phenomenal concepts paradigmatically have the form THAT PHENOMENAL PROPERTY, where the indexical or demonstrative THAT refers to the phenomenal property exemplified in an associated mental sample (presumably an image or quasi-image[3]). For example, suppose that I think in a phenomenal way of something's looking red. On this proposal, the image of red accompanying my thought exemplifies the phenomenal property, RED*, and my thought refers to the same phenomenal property by conceiving of it as that property—the one exemplified in my image.[4] If this account is applied to the concept PHENOMENAL PROPERTY as itself having the form THAT PHENOMENAL PROPERTY, the regress is stopped.

[2] I should add that this proposal may not reflect Block's current view.

[3] The notion of an image or a quasi-image is to be understood broadly here so that it covers a phenomenal memory of pain, for example. The latter is a phenomenal state that faintly echoes real pain, a state that may elicit a mental shudder or grimace.

[4] Here and throughout the paper, I write as if I accept the dogma that phenomenal properties are intrinsic properties of images and experiences. That, of course, is not my real view. See here Tye 1995, 2000. *For present purposes*, whether phenomenal qualities are qualities of experiences or qualities represented by experiences does not matter. The story I have to tell about phenomenal concepts will apply to either view with minor (and fairly obvious) modifications.

Leaving aside the point that it is far from obvious that there is always an associated mental sample when a phenomenal concept is exercised[5], there are two insuperable difficulties for this proposal. One is that a mental sample that exemplifies one phenomenal property will exemplify many. My image, when I think of something's looking red, will not only exemplify RED* but also (let us suppose) SCARLET*, DARK RED*, HAVING A COLOUR*, and so on. Which of the exemplified properties is the one to which the demonstrative concept THAT PHENOMENAL PROPERTY refers? It seems that appealing to a mental sample does not help to fix the reference of the phenomenal concept at all.

A second related difficulty concerns the phenomenal concept PHENOMENAL PROPERTY. What is the relevant sample for this concept? It appears that *any* phenomenal image or quasi-image will do, in which case the problem of too many eligible candidates for reference rears its head again.

11. Perhaps it will be replied that the problem of too many eligible candidates goes away on the supposition that the property to which the demonstrative THAT refers is the phenomenal property (exemplified in the sample) to which the imager is attending. This does not help, however. Attention to a property is not like training the eyes on a point in space. Given the multiplicity of exemplified properties, attention to one of those properties rather than another requires noticing the relevant property. And that involves bringing it under a concept. The appropriate concept here will surely be a phenomenal one. So, the proposal is now circular.

12. The conclusion to which we seem driven as physicalists is that phenomenal concepts refer directly. They have no associated reference-fixers, no descriptive content at all. For concepts of this sort, the referent is presented without the assistance of associated features distinct from the referent which the thinker a priori associates with it. There is no separate guise that the referent takes in the thinker's thought. Intuitively, independent of the truth of physicalism, this seems to me the right approach. If I focus introspectively on the feeling of pain, as I experience it, I form a conception of how it feels, and the concept that enables me to do that is not one that I apply to the feeling by discerning non-phenomenal features (or for that matter *other* phenomenal features) that aid in the identification of its phenomenal character. Intuitively, I know that I am in pain

[5] More on this later.

just by attending to how my state feels, not by knowing something *else* connected to it.

13. The natural picture, it seems to me, is as follows. Our phylogenetic nature determines which experiences we undergo. We are hard-wired to experience various bodily sensations and to undergo various perceptual experiences. We cannot experience what a bat experiences when it uses echo-location, since we lack the appropriate sensory system. We are also equipped by evolution and nature to respond cognitively to our experiences in a certain range of ways once we undergo them. In responding cognitively, we bring the experiences under phenomenal concepts. Which concept is applied may depend on a number of factors: how our attention is directed, previous experiences, learning, attention span. But there are limits set upon the phenomenal concepts available to us by our nature.

I am happy to allow that there could be other creatures capable of undergoing the same experiences as us but who conceive of their experiences differently on a first person basis. For example, they might be capable of much finer grained classifications with respect to their colour experiences than we are. Such creatures are equipped with a different battery of phenomenal concepts, one that no doubt partly overlaps with ours.

In my view, introspection of phenomenal character is a *reliable* process that takes phenomenal character as input and yields awareness *that* a state is present with a certain phenomenal character as output. It is the reliability of this process that underwrites knowledge of phenomenal character. In this respect, introspection of phenomenal character is like introspection of thought contents. Let me explain.

If I think that water is wet, and I introspect, I become aware *that* I am thinking that water is wet. This awareness is not based upon an inference from other propositional states. Nor is it the result of attention to an internal auditory image of myself saying that water is wet, though such an image may accompany my thought. Intuitively, my introspective access to what I am thinking is direct. It seems plausible to suppose that introspection of thought contents is a reliable process that takes as input the content of the thought and delivers as output a belief or judgment that one is undergoing a state with that content.

On this view of introspective knowledge of thought contents, the concept of a thought that *P* is, in its first-person present-tense application, a *recognitional* concept.[6] Those who have mastered the

---

[6] For more on recognitional concepts, see Brian Loar 1990.

concept can introspectively recognize that an occurrent thought that
P is present without going through any process of reasoning. In
cases involving what Tyler Burge has called 'Cogito thoughts' (that
is, cases in which one consciously thinks to oneself that one is thinking that P), there is a conscious act of recognition. But in the typical case, one's recognition of what one is occurrently thinking does
not involve a conscious act. One can recognize that one is thinking
that water is a liquid, when the only conscious thought one is having is that water is a liquid.[7]

In much the same way, we do not have introspective knowledge of
phenomenal character by inferring that character from something
else. We acquire introspective knowledge of what it is like to have
such-and-such an experience or feeling via a reliable process that
triggers the application of a suitable phenomenal concept or concepts. Phenomenal concepts—the concepts that enable us to form a
conception of phenomenal character via introspection—are, in my
view, recognitional concepts of a special sort.

14. My proposal, then, is that phenomenal concepts refer via the
causal connection they have with their referents. In first approximation, a phenomenal concept C refers to a phenomenal quality Q
via C's being the concept that is exercised in an introspective act of
awareness by person P if, and only if, under normal conditions of
introspection, Q is tokened in P's current experience and because Q
is tokened. I say 'in first approximation' here since a further condition is needed to handle the possibility that C not only causally
covaries with Q but also with a further non-phenomenal, indeed
non-introspectively accessible, quality of the experience under
normal conditions.

This difficulty is, of course, part of a more general one for causal
covariation accounts of representation, whether that representation
is conceptual or not. The hair shedding of cats (under normal conditions) is causally correlated with the lengthening of days; and
lengthening days correlate (roughly) with increasing temperature.
Thus, shedding in cats causally covaries with both day length and
temperature. Even so, given what we know of the relevant biological mechanisms, it seems wrong to say that the shedding of hair represents temperature as well as (or instead of) day length.

In the cat case, the causal covariation between the shedding of
hair and increasing temperature arises because the hair shedding
causally covaries with day length and day length covaries with

---

[7] Introspection of thought content is discussed in more detail in
McLaughlin and Tye, 1998.

97

temperature. Were the covariation link between temperature and day length broken (by, for example, keeping cats indoors at a constant temperature or moving them to higher altitudes at the same latitude), the hair shedding would continue to covary with day length (albeit artificial day length for the indoor case generated by varying the hours of artificial light), but not with temperature. For this reason, hair shedding is best taken to represent day length—provided that we are prepared to talk of representation in this context at all.

Intuitively, then, what is needed to supplement the basic causal covariation approach is a further asymmetric dependence condition. For state S to represent feature F not only must S causally covary with F under optimal or normal conditions but it must also be the case that if there is some other feature G such that F covaries with G under optimal conditions then were F to fail to covary with G, the causal covariation link between S and F under optimal (normal) conditions would still hold but that between S and G would be broken.

This qualification handles the case of phenomenal concept C covarying with both phenomenal quality Q and non-phenomenal quality N. P can be held to represent Q and not N so long as it is held that were the covariation link between Q and N broken, C would continue to causally covary with Q but not with N.

15. Perhaps it will be objected that it is surely possible for a concept to refer directly to a phenomenal quality without being a phenomenal concept. Suppose, for example, that the distinctive phenomenal character of pain is a brain state and that Fred is a 21st century neuroscientist who is incapable himself of feeling pain in virtue of a neurological defect he has had since birth. Fred has a device partly wired into his brain that causes him to think that another person is feeling pain when and only when the external part of the device is directed at the other person's brain and the relevant brain state is present there. Fred's thought exercises a concept of pain, but that concept isn't a phenomenal concept. For Fred does not know what it is like to experience pain, and intuitively one cannot grasp the phenomenal character of pain, one cannot have a *phenomenal* concept of pain, without knowing what it is like.

16. This example shows that we need to distinguish the question, 'What is it that makes a phenomenal concept of quality Q be about or of Q?' from the question, 'What makes a phenomenal concept phenomenal?' Not all concepts that refer directly are phenomenal.

Concerning the latter question, the thesis in Tye, 1999 was that a concept that directly refers to a phenomenal quality is phenomenal if and only if it functions in the right sort of way. I denied, however, that this functioning could be specified *a priori* in a way that eschews any phenomenal language. My view was (and is) that the concept of a phenomenal concept is conceptually irreducible: no a priori definition or analysis is possible in non-phenomenal terms. This should come as no surprise. If such an analysis were possible then a suitably cognitively informed automaton, totally without any experiences, would be able to acquire the concept of a phenomenal concept simply by reflecting upon the analysis. Intuitively, however, that isn't possible. Such an automaton could glean no phenomenal notion of an experience; and without such a notion the concept of a phenomenal concept would be beyond its grasp.

This does not have the consequences that we cannot say a priori anything illuminating about the relevant functioning of phenomenal concepts. Quite the contrary. A concept is phenomenal, I maintain, if and only if (1) it is laid down in memory as a result of undergoing the appropriate experiences (barring miracles, etc), (2) it tends to trigger appropriate conscious images (or quasi-images) in response to certain cognitive tasks, and (3) it enables its possessors to discriminate the phenomenal quality to which it refers directly and immediately via introspection.[8] This proposal was originally made in Tye 1999 and it was motivated by what I take to be a priori links between phenomenal concept possession and knowing what it is like (one cannot possess a phenomenal conception of a given experience type unless one knows what that experience type is like) and further a priori links between the latter and certain phenomenal abilities underpinning the stated conditions (abilities to imaginatively recreate the experience, to remember it, to recognize it directly when it comes again). Moreover, the proposal, though non-reductive, is not vacuous or trivial. It imposes real requirements on a concept's being phenomenal, requirements that are not met by most of the concepts we have.

The proposal also entails that phenomenal concepts are, in a certain sense, perspectival. Intuitively, possessing the phenomenal concept PAIN* requires having a certain perspective on pain, the one conferred by experiencing pain oneself (barring miracles, etc). Why should this be? Answer: because the phenomenal concept PAIN* would not be a phenomenal concept at all if it didn't function in the right sort of way, and that functioning brings with it

---

[8] Note incidentally that this account itself entails that phenomenal concepts refer directly.

a distinctive first person perspective on pain. This is why the 21st century pain detector wired into the head of our neuroscientist Fred does not provide Fred with a *phenomenal* concept of pain, and why Mary in her black-and-white room does not have the phenomenal concept RED*. These individuals, given their special conditions, don't have any internal mental representations that function in the appropriate ways.

17. The imagistic dimension of phenomenal concepts deserves further comment.

Consider first the following example of a phenomenal-physical identity claim:

The visual experience of red = brain state B.[9]

One reaction some philosophers have to claims of this sort is that they must be mistaken, since the phenomenology isn't captured by the right-hand side. From the present perspective, this reaction involves a sense/reference confusion. When we think of the referent of the designator on the left-hand side in a phenomenal way, we bring it under a concept that has a distinctive functional role. In reflecting on the identity claim and what is puzzling about it, the phenomenal concept we deploy is apt to trigger in us a visual image of red. In this event, if the identity is true, our brain actually goes into brain state B. But, of course, when we think of the referent of the designator on the right hand side *as* brain state B, nothing like that happens. Exercising the neurophysiological concept is not apt to trigger a visual image of red. It may then be tempting to infer that the right-hand side has left out the phenomenology of the left, that there is a huge gap that the physicalist has failed to close. The conclusion clearly does not follow, however. There is indeed a striking difference in the roles that the concepts play, in their functioning, but not (so far as is shown here) in their referents.[10]

It should be emphasized that the view I am proposing of phenomenal concepts does not require that a conscious image or quasi-image always be present when a phenomenal concept is exercised. Some philosophers take a stronger position. We saw earlier that, according to Ned Block, phenomenal concepts have the structure THAT PHENOMENAL QUALITY, where the

[9] I myself do not accept identities of this sort. In my view, the objective states with which phenomenal states should be identified are complex representational states (Tye, 1995, 2000). In the present context, however, this does not matter.

[10] Cp. Papineau, 1993.

indexical refers to the phenomenal quality exemplified in an associated mental sample. David Papineau (1993) has a similar view. His claim is that our brains are wired to form copies or replicas of the experiences we undergo, and these replicas play a role in fixing the reference of phenomenal concepts. Specifically, Papineau's proposal is that phenomenal concepts have the structure THAT EXPERIENCE, where the demonstrative refers to the experience type exemplified in an associated image or copy of the experience. On Papineau's account, exercising a concept of a phenomenal state involves recreating it or simulating it, and thinking of it as that state, the one tokened in the simulation.

This cannot be correct. For one thing, when I deploy a phenomenal concept in an introspective act—when I introspectively recognize the feel of a tickle, say—the only experiential state present is surely the one I am recognizing, the tickle feeling. There isn't a *further* image or copy of a tickle within my introspective act of recognition or associated with it. If there were, it would be accessible to me via my further awareness that I am engaging in an act of introspectively recognizing a tickle. But no such tickle copy or replica reveals itself to me.

A second problem is that the earlier objection to Block applies to Papineau too. What Papineau calls (following D. M. Mellor (1992)) 'exemplificatory reference by secondary experience' (1993, p. 112) is not reference at all. Consider the idea that when I think of pain in a phenomenal way, I exercise the concept THAT EXPERIENCE (TYPE), where the demonstrative picks out the type of experience tokened in an associated pain image or replica. There is, alas, no such thing as *the* type of experience so tokened. There are many types. My pain replica exemplifies the phenomenal quality PAIN* but it also exemplifies such phenomenal qualities as THROBBING PAIN* or DULL PAIN* or PRICKING PAIN* as well as such phenomenal properties as HAVING A PHENOMENAL QUALITY, HAVING AN UNPLEASANT PHENOMENAL QUALITY, and so on.[11]

Block and Papineau's primary mistake, then, is to suppose that images play a *reference-fixing* role for phenomenal concepts. As far as reference goes, associated images play no role at all. Still, it does seem right to say that sometimes exercising a phenomenal concept triggers an image or faint replica of the relevant experience, and that this connection is one that is essential to phenomenal concepts generally. Why should there be such a connection? What is it about

[11] Appealing to attention with respect to one of the properties does not save the proposal. See (11) earlier.

phenomenal concepts that explains their essential imagistic associations?

18. Consider the following possible model. Suppose that an explorer sees an animal belonging to a hitherto unknown species. He takes a picture of the animal, and assigns a name to the species. He then keeps the photograph in a file with the name written beneath it. On later occasions, in talking about the animal to others, he opens the file, takes out the photo and holds it up as he uses the name.

The name refers to the species, not to the particular animal the explorer saw. The picture is a picture of a member of that species, a token of the type.

Alternatively, the explorer, instead of taking a photograph might carve a replica of the animal in wood. The wooden replica is a replica of a particular animal, though the explorer can certainly use it to represent the species too, as he uses the name to discourse about the species.

We might be a bit like the explorer. Consider the following proposal. Suppose that we each have a phenomenal character detector wired into our heads. The detector is set up to register phenomenal qualities in our experience that are the focus of out attentional mechanisms. The detector does this by outputting a name or simple symbol, a different symbol for each different phenomenal quality. If the phenomenal quality is an unfamiliar one, the device places the name in memory and it makes a copy or a faint replica of the phenomenal token of that quality which is present in our experience. The copy is then placed in memory along with the name. These processes, we may suppose, are automatic and unconscious.

On some occasions, as when we introspectively recognize a phenomenal type, we make no use of the stored copy or image. On other occasions, when the phenomenal type is absent from our experience but we are thinking phenomenally about it, we use the name and we retrieve a copy of a token of the phenomenal type too, an image or quasi-image, which we may then put to cognitive use.

For example, when asked the question, 'Which is darker green, grass or a Scottish fir?,' people typically think about the colour of grass and that of Scottish firs in a phenomenal way. This generates phenomenal images of the two greens, images that are then inspected and compared by the subjects before they reply to the question. Those without the capacity to form such images, visual agnosics, for example, are unable to answer.

19. Two worries remain. First, it may be objected that my account faces a regress problem just as some of the earlier proposal do. For in saying what makes a concept phenomenal I have used phenomenal concepts. These concepts must refer to physical states and properties, if physicalism about phenomenal consciousness is to be true.

My reply is that there is no vicious regress set off by this requirement, since the reference of phenomenal concepts is direct. It is *not* the case, on my view, that in order for a given phenomenal concept to *refer* successfully, other phenomenal concepts must do the same, where these concepts refer successfully only if other phenomenal concepts do, and so on without end.

Nor is there any regress in my account of what makes a concept phenomenal. The account is not proposed as a reductive one. So, the fact that it uses phenomenal concepts does not create a regress. What the use of these concepts reflects is simply the conceptual irreducibility of the concept of a phenomenal concept.

20. The final worry I want to consider pertains to the case of Mary and whether the proposal I have made about phenomenal concepts allows Mary to make any new discoveries about the phenomenal character of colour experience after she leaves her black and white room.

The answer, in brief, is yes. In order for Mary to think a phenomenal thought, she must exercise a phenomenal concept. She does not have phenomenal colour experience concepts in her room. So, when she leaves her room, she starts to have *new* phenomenal thoughts. Content-wise, it must be granted, in one standard sense of the term 'content', these thoughts will not be new, given Mary's complete physical knowledge in her room. For, on my proposal, phenomenal concepts refer directly and thus, the contribution they make to thought content is given by their referents alone—referents that are physical, if physicalism about consciousness is true. But thought-types need not be individuated by their contents alone.

Intuitively, phenomenal thought types play a different role in rationalizing explanations than non-phenomenal thought types. If their contents are identical, then a second factor must account for this difference. And intuitively that factor is simply that phenomenal thoughts exercise different concepts—*phenomenal* concepts (whose difference from non-phenomenal concepts, on my account, is given by their functional role). Accordingly, I claim that the identity of a phenomenal thought type may be traced both to its content and to the fact that it employs concepts that function in a certain characteristic way. This two-factor view of phenomenal thought types permits the physicalist to maintain that there is a perfectly good sense in which Mary discovers that so-and-so is the case after she is released. For she comes to think new thoughts and thereby instantiate cognitive thought-types (knowing-that types) she did not instantiate before, even though, given her exhaustive knowledge of the physical facts, the contents of her thought-types before and after remain unchanged. And if Mary or anyone else knows that p at time t without knowing that p before t, then surely it is correct to say, in ordinary parlance, that the person has made a discovery at t.

21. The theory of phenomenal concepts sketched above seems to me both to respect anti-physicalist intuitions and to give the physicalist everything she needs. It allows for the conceivability of those states of affairs pertaining to experience that are dear to the hearts of anti-physicalists. It preserves the intuition that we know phenomenal character in a direct, non-inferential way. It acknowledges that undergoing a new experience and attending to it yields a discovery, and that this is the case regardless of how much physical knowledge we have. It finds a place for images or faint copies of experiences in the exercise of phenomenal concepts. Moreover, it does all this while holding that the referents of phenomenal concepts are physical. The theory thus discharges a heavy burden on the physicalist; and it leaves those who insist that we still don't have a good account of phenomenal concepts (Levine, 2001) with the burden of explaining why.

References

Dretske, F. 1995. *Naturalizing the Mind* (Cambridge, Mass: The MIT Press, Bradford Books).

Jackson, F. 1982. 'Epiphenomenal Qualia,' *Philosophical Quarterly*, **32**, 127–36.

Levine J. 2001. *Purple Haze: The Puzzle of Consciousness* (Oxford: Oxford University Press).

Loar, B. 1990. 'Phenomenal States,' in *Philosophical Perspectives*, 4, J. Tomberlin, (ed.), (Northridge: Ridgeview Publishing Company).

Lycan, W. 1996. *Consciousness and Experience* (Cambridge, Mass: The MIT Press, Bradford Books).

McLaughlin, B. and Tye, M. 1998. 'Externalism, Twin-earth, and Self-Knowledge' in *Knowing Our Own Minds: Essays on Self-Knowledge*, C. Macdonald, B. Smith and C. Wright (eds.) (Oxford: Oxford University Press).

Mellor, D. H. 1992. 'Nothing Like Experience,' *Proceedings of the Aristotelian Society*, 93.

Papineau, D. 1993. *Philosophical Naturalism* (Oxford: Blackwell).

Perry, J. 2001. *Possibility, Consciousness and Conceivability* (Cambridge, Mass: The MIT Press, Bradford Books).

Sturgeon, S. 1994. 'The Epistemic View of Subjectivity,' *Journal of Philosophy*, 91, pp. 221–35.

Tye, M. 1995. *Ten Problems of Consciousness* (Cambridge, Mass: The MIT Press, Bradford Books).

Tye, M. 1999. 'Phenomenal Consciousness: The Explanatory Gap as a Cognitive Illusion,' *Mind*, 108, 705–25.

Tye M., 2000. *Consciousness, Color, and Content* (Cambridge, Mass: The MIT Press, Bradford Books).

Free Will and the Burden of Proof

WILLIAM G. LYCAN

1. Here are some things that are widely believed about free will and determinism.

(1) Free will is prima facie incompatible with determinism.

(2) The incompatibility is logical or at least conceptual or *a priori*.

(3) A compatibilist needs to explain how free will can co-exist with determinism, paradigmatically by offering an analysis of 'free' action that is demonstrably compatible with determinism. (Here is the late Roderick Chisholm, in defence of irreducible or libertarian agent-causation: 'Now if you *can* analyse such statements as "Jones killed his uncle" into event-causation statements, then you may have earned the right to make jokes about the agent as cause. But if you haven't done this, and if all the same you do believe such things as that I raised my arm and that Jolns [sic] killed his uncle, and if moreover you still think it's a joke to talk about the agent as cause, then, I'm afraid, the joke is entirely on you.'[1])

(4) Free will is not impugned by quantum *in*determinism, at least not in the same decisive way that it is impugned by determinism. To reconcile free will with quantum indeterminism takes work, but the work comes under the heading of metaphysical business-as-usual; to reconcile free will with determinism requires a conceptual breakthrough.

And listen to Laura Waddell Ekstrom on the burden of proof.

...in the absence of an argument to the contrary, it is straightfor-wardly clear to most all of us as we adopt the practical deliberative point of view toward our own future that the follow-ing is true: I am free in what I do at the next moment only if I am not necessitated to do just what I do by the past and the natural laws.... The compatibilist, then, needs a positive argument in favour of the compatibility thesis.[2]

What is interesting is that each of these claims is tacitly granted by many free-will compatibilists as well as (obviously) by

[1] 'Comments and Replies,' *Philosophia* 7, Nos. 3–4 (July 1978), 597–636, p. 623.

[2] *Free Will* (Boulder, CO: Westview Press, 2000), p. 57.

William G. Lycan

incompatibilists. The compatibilists take up the burden and labour to overcome the supposed conceptual obstacles.

I maintain that (1), (2) and (3) are just false. I believe (4) is false as well—though perhaps not *just* false.

It's actually worse than that. Here is a confession: I have always been free-will-blind. I don't get it. I don't see what the big problem is supposed to be. (My talk today may have the unintended effect of persuading some of you that that's right: that I *just don't get it*.) I am a natural-born, cradle compatibilist. Ted Honderich suggests[3] that even if we are Soft Determinists, each of us still *desires* a measure of libertarian agent-causation, or can easily be made to; the real problem is attitudinal. But if I have such a desire, it operates at a level deeper than introspection can penetrate.

Of course I know that there are serious arguments for incompatibilism. Some are simple, some more complicated, some very complicated and ingenious. But I have never found any of them at all convincing. My purpose in this paper is to try to show that that response is right and proper, and that there are good general dialectical reasons for rejecting all incompatibilist arguments. (To my title I might have added the subtitle, 'in which it is shown that compatibilism is not only true, but the only position rationally available to impartial observers of the issue.')

Ground rules: For the sake of argument, I shall assume that determinism is true. I myself believe that it is not true; but let us assume it, because my main thesis is the compatibility of freedom *with determinism*, and because if I am right in rejecting (4), indeterminism would not help anyway. Also, *if* no incompatibilist argument succeeds, there is no reason to think that indeterminism would make us any freer.

By 'free' I shall mean free in whatever sense is germane to moral responsibility, that is, such that one is morally responsible for only those of one's actions that were free actions. (I know this usage is not inevitable.[4])

---

[3] *How Free Are You?* (Oxford: Oxford University Press, 1993); 'Determinism as True, Compatibilism and Incompatibilism as Both False, and the Real Problem'
(http://www.ucl.ac.uk/~uctytho/dfwVariousHonderichKanebook.htm).

[4] For example, Ekstrom (op. cit., p. 8) eschews it, arguing plausibly that the exact relation between freedom and moral responsibility is unclear and disputable. But the alternative seems to be either metaphor or characterization vapid enough to be all too obviously available to the compatibilist ('our actions are truly attributable to our selves..., ultimately *up to us*' (Ekstrom, p. 3)).

Free Will and the Burden of Proof

2. I begin with a general methodological point about modality: Compatibilism, not just about free will but generally, on any topic, is the default. For any modal claim to the effect that some statement is a necessary truth, I would say that the burden of proof is on the claim's proponent. A theorist who maintains of something that is not obviously impossible that nonetheless that thing *is* impossible owes us an argument. And since entailment claims are claims of necessity and impossibility, the same applies to them. Anyone who insists that a sentence S_1 entails another sentence S_2 must defend that thesis if it is controversial. If I tell you that 'Pigs have wings' entails 'It snows every day in Chapel Hill,' you need not scramble to show how there might be a world in which the first was true but the second false; rather, you would rightly demand that I display the alleged modal connection. And of course the same goes for claims of incompatibility.

The point is underscored, I think, if we understand necessity as truth in all possible worlds. The proponent of a necessity, impossibility, entailment or incompatibility claim is saying that *in no possible world whatever* does it occur that so-and-so. That is a universal quantification. Given the richness and incredible variety of the pluriverse, such a statement cannot be accepted without argument save for the case of basic logical intuitions that virtually everyone shares.

3. Let us turn specifically to (1) and (2). The second thing to notice here is that 'incompatible' cannot mean, *logically* incompatible. No one can start with determinism and derive in the predicate calculus any reasonable translation of the denial that anyone's action is ever free. What 'incompatible' must mean is, jointly incompatible with some further principle. I have argued elsewhere[5] that such a further principle is likely to be speculative and suspiciously philosophical, and I shall develop that point below.

The principle cannot be just the truth-functional conditional from determinism to the negation of free will or vice versa, because the incompatibilist is saying more than that determinism and free will do not in fact both obtain. The principle must be independently motivated and entail that they do not both obtain. I shall argue below that any such principle will be dubious.[6]

[5] *Consciousness* (Cambridge: Bradford Books/MIT Press, 1987), Chapter 9.

[6] N.B., I will not contend, as some compatibilists have in attacking incompatibilist arguments, that the principle *begs the question.*

William G. Lycan

Not so fast, though. It is not quite so obvious that 'incompatible' cannot mean logical incompatibility. In response to my previous work aforementioned, James Tomberlin has made a clever and doughty move.[7] Taking my allusion to the predicate calculus at face value, he pointed out that there are richer logics, notably modal logics, which reveal more logical incompatibilities than can be demonstrated in predicate logic. $\Box P$ & ~P, $\Diamond P$ & $\Box$~P, and P &~ $\Diamond P$ are all logical contradictions within the meaning of the act even though they cannot even be directly formulated in the predicate calculus. (Of course they can be *translated into* the predicate calculus by appeal to an ontology of possible worlds, and in that derivative sense shown valid by use of predicate logic.) Thus, for all I have shown, it is possible that determinism and freedom can be formulated in such a way that they prove to be logically, because modal-logically, incompatible after all, and no extraneous principle, dubious or not, will be needed.

Here, in brief, is how Tomberlin's argument goes (pp. 128–30). He assumes for *reductio* that 'Although Bob did A freely, his doing A has a determining cause [C].' He gradually translates that assumption into the vernacular of possible worlds, and proceeds to derive both '[F]or any possible world, if C obtains, Bob does A [in that world]' and '[T]here is some physically possible world such that although C obtains, Bob does not do A,' which predicate-calculus contradiction reduces the original assumption to absurdity. The derivation proceeds, concessively, through a premise corresponding to the traditional compatibilist hypothetical analysis of 'could have done otherwise,' though that premise is not itself translated into possible-worlds talk. So Tomberlin's thesis is that even if that ostensible pillar of compatibilism is granted, the original assumption is still refuted via the predicate calculus and incompatibilism is thus established.

The trouble with Tomberlin's argument, I have argued elsewhere,[8] is that although each of its premises is perfectly true and one might casually think that the conclusion follows from them, the tendentiousness lurks in the untranslated premise, which reads: 'In C Bob would have done otherwise =*df* In C, if he had chosen to do otherwise and..., then Bob would have done otherwise' (p. 129, ellipsis original). To make the argument demonstrably valid, we have to finish the job and explicate that premise in terms of

[7] 'Whither Compatibilism? A Query for Lycan', *Philosophical Papers* **17**, No. 2 (August 1988), 127–31.

[8] 'Compatibilism Now and Forever: A Reply to Tomberlin', *Philosophical Papers* **17**, No. 2 (August 1988), 133–9.

possible worlds. If we do so in the normal way, according to roughly Stalnaker-Lewis 'similarity' semantics and making the most natural judgments of similarity, the resulting formula does not combine with the previous premises to entail the needed contradiction. (If we suspect that the hypothetical analysans should be treated as a backtracker,[9] and apply a natural similarity analysis for backtrackers, the resulting translation leaves the argument even more obviously invalid.) So Tomberlin has failed to deduce a contradiction from the original assumption.

A similarly a priori and very ingenious modal incompatibilist argument has recently been devised by Ted A. Warfield.[10] There is some question whether the argument is in fact valid even as already formulated into modal notation,[11] but in any case, two English sentence-schemata originally offered by Warfield have to be translated into modal notation in such a way as to make it valid. (The schemata are 'P is true and there's nothing anyone is free to do in the circumstances that even might result in ~P' and 'P is true and there's nothing anyone is free to do in the circumstances that would definitely result in ~P' (p. 173).) I would contend that the translations needed to make the argument valid would have to be tendentious in the characteristically philosophical way, though I cannot argue that here (or even sketch Warfield's complex modal argument).

Thus, the incompatibilist's tendentious assumption need not take the form of a principle (though one can always reconstruct it as such). In these would-be purely modal arguments it can take the form of either a failure to translate in detail, leaving a gap in the argument, or a highly disputable translation.

So, vs. (1) and (2): (1) is false because nothing is 'prima facie incompatible' with anything unless there is a marked air of *logical* contradiction. (2) *might* yet be shown to be true, but induction over spirited and ingenious attempts by excellent philosophers argues otherwise.

[9] In the sense of David Lewis' 'Counterfactual Dependence and Time's Arrow', *Noûs* 13, No. 4 (November 1979), 455–76. The idea derives originally from P. B. Downing, 'Subjunctive Conditionals, Time Order, and Causation', *Proceedings of the Aristotelian Society* **59** (1959), 125–40.

[10] Causal Determinism and Human Freedom Are Incompatible: A New Argument for Incompatibilism', in *Philosophical Perspectives 14: Action and Freedom*, J. Tomberlin (ed.) (Atascadero, CA: Ridgeview Publishing, 2000), 167–80, pp. 172–77.

[11] Michael Kremer, 'How Not to Argue for Incompatibilism', MS, University of Notre Dame.

4. Against thesis (3): Incompatibilists often challenge compatibilists to say what 'free action' means, if it does not mean an action that is physically undetermined. (Recall our opening quote from Chisholm.) And compatibilists have leaped to respond; Stace and Ayer, for example, offered their infamous hypothetical analyses of 'free action',[12] according to which my action was free iff, roughly, had I wanted/chosen otherwise, I would have done otherwise. Such analyses were promptly attacked by Austin, Chisholm, Keith Lehrer and others.[13]

I think the compatibilists have made a big strategic error. If my previous points, against (1) and (2), are right, the compatibilist has no obligation to offer any competing *analysis* of 'free action'. I believe the compatibilists should have balked, and merely insisted that *there is* a perfectly good sense of 'free' in which we act freely despite our actions' being the determined result of pre-existing conditions.

Notice, I said they *should* have balked, not just that they would have been within their dialectical rights to have done so. Notice particularly that in capitulating and consenting to offer analyses, they opened themselves to a kind of attack whose dialectical force is weak but whose rhetorical force is strong: Their opponents could and did vigorously attack the analyses, thereby making it look as though there were something wrong with the compatibilist position in itself.

Think about it. On *any* philosophical topic, the person who propounds an analysis is going to get creamed. Philosophical analyses virtually never work, but are lacerated by counterexample after counterexample. So by agreeing to propose a particular analysis of 'free action', our compatibilist is entering a contest s/he cannot hope to win—*not* because there is anything wrong with compatibilism or because 'free' really does mean whatever the incompatibilist thinks it does, but only on the entirely general

---

[12] W. T. Stace, *Religion and the Modern Mind* (New York: Lippincott/Harper and Row, 1952); A. J. Ayer, 'Freedom and Necessity', in *Philosophical Essays* (London: Macmillan, 1954), 271–84.

[13] J. L. Austin, 'Ifs and Cans', *Proceedings of the British Academy* **42** (1956), 109–32, reprinted in *Philosophical Papers* (Oxford: Oxford University Press, 1961); R. M. Chisholm, 'J. L. Austin's Philosophical Papers', *Mind* **73**, No. 289 (January 1964), 1–26; K. Lehrer, 'Preferences, Conditionals and Freedom', in *Time and Cause*, P. van Inwagen (ed.) (Dordrecht: D. Reidel, 1980), 187–201.

grounds that in the game of philosophical analysis, the analysts' opponents nearly always win.

Compare J. J. C. Smart and his famous 'topic-neutral translations' of mental ascriptions.[14] They were offered in response to each of three objections to Place and Smart's Identity Theory of mind: the claim that mental ascriptions simply entail the existence of non-physical states or events, the claim that the Identity Theory violated Leibniz' law, and the more complicated 'Objection 3,' attributed to Max Black in Smart's footnote 13. Smart contended that mental ascriptions are topic-neutral, in that they entail neither that the states and events ascribed are nonphysical nor that they are physical. (Never mind whether this would in fact have blocked the second and third objections.) Smart sought to show that mental ascriptions are topic-neutral by providing synonyms or paraphrases of them that are both adequate as paraphrases and obviously topic-neutral. (Notoriously, 'I see a yellowish-orange after-image' became 'There is something going on which is like what is going on when I have my eyes open, am awake, and there is an orange illuminated in good light in front of me, that is, when I really see an orange.')

Allies and critics alike seemed to find this entirely appropriate. David Lewis and David Armstrong offered plainly topic-neutral meaning analyses of their own; Michael Bradley, Frank Jackson and other critics attacked Smart's paraphrases, to good effect.[15] But, first, why should we expect that an English expression that is in fact topic-neutral must also have a distinct synonym in English that is more obviously topic-neutral? Second, as above, why should we expect philosophical analysis here to produce greater consensus than it practically ever does? And, third, remember our dialectical points against (1) and (2): In a controversial case, non-entailment—hence, here, topic-neutrality—is the default. The burden is on Smart's opponent to show that mental ascriptions do entail the existence of nonphysical items.

Smart made the strategic (not philosophical) error of venturing onto extremely dangerous ground when he was quite safe where he

[14] 'Sensations and Brain Processes', *Philosophical Review* **68**, No. 2 (April 1959), 141–56. For discussion of the 'topic-neutrality problem' generally, see Chapter 2 of my *Consciousness*, loc. cit.

[15] D. K. Lewis, 'An Argument for the Identity Theory', *Journal of Philosophy* **63**, No. 1 (January 1966), 17–25; D. M. Armstrong, *A Materialist Theory of the Mind* (London: Routledge and Kegan Paul, 1968); M. C. Bradley, 'Sensations, Brain-Processes, and Colours', *Australasian Journal of Philosophy* **41**, No. 4 (December 1963); F. Jackson, *Perception* (Cambridge: Cambridge University Press, 1977).

was. So too the free-will compatibilist who offers an irenic analysis of 'free action'. Let's not do it. And let's not be bothered by the failures of others' analyses. Chisholm was wrong: There is no joke on us.

5. Against (4): If (1)–(3) are not true, then there is no conceptual problem about free will and determinism; so there is no further asymmetry to underwrite (4). (I nearly wrote, 'then there is no prima facie problem about free will...,' but that would have been silly. Of course there is a prima facie problem about free will and determinism, or so much would not have been written about it and we would not be holding this session today. What there isn't is a conceptual problem.)

The reason I earlier expressed doubt about whether (4) is *just* false is the following line of reasoning. Just suppose, contrary to this paper's contention, that free will and determinism are incompatible, so that if determinism is true then there cannot possibly be free will. Then, despite standard claims that in that case interpolating physical randomness would not help, it is still theoretically possible to work out a libertarian theory of agent-causation sitting atop physical indeterminism, that would allow and account for free will. So in principle, indeterminism still goes better with free will than does determinism. (I am not persuaded by that argument, but I do not want to pursue the matter here.)

6. Now I am going to offer a Moorean argument for compatibilism, much the sort of argument Moore would use against idealists and other anti-realists and skeptics.[16] In considering an anti-realist view, he would first derive from it a very specific negative consequence regarding his own everyday experience. For example, take the idealist claim that there are no material objects. From it, Moore would deduce that he himself had no hands—hands being clear cases of material objects.

Of course the idealist had defended the nonexistence of material objects. Let's suppose that the defence had taken the form of a deductively valid argument. The argument must of course have had ultimate premises, themselves undefended. So it is an argument that looks schematically like this:

[16] The strategy is more fully expounded and defended in my 'Moore Against the New Skeptics', *Philosophical Studies* **103**, No. 1 (March 2001), 35–53.

(P1)...
(P2)...

.

.

[steps]

.

.

_____

∴ (C) There are no material objects. QED.

—to which we may add as a corollary,

∴ (C′) I do not have hands.

We are supposing the argument to be valid. But that is to say only that each of the sets {P1,...P_n,~C} and {P1,...P_n,~C′} is inconsistent. The idealist of course wants us to accept the premises and therefore to accept C and C′ on the strength of them. But nothing about the argument itself forces us to do that, since if we wish to deny its conclusion we have only to reject one of the premises. Any argument can be turned on its head.

Elsewhere[17] I have argued more generally that no deductive 'proof' can be anything more than an invitation to compare plausibility: Of the propositions P1,... P_n, and ~C′, which is the least plausible or credible? The proof affords no deeper investigation.

Applying the crucial question of plausibility comparison to any specific argument for idealism concerning the external world, Moore thought its answer was painfully obvious. Since the reality of material objects is directly entailed by something Moore already knows to be true, that he does have hands, the culprit must be one of the other members of the inconsistent set; it must be one of the premises that is false. It may be interesting to try to decide which one, but that is not necessary in order to vindicate our commonsense belief in the reality of material objects.

To put it that way sounds arbitrary and question-begging, and of course Moore has been widely accused of both faults. Why should he get to choose ~C′ over the argument's premises and protect it against them? That comes close to merely announcing that the idealist is wrong.

The nonrhetorical answer to the foregoing rhetorical question is this: At least one of the argument's premises is sure to be distinctively abstract and philosophical, accepted only because it somehow

[17] _Judgement and Justification_ (Cambridge: Cambridge University Press, 1988), Chapter 6.

appeals to the idealist. And remember that a deductive argument is only a plausibility comparison. In this example, the comparison is between (a) 'Here is one hand and here is another' and (b) a purely philosophical premise such as McTaggart's assumption that every existing thing has proper parts that are themselves substances. You be the judge. How *could* a proposition like (b) be considered as plausible as (a)? How could you possibly be more confident that every existent thing has proper parts that are substances, than that you have hands?

The epistemic credentials of metaphysical premises (often called 'intuitions') are obscure. It is hard to say why a given metaphysician should be strongly attracted to a particular such premise, such as (b), when doubtless we can find another metaphysician—perhaps only in another part of the world or another era, but possibly just next door—who firmly rejects it. By contrast, Moore has excellent grounds for the competing proposition (a): He remembers seeing and feeling his hands on millions of occasions, and he can do so again at will. A forced choice between (a) and (b) has got to favour (a).

7. Before we get back to free will, here are six important caveats regarding Moore's technique: First, whatever one now thinks of Moore's response to the idealist—in particular, even if one is not convinced of the plausibility comparison—Moore has not *begged the question* against the idealist. In judging that one of a pair of propositions is more credible than the other, one may be mistaken, but it is no dialectical offense (unless, perhaps, the other proposition is just the negation of the first, which is not the case here).

Second, it would not help the idealist to claim that her/his philosophical premise is *analytic*, or a somehow 'conceptual' truth, and so not in need of defence. Even if one is unpersuaded by Quine of the nonexistence of such truths, the appeal will not help the idealist here, for no one who reasonably thinks that the premise is false is going to be converted by the bare assertion that the principle is conceptually true.

Third, contra many of Moore's critics over the years, Moore is not clinging to his commonsense beliefs come what may and treating common sense as sacred and invulnerable to criticism. Moore never held that common sense is irrefutable. Commonsense beliefs can be corrected by careful empirical investigation and scientific theorizing, which is what happened in, e.g., the case of the earth's shape and motion. The point against the idealist is that *philosophers* are not empirical investigators or scientists. McTaggart provided no evidence for his claim that every existent thing has proper parts that are substances; it just seemed true to him, for some reason. Though common sense must yield to evidence, it need not yield to bare metaphysical pronouncement.[18]

Fourth caveat: It's important to see that the argument contains no premise *about* commonsense propositions themselves, e.g., not that we should give commonsense beliefs considerable weight, or that commonsense beliefs are prima facie justified, or that (good God) they have a 'right of ancient possession'[19]. It is not that 'I have hands' etc. are known or justified in virtue of their being common-sense propositions. It is just that they are individually more plausible than are the premises of any philosophical argument intended to show that they are false. (A later philosophical *explanation of* their plausibility might advert to their being commonsensical, though I myself take a different line.)

Fifth, do not be too quick to dismiss Moore's method as shallow and superficial, disrespectful of our need for a deep philosophical critique of common sense. There is an old and well-entrenched idea that philosophy can get above, or beneath, the body of belief constituted by common-sense-plus-science, and subject that body as a whole to deeper rational examination. I reject that idea, essentially on the grounds of what I have said earlier about the unprobative-ness of deductive arguments; I have criticized it more extensively elsewhere.[20]

And, sixth: To make my point, I do not need a *theory of* plausibility/credibility. Granted, the psychological basis and normative authority of 'plausibility' judgments are important philosophical issues, but they are just that: philosophical issues. Actual plausibility comparisons made in real life do not depend on having a well justified theory of plausibility—else only professional epistemologists could make them. That people often ride the bus is more plausible or credible than that a BMW will do over 120 mph, or that more people drive vintage Jaguars than drive Chevrolets, or that there is life somewhere else in our galaxy, or that the cause of an idea must have at least as much formal reality as the idea itself has objective reality. I do not have to have any philosophical theory of plausibility in order to be entirely justified in making such

[18] In saying this, I am not assuming a clear distinction between theoretical science and metaphysics, nor do I believe in any such distinction. But that is to say only that there are borderline cases.

[19] Keith Lehrer, 'Why Not Skepticism?', *Philosophical Forum* 2, No. 3 (Spring 1971), 283–98 (quoting Thomas Reid).

[20] 'Moore Against the New Skeptics', loc. cit.

judgments, any more than I have to have a philosophical theory of meaning in order to know what my wife has just said.[21]

8. And finally we can state the argument for free-will compatibilism.

I used to claim that a qualified, macro-event-level version of determinism is itself common sense.[22] That has proved to be problematic, for it may be a case in which a commonsense proposition, even the qualified version of determinism, is refuted by compelling argument based on indeterminist science. But I need not stand by that claim. For purposes of my Moorean argument, all determinism needs to be is: not an affront to common sense.

In any case, the incompatibilist must assume determinism for the sake of argument. And whether or not it is true, numerous commonsense claims of free action always will be more plausible than are the *purely philosophical* premises (or translation lore etc.) of any argument designed to convince us of incompatibilism. So we reject at least one of those premises in each case. Since the incompatibilist argument fails and compatibilism is the default (cf. again the general methodological point, section **2** above), compatibilism rules. Thus, to say the least, it is hard to imagine how compatibilism could be rationally discredited.

9. Two more caveats are immediately needed.

I am not saying that *compatibilism* is a commonsense view. Ekstrom considers such a claim;[23] I am not sure whether she rejects it, though she certainly denies that it is a good reason for embracing compatibilism. I firmly reject it. Compatibilism is a controversial philosophical thesis. (Nor do I buy the '*Mind* argument' that incompatibilist accounts are incoherent.[24])

Further, in insisting that some of our actions are free, I am not

---

[21] Which is not to say that I don't have such a theory, see *Judgement and Justification*, loc. cit. Chapter 7.

[22] *Consciousness*, loc. cit., pp. 113–14.

[23] Op. cit., pp. 56–57.

[24] R. E. Hobart, 'Free Will as Involving Determinism and Inconceivable Without It,' *Mind* **43**, No. 169 (January 1934), 1–27; P. H. Newell-Smith, 'Free Will and Moral Responsibility', *Mind* **57**, No. 225 (January 1948), 45–61; and J. J. C. Smart, 'Free-Will, Praise and Blame', *Mind* **70**, No. 279 (July 1961), 291–306; also, Ayer, op. cit. I believe the term 'the *Mind* argument' was coined by Peter van Inwagen, in *An Essay on Free Will* (Oxford: Clarendon Press, 1983); he distinguishes three different 'forms' or 'strands' of it.

committing the magician's-assistant fallacy, i.e., taking the fact of failing to introspect determining causes of my actions as a successful introspecting that the actions are free. Nor am I making any other (direct) appeal to phenomenology.

10. I contend, then, that every incompatibilist argument is bound to fail. That is not to say that each will fail in the same way. But to get a feel for the failure, let us take a quick look at one example, an influential and apparently powerful incompatibilist argument, the 'Consequence argument' due variously to Carl Ginet, David Wiggins, Peter van Inwagen and James Lamb.[25] For convenience, let us focus on van Inwagen's 1983 version: [26]

$\Box$ S

$\Box$ (S $\supset$ A)
_____

$\therefore$ $\Box$A,

where the box is interpreted as 'unalterability' of some sort, A is the performance of an arbitrarily selected future action of mine, and S is a total efficient cause of A existing before I was born. (Here as always we assume determinism, in this case for conditional proof.) The argument's appearance of validity is unmistakable. And if we construe the box as, unalterability *by me* in particular, its conclusion denies me free will.

Michael Slote argues that although this inference is attractive because $\Box$ is felt to be 'agglomerative' ($\Box$X, $\Box$Y $\vdash$ $\Box$ (X & Y), agglomerativity fails for some real-life modalities.[27] (He focuses on

[25] C. Ginet, 'Might We Have No Choice?' in *Freedom and Determinism*, K. Lehrer (ed.) (New York: Random House, 1966), 87–104; D. Wiggins, 'Towards a Reasonable Libertarianism', in *Essays on Freedom of Action*, T. Honderich (ed.) (London: Routledge and Kegan Paul, 1973), 31–61; P. van Inwagen, 'The Incompatibility of Free Will and Determinism', *Philosophical Studies* **27**, No. 3 (March, 1975), 185–199, and *An Essay on Free Will*, loc. cit.; J. Lamb, 'On a Proof of Incompatibilism', *Philosophical Review* **86**, No. 1 (January, 1977), 20–35.

[26] There are now a number of interestingly different versions of the Consequence argument, subject to somewhat different sets of objections. These are nicely catalogued and discussed by Ekstrom, op. cit., Chapter 2. I criticize van Inwagen's version more extensively in Chapter 8 of *Modality and Meaning* (Dordrecht: Kluwer Academic Publishing, 1994), though that discussion is marred by some vicious copy-editing errors.

[27] 'Selective Necessity and the Free-Will Problem', *Journal of Philosophy* **79**, No. 1 (January, 1982), 5–24.

William G. Lycan

agglomerativity because he thinks van Inwagen's inference proceeds by agglomeration followed by closure under necessity, but as we shall see, this interpretation is inessential to the objection.) Consider, e.g., *nonaccidentalness* in the everyday sense. Slote explicates the nonaccidentalness of an event in terms of the event's being the outcome of what he calls a 'routine plan' (RP). (In virtue of the plan, the event was quite normal and to be expected.) Now (p. 15), one day in a bank there is an accidental meeting between Jules and Jim. Each of the two has been sent to the bank 'as part of a well-known routine or plan of [respective] office functioning.' Thus, it is no accident that Jules arrives at the bank when he does, and it is no accident that Jim arrives at the bank when he, Jim, does. But it is entirely accidental that both are there at the same time. Jules' presence in the bank was necessitated by RP1 and Jim's presence there was necessitated by RP2, but there is no RP that necessitated the simultaneous Jules'-presence-and-Jim's-presence, because in particular the amalgam RP1+RP2 is not itself a RP.

$\square_{\text{RP1}}$ (Jules arrives at the bank at t_b)
$\square_{\text{RP2}}$ (Jim arrives at the bank at t_b)

—but nothing of the form $\square_{\text{RP}n}$ (Jules arrives at the bank at t_b & Jim arrives at the t_b) follows, because there is no such RPn. Agglomeration fails.

The case of the Consequence argument's premises is parallel, except for being a modalized Modus Ponens rather than modalized Conjunction Introduction. The analogue of an RP is what I shall call a 'me-excluding determinant.' Why is S, the total efficient cause of A existing before I was born, unalterable by me? Because it was in place quite independently of my desires, wishes, intentions, for that matter beliefs, and whatever other conative structure would be relevant (hereafter just 'my CS'), because I neglected to exist at the time. Why is the material conditional S ⊃ A unalterable by me? Because it is a logical consequence of the laws of nature, and both logic and the laws hold quite independently of my CS. It is in that sense that S and S ⊃ A are me-excluding determinants (MEDs).

But the individual MEDs differ as between van Inwagen's first premise, $\square$S, and the second, $\square$ (S ⊃ A). We have

$\square_{\text{MED1}}$S
$\square_{\text{MED2}}$(S ⊃ A)

But nothing of the form $\square_{\text{MED}n}$ A follows, because there is no such MEDn. In particular, the amalgam S & (S ⊃ A) is not a MED, for it does not determine A in a way that bypasses my CS. Since A is a future action of mine, A is hardly unaffected by my CS. In fact, my CS is an, if not the, prominent element of A's total efficient cause. To be unalterable by me is to be determined or necessitated in a certain way, viz., in a me-excluding way. S and S ⊃ A are necessitated in that way, but A, though necessitated in other ways, is not necessitated in that one. The inference-pattern fails.

To put it back in terms of agglomerativity for Slote's sake: In general, even where Z is entailed by the conjunction X & Y, that X is determined by a MED and Y is determined by a MED does not entail that Z is determined by a MED. So □A cannot be derived.

11. 'Oh, spoken like a good Soft Determinist!,' van Inwagen might reply.[28] Indeed, my moves in this paper against Tomberlin's and van Inwagen's arguments may have sounded at every turn as though I had said, 'Let's all remember that Soft Determinism is true, and just stiffarm whatever contrary claim we have to in order to save our view.' Van Inwagen's argument schema seems valid to him on what he considers any reasonable interpretation of the box; modalities such as mine that fail to support the schema are conspicuously already congenial to the Soft Determinist. Van Inwagen admits that his argument will never convince the die-hard compatibilist,[29] but for his part he cannot hear any Soft-Determinist-leaning interpretation of the box as a reasonable interpretation. It is at best a stalemate.

I believe it is no stalemate, and that Slote and I win. First, our objection to the Consequence argument does not presuppose compatibilism, let alone the truth of Soft Determinism. Our objection is that the argument employs modalities that are, like virtually every other modality expressible in English, relative modalities, and that on one entirely reasonable interpretation the argument's premises are true and its conclusion false. Granted, the interpretation is guided by a conception of action that is indeed congenial to Soft Determinism. (And I admit here and now that that will be my offstage strategy in responding to every incompatibilist argument.) But it does not follow that the objection presupposes the compatibility of free will with determinism; it does not. Of course, so far as I can see, van Inwagen's controversial inference does not presuppose incompatibilism either, so this first

[28] Van Inwagen did reply to Slote essentially in that way, in an unpublished note, 'Modal Inference and the Free-Will Problems.'

[29] 'Reply to Christopher Hill', *Analysis* **52**, No. 2 (April 1992), 56–61, p. 58.

point does not show that we are not in stalemate. But if we are in stalemate, it does not take the form of mutual question-begging.

Second, I have pointed out that, so far as has been shown, the Consequence argument is invalid. To respond, van Inwagen or another incompatibilist would have to either add another premise, or block my counter-interpretation in some principled way. And, as before, the premise or principle thus introduced would have to be more plausible than the commonsensical claim that I did A freely in the sense germane to responsibility. My doubt that the incompatibilist can do that is my reason for denying that we are in stalemate. Remember that the compatibilist bears no corresponding burden; if some conclusion does not obviously follow from some premise, we can only wait to see why the proponents of entailment think it does follow.

In 'Reply to Christopher Hill' (ibid.), van Inwagen offers a sensible dialectical model (p. 58): Think of the issue as a debate conducted by a compatibilist on one side and an incompatibilist on the other, but before an audience that is agnostic on the issue. Each of the two debaters is trying to convert, not necessarily the opposing debater, but the hitherto neutral listeners. So, as the incompatibilist debater, van Inwagen need not restrict himself to premises that would be acceptable to the compatibilist, but must only present an overall case, including replies to the compatibilist's opening points, further rejoinders, etc. that will or should sway the agnostics. In like wise, the compatibilist may use premises that would be unacceptable to the incompatibilist, so long as they are likely to be granted by the neutral audience.

That is a good test. And the ultimate point of my Moorean argument is to show that the audience will always be forced to choose between, on the one hand, a host of commonsense propositions about their and others' doing things freely, and on the other, a purely philosophical principle that is controversial even among philosophers. In the nature of things, I have argued, philosophy will always lose that one. Compatibilism still rules.[30]

[30] I thank Jim Tomberlin for his stimulating article cited above. Thanks also to Fritz Warfield for the talk and subsequent conversation that inspired this paper. I am grateful to Anthony O'Hear and Tim Crane for putting together 'Free Will day' at University College London, and to the Royal Institute audience for spirited and helpful discussion.

Materialism and the First Person

GEOFFREY MADELL

I

Here are some sentences from Fred Dretske's book *Naturalising the Mind*:

> For a materialist there are no facts that are accessible to only one person… If the subjective life of another being, what it is like to be that creature, seems inaccessible, this must be because we fail to understand what we are talking about when we talk about its subjective states. If S feels some way, and its feeling some way is a material state, how can it be impossible for us to know how S feels? Though each of us has direct information about our own experiences, there is no privileged access. If you know where to look, you can get the same information I have about the character of my experiences. This is a result of thinking about the mind in naturalistic terms. Subjectivity becomes part of the objective order. For materialists, this is as it should be.[1]

I think Dretske is right: for the materialist, there can be no such thing as privileged access. But the denial of privileged access looks wildly implausible. A being incapable of feeling pain can have access to all the physical facts relating to pain, but not have the faintest idea what pain feels like; and so for all sensations. No amount of knowledge of the physical facts will allow one to understand what the experience feels like, a fact that has become known as 'the explanatory gap'. What I want to look at is an approach shared by a number of materialists which argues that knowledge which is essentially perspectival, first-personal, and of that which is inaccessible to the observer, can be accommodated in a materialist position. This is an approach which is shared by Michael Tye, William Lycan, Owen Flanagan, Brian Loar, Scott Sturgeon, and others. The essence of it goes like this:

Fred, in Frank Jackson's well-known story, has superfine colour discrimination.[2] He distinguishes between two shades of red where

[1] F. Dretske, *Naturalising the Mind* (Cambridge, Massachusetts: The MIT Press, 1997), 65.
[2] See F. Jackson, 'Epiphenomenal Qualia', reprinted in W. G. Lycan (ed.), *Mind and Cognition* (Oxford: Basil Blackwell, 1990), 470–2.

the rest of us only see one shade. We can see that there is some physical basis for this, both in Fred's cranium and in the red part of the colour spectrum. But we have no idea what Fred's experience is like. Why not? Because, Flanagan points out, we are not connected up either internally or to the outside world as Fred is (though he doesn't actually mention Fred by name).[3] If introspection is a form of self-scanning, as Lycan claims, then the explanatory gap, the lack of tracings and explanations of the sort demanded, is just what you would expect. I know my own pain by introspection, and no one else can know the same fact by being in the same functional state. Only I can scan my own internal states.[4] Tye also sees the essential point to be that phenomenally conscious states are 'perspectivally subjective in the following way: each phenomenal state S, is such that fully comprehending S as it is essentially in itself, requires adopting one particular point of view or perspective namely that provided by undergoing S'. A phenomenal concept such as RED 'is exercised when one becomes aware by introspection of what it is like to experience red'[5]; and: 'no amount of a priori reflection on phenomenal concepts alone will reveal phenomenal-physical connections, even of a contingent type'.[6]

According to this approach, then, the phenomenal character of experience, the 'explanatory gap' presented by the evident failure of physical description and explanation to account for that phenomenal character, and the fact that this character is something to which the subject has privileged and private access, are all matters to be accounted for by the perspectival nature of phenomenal concepts. 'The inexplicable nature of qualia-based subjectivity', says Scott Sturgeon, 'is best explained by epistemic features for our qualitative concepts. Nothing ontologically funny is required... From the fact that no explanation is possible for qualia-based subjectivity *it simply does not follow* that the properties captured by our qualitative concepts are distinct from those captured by other concepts'.[7]

Lycan connects all this explicitly with the irreducibility of first person reference. 'My mental reference to a first-order

[3] O. Flanagan, *Consciousness Reconsidered* (Cambridge, Massachusetts: The MIT Press, 1992), 91, 116.

[4] W. G. Lycan, *Consciousness and Experience* (Cambridge, Massachusetts: The MIT Press, 1996), 54–68.

[5] M. Tye, 'Phenomenal Consciousness: The Explanatory Gap as a Cognitive Illusion', *Mind* **108**, No. 432 (October 1999), 710.

[6] Tye, 713.

[7] S. Sturgeon, 'The Epistemic View of Subjectivity', *Journal of Philosophy* **91**, No. 5 (May 1994), 235.

psychological state of my own is a tokening of a semantically primitive Mentalese lexeme. My mental word is functionally nothing like any of the complex expressions of English that in fact refer to the same (neural) state of affairs... And since no one else can use that mental word... to designate that state of affairs, of course no one can explain... why that state of affairs feels like [*that* or *semantha*] to me. Introspection involves a very special mode of presentation, primitive and private' (Lycan's brackets).[8]

The subjectivity of experience, and, in particular, the fact that no physical description can explain the phenomenal character of sensation, is thus taken to be fully accounted for by the perspectival nature of phenomenal concepts, and by the nature of self-monitoring and self reference.

II

I think this position is totally untenable. There is, I shall argue, no way in which phenomenal, or perspectival, or first-person awareness can be accommodated in a materialist framework. Materialists do not understand what first-person knowledge is, and they do not understand what the first person is.

Before I continue, let me point out that the position outlined is one of 'robust' physicalism, as Tye calls it. That is, we are wholly composed of physical elements whose nature is pretty well known. There are no mysterious inscrutable properties of the physical, nor any mystery about the connection between the mental and the physical; and we don't have to wait on some fundamental revolution in our understanding of the physical. We are, Lycan tells us, rather large collections of small physical objects.[9]

The first question we must ask is prompted by Dretske's comment. How is it possible to accommodate a private realm, inaccessible to the observer, in a wholly material world? Whatever the physical is, there can surely be no aspect of it which is in principle closed to public scrutiny. If its feeling like *that* to me is something in principle inaccessible to public scrutiny, then it can't be physical, or so one would suppose. To suggest otherwise leaves one without an understanding of what it could mean to call anything physical.

What has gone wrong here? Part of it, I suggest, is a disposition to suppose that the question reduces to one about ownership. My

[8] Lycan, 64.
[9] Lycan, 45.

mode of access to the posited neural states is *self*-scrutiny, or *self*-monitoring. No one else can have *that* mode of access to the posited neural state. But then, no one else can have my smiles or frowns, or undergo my death. So, Tye tells us, 'The fact that you cannot undergo my pains... [is] no more mysterious... than the fact that you cannot undergo my death'.[10]

But this cannot be the answer. The issue is not about necessary ownership, nor even about necessary ownership of a mode of access, but about privileged access. My frowns, smiles or death are items in the public world. My phenomenal states are not.

That my scrutiny or monitoring of some posited state is *self*-monitoring goes no way towards accounting for the necessary privacy of what is being monitored. The refrigerator monitors its own temperature, but no one supposes that what it monitors is necessarily private to that refrigerator, that it has privileged access to its own temperature, even though nothing else can monitor that refrigerator's temperature in the way that that refrigerator does. There is nothing about self-monitoring, or about what is thus monitored, that is necessarily hidden from the observer. What needs to be explained is how a self-monitoring, admittedly vastly more complex than that of the refrigerator, can be such as to result in, or have as an aspect, something in principle inaccessible to the observer. That looks to be simply incompatible with physicalism, as Dretske observed.

But the need for an explanation of the required sort can never be satisfied. No reflection on the physical facts, no matter how detailed and comprehensive, can reveal why, when some putative neural state is the object of self-scrutiny, it feels as it does, or even why it should feel any way at all. And this is fully admitted by proponents of the position under discussion. As Tye says, 'each phenomenal state *S*, is such that fully comprehending *S* as it is essentially in itself, requires adopting one particular point of view or perspective namely that provided by undergoing *S*'.[11] And, as Lycan points out, no one can explain why that state of affairs feels like *that* to me.

Since no description or inspection of the physical facts will explain why any neural state feels like *that*, we clearly have an 'explanatory gap'. But the gap cannot be dismissed as something that does not count against materialism, or almost counting in its favour, as Lycan claims, nor as a 'cognitive illusion', as Tye claims.

[10] M. Tye, *Ten Problems of Consciousness* (Cambridge, Massachusetts: The MIT Press, 1996), 92.

[11] Tye, 'Phenomenal Consciousness', 708.

It is fatal to materialism. It cannot be enough simply to point to the claimed special nature of phenomenal concepts as essentially per-spectival. The notions of perspective, of self-scanning or monitor-ing cannot support the implication that such scanning focuses on something intrinsically hidden from the observer, as I have pointed out. Until it is explained how what looks like Cartesian privacy can be reconciled with materialism (and I see no prospect of that), simply referring us to 'the special, perspectival, nature of phenomenal concepts' is of no use at all.

III

Most of the discussion of the so-called explanatory gap has focused on a rather different aspect: the claimed identity between the phenomenal and the physical. A full understanding of the micro-structure of water allows one to infer that where that micro-struc-ture is realized, the relevant surface properties are also realized. But no understanding of neural states will allow one to infer that where neural state N is realized, so also will phenomenal state P. So the claimed necessary identity between the physical and the phenomenal looks to be brute, 'metaphysical' necessity, which crit-ics such as David Chalmers claim to be quite unacceptable.[12]

I think Chalmers is right to reject the notion of brute metaphys-ical necessity. A standard claim is that the necessary identity of water with H_2O is a posteriori, metaphysical necessity. Well, so be it, but that gives no credence to the claim that neural state N is iden-tical with phenomenal state P as a matter of metaphysical necessity. That water is H_2O is discovered a posteriori, but the identity is fully revealed. There is no such discovery in the case of the claimed identity between neural and phenomenal state; we discover only a correlation. And, as I noted earlier, in the case of water, under-standing the micro-structure enables one to infer the presence of the relevant, watery surface properties. By contrast, no inference from physical to phenomenal properties is possible. Recourse to the paradigm of the necessary identity of water with H_2O is therefore of no avail. The claimed necessary identity of physical and phenomenal state looks as brute as can possibly be, an impression strengthened by the fact that proponents of the materialist view in question all allow, to a greater or lesser extent, the possibility of

[12] See D. Chalmers, *The Conscious Mind* (Oxford: Oxford University Press, 1996), 136–43.

inverted qualia, changed qualia, and absent qualia, though these possibilities are deemed merely 'epistemic', on a par with the possibility of water being something other than H_2O. The impression is given, therefore, that it is simply arbitrary that phenomenal state P is identical with neural state N, and there's nothing one can do to make this any more intelligible.

IV

Some materialists, understandably blanching at this outcome, suggest that escape from it is to be found in acknowledging the intentionality of sensations. We could, Lycan says, hold to the line that, although inverted spectra are not only imaginable and 'conceivable' in every psychological sense, but logically possible as well, they are no more metaphysically possible than is the distinctness of water from H_2O. This tough line is defensible, and may well be correct, but, he says, it is not *fun*.[13] The emphasis from this point is on the intentionality of qualia, their representative nature. Qualitative differences between sensations, it is claimed, do not outrun intentional differences, the 'colours' involved in visual experiences being just the physical colours of represented physical objects. And a recent review of a book of Tye's articles also suggests that the way to avoid the conclusion that the identity of phenomenal and physical states can only appear arbitrary is to accept that 'what is definitive of phenomenal character F is its transparent presentation of the colour property C—redness, say—of macroscopic things in the world'.[14]

But this suggestion provides no escape for the materialist. First of all, if it really is the case that 'qualitative differences do not outrun intentional differences', then it is difficult to see why anyone should have thought that there is a problem of an explanatory gap between the physical and the phenomenal at all. If phenomenal states are transparent presentations of some physical reality, directly representative of that reality, how could there be such a gap? As Lycan points out, a proper description of the micro-properties of water fully explains the visible properties of water; that's to say, the visual impression does seem to be a direct or transparent presentation of the physical reality. And, even more simply, an object is described as square and so big, and, lo and behold, that is what my visual

---

[13] Lycan, 79.

[14] See B. Brewer's review of M. Tye's *Consciousness, Colour and Content* in *Mind* **110**, No. 439 (July 2001), 871.

impression presents. But, as in fact Lycan himself reminds us, 'vision is a radically atypical and unrepresentative sense modality'.[15]

It is atypical because it is not possible to construe the sense of taste and smell as intentional or representative in anything like the way that visual impressions might be so construed. My visual impression of the object is a presentation of the object as correctly described. But it really makes no sense to say that my sensation of taste or smell matches the physical description of the object, or some aspect of the object. No description of any physical property can reveal why it tastes or smells as it does, or why it should have any taste or smell at all. The best that those who press the 'intentionality of sensation' line can do is to point to a causal link between molecular properties and smell or taste sensations—obvious enough, but really giving no ground for talk about smell or taste sensations as intentional or representative. Visual impressions are, if you like, directly recognitional: direct apprehensions of the object seen. If phenomenal experiences such as taste and smell are directly recognitional, as Loar, for example, claims phenomenal properties as a whole to be,[16] they nevertheless give very little idea of the physical properties supposedly directly recognized. My visual impression gives me the information that there is a large, square object in front of me. By contrast, my experience of the taste of a malt whisky gives me only the information that I'm having a certain experience of taste; even that it's the taste of malt whisky is information not conveyed by the experience of the taste. Overall, there is no escape from the problem poised by the explanatory gap for the materialist by pressing the idea that sensations are intentional or representative. In particular, there is no escape from the charge that it looks to be just arbitrary, something not further explicable, that neural state N is identical with phenomenal state P.

Perry suggests that the Molyneaux problem offers support for the materialist. Someone who is blind and able only to feel the shape of objects, would not be able to deduce a priori that the object he feels will present a certain visual shape.[17] Both in the Molyneaux case and in the case of the identity between the physical and the phenomenal, therefore, we have identities which cannot be determined a priori.

But the suggested parallel does not help the physicalist. First, the person who gains his sight now has two sensations, and there is no

[15] Lycan, 114–5.

[16] B. Loar, 'Phenomenal States', *Philosophical Perceptives*, 4 (Atascadero, California: Ridgeview, 1990), 81–108.

[17] J. Perry, *Knowledge, Possibility and Consciousness* (Cambridge, Massachusetts: The MIT Press, 2001), 205–6.

question that *these* are not identical, as Perry allows. It is the object sensed in these two ways which is one and the same identical object. The physicalist, by contrast, claims that the sensation is identical with the physical set-up. Second, whatever the recently sighted person may say, it is clear that he, like us, will come to see that a thing felt as square must look square. But we can never understand why the physical set-up has got to feel as it does. That remains sheer, brute 'metaphysical' necessity. We cannot escape from this by insisting that the apparent duality consists only in there being two ways of knowing the same physical reality. Whether the connection is a priori or not, the Molyneaux case does not present us with an explanatory gap. A full description of the object's shape will explain why it looks as it does, shapewise. No description of the physical facts, indeed no scrutiny of the physical reality itself, will reveal why it tastes or smells as it does.

V

I have argued that the notion that the subjectivity of the mental, and one's privileged, first-personal access to the nature of one's phenomenal states, can be accounted for as an implication of the perspectival nature of such knowledge, and in a way which is perfectly compatible with materialism, is quite untenable. I repeat that the claim that some aspect of knowledge is intrinsically private is an amazing one for materialists to be seen to defend. I now want to argue that the notion of perspectival, or first-personal, knowledge is in any case one that the materialist quite fails to understand. The materialist cannot account for first-person knowledge because they cannot account for the first person. There can, therefore, be no such thing as perspectival knowledge in a materialist world.

Self-regarding attitudes, Lycan says, differ functionally from other attitudes directed upon the very same state of affairs, though they have the same truth conditions, that state of affairs itself. I know that *I myself* weigh 12 stone while you may know only that GM weighs 12 stone, but it is, on Lycan's view, the same fact that we both know. There is no extra fact that is known or believed by me. Anyone besides me can use the word 'I' to designate themselves, and anyone else can use some word to designate me, but no one else can do both (only I can use 'I' to designate G.M.) If I refer to a mental state of my own, no one else can use the same, first-personal, term to designate the same state of affairs, and so no one can explain why that state of affairs feels like *that* to me. Introspection involves a very special mode of presentation, primitive and private.

Note, first, that while in the example about weight it does indeed seem to be the same fact that we both know when I know that I am 12 stone and you may know that GM is 12 stone, in the case of first-person reference to sensation there is something that only I can know, viz., that the state in question feels like *that*. The innocuous point about self-reference cannot account for this aspect, one which, as I've said, the materialist ought to find disturbing.

But that is only a preliminary point. The more substantial point is that the irreducibility of first-person reference, or representations *'de se'*, is not the innocuous feature Lycan and others suppose it to be. True, only I can use 'I' to designate GM; self-regarding attitudes are irreducible. But it cannot be supposed that the possibility of self-reference is something requiring no explanation.

Nagel famously argued that a complete description of the physical world leaves a vital bit of information unaccounted for: which of the billions of persons described is *me*. It seems to me a delusion to suppose that this point can be turned aside simply by reminding us that self-regarding attitudes are irreducible. On the contrary, the very possibility of self-regarding attitudes stands in need of explanation. And that explanation must provide an answer to Nagel's point, not simply something that attempts to turn it aside.

I do not think that the materialist can provide an answer to Nagel's point. It's pretty clear on reflection that the materialist's conception of perspective, and hence of perspectival knowledge, must be akin to the notion of a computer's perspective on its own workings, or even the refrigerator's monitoring of its own temperature. We, like them, it is supposed, are assemblies of physical elements, and each of us has an individual perspective both on the world and on our own internal states. There are about six billion humanoid 'rather large collections of small physical objects' (which is what we are in Lycan's view) in the world. The great majority of them indulge in self-monitoring of their internal states, just as refrigerators do, though in a rather more complex manner, and also in giving utterance to a first person word: 'I', or some equivalent. There must be a question for the materialist: what is for some seemingly arbitrary one of these collections of small physical objects to be *me*. It is utterly unclear what sort of answer the materialist could give to this question. That each of them engages in self-monitoring and self-reference offers not a hint of an answer.

David Chalmers gets on to this point, suggesting that 'the indexical fact [that some person is *me*, some point of view *mine*] may have to be accepted as "primitive"[18]. But then he claims that this unexplained fact is 'thin' compared with the 'facts about consciousness in all its full glory', and that admitting it would require less revision of our materialist world view than would admitting irreducible facts about conscious experience. I don't agree. *All* conscious experiences are irreducibly mine or not mine. This is not some 'thin' fact. Unless the materialist can make sense of this their strategy for accommodating qualia and phenomenal experience within a materialist framework collapses. Talk of such knowledge or awareness being 'perspectival' will be of no avail unless materialism can explain what it is for some apparently arbitrary perspective to be mine. Or rather, talk of 'perspectival' knowledge will be of no avail for materialists unless they can explain how the indexical fact that some particular perspective is *mine*, some particular assembly of physical elements is *me*, can be accepted as a primitive, irreducible or non-derivative fact. It seems pretty clear that materialism can offer no such explanation. For the materialist, any decent computer or indeed any decent refrigerator has a perspective on its own internal states, and any camera has a perspective on the world. But nothing akin to that sort of perspective can be irreducibly mine or not mine.

It is, therefore, a total misreading of Nagel's concern to suppose that it can be turned aside as pointing to no more than the irreducibility of first person to third person reference, and to regard this latter as an innocuous 'conceptual' point. Of course first-person reference is so irreducible, but this isn't a self-standing 'conceptual' point, having no ontological implications. Our possession of the first-person concept stands in need of some sort of explanation. Materialists cannot simply help themselves to it.

At one point Lycan imagines that he has become amnesiac or the like. Lots of evidence is collected and presented to Lycan about who he is, but, Lycan says, it's all third-person-descriptive. No one else can *explain why* W.G,L. or the person who is *F,G...* is *me*. Yet these persons are in fact both me. But the materialist *does* have to explain, if not *why* G.M. is me (which is surely not the relevant question), at least what it can *mean* for some small segment of the physical world, the G.M.-part, to be me. And there is no explanation to be offered.

VI

So far, I have argued that materialists attempts to accommodate phenomenal knowledge are totally unsuccessful. The startling claim

[18] Chalmers, 85.

is made that the notion of self-monitoring, or perspectival nature of phenomenal concepts, offers an account of why no one can explain why neural state N feels as it does; and so Cartesian privacy is reconciled to materialism. But no such reconciliation is possible, as Dretske saw. Further, the 'explanatory gap' between the physical and the phenomenal demands that the claimed identity between them is a matter of brute 'metaphysical' necessity, in a way which is a utterly remote from the usual paradigm of metaphysical or a posteriori necessity, that of the identity of water with H_2O. And recourse to the supposed representative nature or intentionality of sensations won't help, since sensations are not, in my view, intentional at all. Lastly, the whole structure of argument rests on the claim that subjective knowledge is perspectival, or pro-nominal (Lycan's word) or first-personal. But the notion of perspectival or first-person, knowledge rests on acceptance of a primitive indexical fact, the irreducible fact that one perspective is mine, one person is me. And that is not compatible with the objective standpoint of materialism.

More broadly, materialists cannot simply help themselves to concepts such as those of phenomenal knowledge, perspectival knowledge and pro-nominal or first-personal awareness and then claim that those features which seem to offer a threat to materialism are merely conceptual or epistemic, and have no ontological implications.

VII

I have been considering the failure of materialism to account for phenomenal knowledge, a failure, in fact, to understand or account for the first-person perspective. I now want to consider another way in which this failure shows itself, and that is in the failure to grasp what it is to ascribe emotion, either to oneself or to others.

Understanding the ascription of emotion is first-personal understanding, or so it seems to me. Ascribing emotions to others is, in the first instance, a matter of bringing the template of one's emotional experience to the behaviour of others. What it cannot be, I think, is a matter of discerning that the behaviour of another realizes some pattern of physical events, no matter how high-grade we take that pattern to be.

In Dennett's discussion on this sort of issue, we find him suggesting that there is after all some 'real pattern' which is common to, for example, all the possible finger motions and vocal chord vibrations, which together constitute the indefinitely many different ways a stockbroker might have taken to place an order for 500 shares in General Motors.[19] Similarly, there is some very high-grade physical pattern which is common to all the games of chess which, let's say, have been played to a conclusion. We don't simply have a vast number of different movements, with no pattern to be discerned. There is a pattern to be discerned. It's not a visible pattern, rather it's a high-grade, 'intellectual' pattern. But it's there, realized in the physical world. What's more, both the pattern common to all cases of buying 500 shares in General Motors and the pattern common to all games of chess played to a finish might be discerned without recourse to intentional notions—without, that is, any reference to the possible intentions and desires of any agent. In fact, we can dispense with Dennett's 'intentional stance' altogether, so far as examples of this sort are concerned.

But emotional understanding, the ascription of emotion to others, cannot be like this. There is no physical pattern common to every possible expression of indignation, or behaving to express gratitude or out of remorse, or to very possible case of taking oneself to be humiliated and seeking revenge. There is, of course, some real pattern here, but it's not a physical pattern. The pattern is simply that every instance can be seen as an expression of indignation, remorse, or whatever. And to discern that pattern requires first-personal experience of the relevant state of conscious, knowledge of what it is to be indignant, to feel grateful, or full of remorse.

It's a common claim that psychological categories are irreducible to physical categories. They certainly are, but materialists commonly suggest that the reason for this is that the states in question can be multiply realized. The notion of a thermostatically-controlled water heater can be variously realized, Papineau tells us; and so can psychological categories.[20] Well, no. There clearly is something physically common to all thermostatic water heaters: they all boil water and cut off when the job is done; and that's a physical similarity.[21] There's no such physical similarity in the case of

---

[19] D. Dennett, 'True Believers', in his *The Intentional Stance* (Cambridge, Massachusetts: The MIT Press, 1987), 26.

[20] D. Papineau, 'Irreducibility and Teleology', in D. Charles and K. Lennon (eds), *Reduction, Explanation and Realism* (Oxford: Clarendon Press, 1992), 60–4.

[21] Papineau actually says that there is nothing physically in common to all thermostats *apart from* their all turning the heater off when the water gets hot enough. That crucial qualification undermines the suggested parallel with psychological concepts.

expressions of emotion. In any case, to accept the idea of multiple realizability is to accept that this or that token of physical elements and events is an actual realization of the concept—of thermostatic water heater, or whatever. But I don't have the faintest idea what it could mean to say that my indignation at the treatment of a friend is realized as some particularly complex pattern among 'small physical objects'. Emotional understanding is a species of first-personal understanding of states of consciousness. It is not a matter of detecting some pattern of physical events, no matter how complex or 'high-grade', either in oneself or in others.

VIII

I want now to consider a different, though clearly related, line of argument. Adrian Cussins some years ago raised the following issue. The materialist seems to be committed to the claim that many stretches of human behaviour are capable of being explained in two different ways. To take one example (not in fact Cussins'): There is an explanation couched in terms of ordinary psychological or intentional notions which explains why someone, receiving an invitation to a dinner, is reluctant to accept because he learns that one of the guests is to be X and X has behaved badly towards him in the past. But on the other hand he has cause to be grateful to the person who is giving the dinner, and doesn't want to disappoint him. The decision is tricky, but eventually he decides to go, and turns up at the appointed hour. There is also an explanation of just the same sequence of behaviour couched in the terms of neurophysiology. Each explanation is quite independent of the other, but each explanation is a complete and sufficient explanation of the stretch of human behaviour in question. Isn't it a miraculous coincidence that one and the same stretch of behaviour is capable of two quite independent but equally sufficient explanations?

Cussins' response is that this is not a miraculous coincidence at all. He says, '*It is the nature of human cognition that that is how things are.* It is because humans have the cognitive nature that they have that their physiology meshes with folk psychology; that the two march in step' (Cussins' italics).[22] And so, we are to suppose, the explanation of one's behaviour in terms of being motivated by emotions such a resentment and gratitude, an explanation which, I

---

[22] A. Cussins, 'The Limitations of Pluralism', in *Reduction, Explanation and Realism*, p. 198.

have argued, rests on first-personal understanding, is paralleled by a sufficient explanation in terms of neurophysiology. That, Cussins claims, is not a miraculous coincidence at all.

But it is. It would indeed be a miraculous coincidence if the behaviour of one we see to be motivated by, say, resentment, jealousy, the desire for revenge, on the one hand, or by feelings of gratitude was capable of being sufficiently explained in neurophysiological terms, terms which make no reference to intentional states of consciousness at all. We *know* that the behaviour of the individual in question makes sense *only* as motivated by resentment, jealousy, or the desire for revenge. What could account for this view that there might be no problem here?

Almost certainly, it is the model of the mind as a computer. Taking a well-known example of Dennett's, we might be disposed to argue that the behaviour of a chess-playing computer can indeed be given two equally sufficient explanations, one in terms of the physical design of the computer including its software, and the other in terms of intentional states. We can take the 'intentional stance' in relation to the computer. Each explanation is sufficient, and quite independent of the other. Two sequences of events can therefore be explained in two utterly different ways, the one 'physical' the other intentional, and of course that is not a miraculous coincidence at all.

But to take this as a paradigm for the explanation of human behaviour would be a serious mistake. It is one thing to be able to construct a symbol-crunching machine like a chess-playing computer and go on to point out that its behaviour can be explained and predicted in two utterly different ways, but quite another thing to suggest that the behaviour of an individual moved to act from jealousy or gratitude could be explained in a way which makes no reference to jealousy or gratitude, or to any other thought or emotion. To act from gratitude is to be prompted to act by a conscious state of emotion. It is to act in a way which, one would have thought, can only be seen as an expression of gratitude; that is, it is to act in a way such that the sole explanation of that behaviour is by reference to the emotion of gratitude. The suggestion that the intentional explanation is just one of two possible explanations of the behaviour, and one that might be temporarily set aside in favour of an explanation in terms of a neurophysiological account, looks quite unacceptable. Talk of 'embodied cognition' will not advance matters here; it can only raise the question, what exactly is being cognized? In the chess example, the answer is unproblematical; symbols, and the rules for manipulating them. But in the case in question, the answer can only be: that one has been the recipient of a benefit for which one is grateful, or of a slight which one resents. I suggest that no sense can given to the claim that such cognition is embodied or realized in some particular configuration of physical elements. Here and elsewhere the computational model of mind goes sadly awry.

In fact the example Cussins himself chooses to illustrate the point raises exactly the problem I have just outlined. A mother holds her child close to the edge of the canyon so that the child can see the view; neurophysiology offers a complete alternative explanation which makes no reference to intentional states. And, Cussins claims, it is not at all miraculous that these two predictions march in step. Really? The trouble is that reference to such factors as the mother's concern and love for her child seems essential to the prediction and explanation of her behaviour, and it is quite unclear, therefore, how any purely physical explanation can be a sufficient account of what goes on.

The conclusion to be drawn from this case is the same as that which emerged from the discussion of Dennett's claim about 'real patterns'. If the intentional and the physical explanation march in step, that indicates that what is picked out by the intentional explanation is a functional/physical pattern, a pattern which could well have been discerned without recourse to intentional explanation at all. First-person understanding is something, therefore, that might be dispensed with. But to explain someone's behaviour as arising from a desire to humiliate someone, or to express gratitude to someone, or as issuing from remorse, is to explain that behaviour as a realization of a pattern which is *not* one that can be picked out from any physical viewpoint, and for the discernment of which first-personal experience and understanding is indeed indispensable. That is to say, different expressions of the desire to humiliate someone, or to express gratitude to someone, will certainly have something in common, but what they have in common will not be a physical pattern, no matter how high-grade. There is no such pattern, and a corollary of this is that the explanation of the individual token of (say) acting to humiliate someone cannot run parallel to a complete non-intentional explanation in physics or neurophysiology. And this point in turn is a corollary of the basic point that the claim that (say) one's feeling of indignation or gratitude is token-identical with an assembly or configuration of physical elements remains, in spite of all efforts to make sense of such claims, an unintelligible one.

Geoffrey Madell

IX

To deny the possibility of the intentional explanation of human behaviour running in parallel with a sufficient explanation in the physical sciences is, of course, to reject the principle of causal closure. So be it. Materialism fails not only to account for our knowledge of phenomenal states, but also to account for behaviour motivated by intentional, often emotional, states of consciousness.

In spite of this, the dominant view seems to be that our common-sense psychological explanation is not incompatible with materialism, and many find it inconceivable that this might be otherwise. Kim, for example, says, 'I don't see principled obstacles to a functional account of intentionality. Let me just say here that it seems to me inconceivable that a possible world exists that is an exact physical duplicate of this world but lacking wholly in intentionality'.[23] There are two points to be made about this claim. First, simply to claim that it is inconceivable that there is such a world falls way short of establishing that there are no 'principled obstacles to a functional account if intentionality'. In fact, the fundamental obstacle remains: we have no way of understanding how one's indignation, pride, joy, or whatever, could be realized as the behaviour of an assembly of physical particles. Until we have this, we cannot treat the suggested impossibility of a physical duplicate of this world which lacks intentionality as giving any support to a functionalist/materialist account of the mental.

My second point is that the claim that an exact physical duplicate of this world which lacks intentionality is impossible can be accommodated in a way which offers no support to a functionalist physicalism at all. An interactionist dualist could easily agree with this claim.[24] There cannot, for the dualist, be a duplicate world which lacks intentionality, since in removing intentionality from the world we are removing conscious states which are often causally responsible for behaviour. A physical duplicate of this world which lacks intentionality would require that many physical events in that world have no cause; for it is a world from which the mental cause of many items of behaviour has been removed. Clearly, these mental causes cannot be replaced by physical causes, for that would mean that this world is no longer a physical duplicate of ours. I therefore make no

[23] J. Kim, *Mind in a Physical World* (Cambridge, Massachusetts: The MIT Press, 1998), 101.

[24] Kim actually allows that abandoning physicalism in favour of substantival dualism is a serious option, and one that will entail the rejection of mind-body supervenience. See Kim, op. cit., 119.

use of, and in fact reject, the notion of a zombie, defined as David Chalmers does as a creature physically just like you or me but entirely lacking in consciousness. This speculation plays a large part in Chalmers thinking. In fact, it is epiphenomenalism under another name, though Chalmers is a bit shy about recognizing that. Anyway, it seems to me an untenable notion.

X

Materialism, I have argued, is undermined by its failure to understand the first-perspective in a number of ways. It cannot make sense of first-person knowledge of sensations; it cannot make sense of the fact that one perspective is *mine*, that one particular person is *me*. And it can have no understanding of the determination of behaviour by intentional states of consciousness (emotions, e.g.), an understanding which rests on a grasp of the first-personal perspective. These latter considerations, of course, point in the direction of interactionist dualism. There may be some sort of monistic account of the person (though I know of no attempt to give one which strikes me as remotely plausible), but it seems to me certain that 'robust physicalism' cannot provide such an account.

Language, Belief and Human Beings

DAVID COCKBURN

1. We may think of the core of Cartesian dualism as being the thesis that each of us is essentially a non-material mind or soul: 'non-material' in the sense that it has no weight, cannot be seen or touched, and could in principle continue to exist independently of the existence of any material thing. That idea was, of course, of enormous importance to Descartes himself, and we may feel that having rejected it, as most philosophers now have, we have rejected what is of greatest philosophical significance in Descartes' conception of the self. That would, I believe, be a mistake. Something akin to the Cartesian mind-body contrast still has a pervasive grip on philosophical thought across a whole range of issues. The contrast is, I believe, reflected in common philosophical versions of the contrasts between mind and body, fact and value, reason and emotion, word and deed, reason and persuasion, and no doubt others. My central concern in this paper is, however, a familiar philosophical understanding of the relation between, on the one hand, belief and its articulation in words and, on the other, action or feeling.

2. We are, in practice, ready to ascribe beliefs to others on the basis of their observed behaviour. Of course, these ascriptions are dependent, in varying degrees, on our knowledge of the individual's context; but given that context we sometimes, without hesitation, judge on the basis of his or her behaviour that, for example, he thinks the building is about to collapse, or she thinks her husband has arrived home. The term 'behaviour', as I am using it here, should be understood to include not only intentional actions—his running away, or her rushing to the door—but also the non-intentional expressive behaviour in which our actions are embedded: his manifest fear or her obvious joy, for example. I should note too that, just as I am using the term 'behaviour' to cover *more* than intentional action, I am using it in a way such that it includes *less* than everything that can be observed of another. For I am using it in the sense in which we may contrast what a person *does* with what she *says*: the sense in which we may, for example, judge that her words 'It's quite safe', spoken of the branch on which her young child is perched, are belied by her behaviour—by her obvious fear for example.

David Cockburn

There is, in general, a fair measure of harmony between a person's behaviour, her circumstances, and what she says. She takes an umbrella, it is raining, indeed very obviously so, and, when asked how the weather is, she replies 'It is raining'. But that harmony sometimes breaks down in more or less dramatic ways. For example, while the fact that her husband is systematically unfaithful to her is staring her in the face, her behaviour is marked by no recognition of this and she would fiercely deny his infidelity if asked about it. Again: while he says, as all those around him do, that the very old plane in which he is flying is completely safe his words are belied by his obvious terror. In some of these cases we may feel unclear just what to say that the person believes. And if a particular person's life displayed a systematic breakdown of the harmony of which I have spoken there would, I take it, come a point at which we would, in practice, have difficulty in ascribing any beliefs to him. Closely linked with that, there would come a point at which we would have little idea what to make of any of his words; for, to put it very crudely, his words, for example, 'It is raining' would tell us nothing useful either about the weather or about him.

I intend those remarks to be no more than a roughly accurate picture of certain features of how our talk about what a person believes operates, in practice, in our lives. My interest in this paper is with the relation between that and ways in which philosophers sometimes speak of belief and meaning. The suggestion that I will develop can be summarized in this way. A central feature of the imagery involved in Descartes' metaphysics of the self is the way in which the ascription of beliefs is quite independent of the fact that the one who has beliefs has a *life*. Indeed, it would be more accurate to say that, on Descartes' view, that which has beliefs—this being a mind that is lodged in a body—does *not* have a life: in the sense in which a life is something that involves activity of a human being in the world of trees, tables and other human beings. The continuing grip of Cartesianism is seen in the new philosophical landscape dominated by the theory of meaning in the way in which discussions of meaning characteristically involve no acknowledgement that those who speak have a *life*. This is reflected in the exclusive primacy given to the *linguistic* expression of belief—a primacy that is combined with an idealising distortion of such expression. With this goes a failure to acknowledge ambiguities in our lives that regularly frustrate straightforward ascriptions of belief; and a failure, too, to acknowledge a sense in which much of our thought is marked by a lack of recognition of facts that are staring us in the face.

3. From a Cartesian perspective, the way in which I spoke of a 'harmony', or its absence, between a person's behaviour, her circumstances, and what she says—and of the connection of that harmony with our ascriptions of belief—will appear potentially misleading. For, given that perspective, it has to be acknowledged that, as they say, it is 'in principle' possible that the whole of a person's system of beliefs is, in the terms that I have employed, *radically* out of line both with how things actually stand—that is, they are all false[1]—and with his behaviour. Indeed, to express the latter point like that fails to do justice to the character of Descartes' mind-body divide. For, given that divide, it makes no sense to speak of a belief as either in, or out of, line with a certain pattern of behaviour. As with all mental states, any systematic connection between a belief of a particular form and its expression in behaviour is entirely contingent. For example, the connection between my belief that someone is in pain and my helping her or manifesting pity towards her is no more 'intelligible' than would be a connection between that belief and any other pattern of behaviour. There is nothing in the nature of a particular belief that, as we might say, fits it for a certain pattern of expression.

Now contemporary discussions of thought and language are driven, in large measure, by a perceived need to avoid the two apparent sceptical gaps that the Cartesian imagery opens up. It is taken to be clear, first, that we must leave no room for the *general* sceptical possibilities that are opened by Descartes' picture of the relation between thought and world; and second, that we must leave no room for the more specific sceptical possibilities about the beliefs of others that are generated by Descartes' picture of the relation between thought and its expression. These aims are achieved, by philosophers who may share little else, by giving a certain form of priority to the linguistic articulation of belief. A person's beliefs are seen *directly* in what she *says*: in the propositions to which she is prepared to assent. And the central constraint on our interpretation of her words—on the meanings that we ascribe to them—is that most of what she says should turn out to be true (or, at least, well grounded).

4. This combination of ideas (though not, at least explicitly, the motivating concern with scepticism) is nicely exemplified in

---

[1] There are familiar difficulties about the force of the word 'radically' there. Roughly: even to be *wrong* about some things—for example, the colour of George Bush's hair—I must be right about an awful lot. But this kind of point does not bear directly on my central concerns in this paper.

David Cockburn

Davidson's influential treatment of radical interpretation. Davidson, following Quine and followed by many others, assumes that the basic evidence available to the radical interpreter consists in, and is exhausted by, the speaker's willingness to assent to or dissent from individual sentences concerning features of the speaker's immediate environment. The basic evidence is, then, of the following form:

> Kurt belongs to the German speech community and Kurt holds true 'Es regnet' on Saturday at noon and it is raining near Kurt on Saturday at noon.[2]

We identify which sentences Kurt holds true through what he says: most significantly through his sincere utterances of the words 'Es regnet', and, perhaps, through his assent to and dissent from the words—for example, 'Es regnet' or 'Yo, gavagai'—that we feed to him.

A striking feature of this approach is the paucity of the understanding of verbal behaviour that is included within the 'basic evidence'. One dimension of this is seen in the fact that there is no suggestion that a notion of *conversational relevance* might have some role to play in our interpretation of another's speech. Assuming, rather charitably, that we have some way of picking out assertions that are descriptions of features of the speaker's immediate environment, it is, one might have thought, going to be extremely difficult to hazard a guess as to what the speaker might be speaking about if we make no assumptions at all about *which* features of his immediate environment might be of some interest to him or those to whom he is speaking.

Of particular significance here will be those features of his environment that might have some bearing on the actions or feelings of the one addressed. The point about conversational relevance is, then, closely connected with a noteworthy feature of much contemporary philosophy of language. This is the fact that there is little reference to the ways in which linguistic articulations of beliefs may feature in offering reasons for action and feeling: to the way in which, for example, I may offer the fact that, as I express it, 'He is in pain' as reason for helping him and pitying him—as I don't, without special explanation, offer the fact that 'He has brown hair' as a

---

[2] Donald Davidson, 'Radical Interpretation', in his *Inquiries into Truth and Interpretation* (Oxford University Press, 1984), 135.

reason for helping and pitying him[3]. This point is, in turn, closely linked with the absence, in the image of the radical interpreter's resources, of any reference to ways in which *non*-verbal behaviour might have a role to play in providing an independent basis for determining what a speaker believes; and so for interpreting the words in which he articulates his beliefs. While it is true that, as Davidson notes, there are sophisticated beliefs that cannot be attributed independently of a grasp of the language in which they are articulated[4], at the level of '*basic* evidence'—our most fundamental attempts to make sense of another human being and her words—is not non-verbal behaviour a crucial guide to her beliefs? We can see, in her obvious terror, that she thinks there is something very dangerous in the woods out of which she has just emerged; and that—combined with the fact that she is addressing someone to whom the danger might be of some immediate relevance—provides a crucial basis for our attempts to interpret what she is saying. (She is probably not, at any rate, remarking on the clemency of the recent weather.)

It is assumed, in the general approach exemplified by Davidson, that we can at least characterize our use of words to say how things are independently of the fact that we have lives with others with whom we share certain interests, certain conceptions of what is important, of what bears on our actions and feelings in particular ways, and so on. Thus the radical interpreter can—perhaps must—identify *what* these alien speakers are saying quite independently of having any sense of the conversational context that makes it relevant to say it. With this, we can, on this view, make sense of the idea that an individual has mastered the use of a language to say how things are quite independently of having any sense of what it might be relevant to say at a particular time. Now I am not certain how we are to imagine this. Are we to think of a person producing sentences whenever they are true, or at least has grounds for thinking them true—over and over, and whether or not there is anyone to whom his words are addressed? But whatever we are to imagine, if the words

[3] While it is sometimes acknowledged—in passing, I think it fair to say —that this too is an aspect of our use of words that is relevant to claims about what we mean by them, it is suggested (for example, by Dummett) that this is a 'secondary' aspect of use that flows from, and so can be taken care of after we have got clear about, the central feature of use: that is, to say how things stand. Robert Brandom's recent book, *Making it Explicit* (Harvard University Press, 1994), is, up to a point, an interesting exception to this tendency.
[4] Op. cit. note 2, 134–5.

pour out quite independently of whether or not they could conceivably bear on any issue at hand, we will be imagining someone who may be a useful source of information, but with whom we would never dream of trying to *talk*.

It might be supposed that the problems here are eased by the suggestion that the radical interpreter might feed the native sentences, and, assuming that he is of a cooperative nature and that we have somehow managed to identify signs of assent to and dissent from what we say, we can test our hypotheses about the meanings of his words: for example, we say 'Gavagai' pointing at a rabbit and he nods. But now it is important to remember that the point of considering the radical translator among the natives is not to provide a practical manual for anthropologists (who I suspect turn to other quarters for advice), but to show us something about what it is to speak a language in which words mean the particular things that they do. And given that *that* is the aim we must ask: why should it be supposed that a consideration of this utterly artificial kind of conversation (if it deserves that name)—one in which one person feeds another sentences to which the other nods or shakes his head—should show us anything of interest about what it is to *talk*?

This image of the radical interpreter is presented by Davidson as an image of the relation in which each of us stands to all other speakers. Behind this image we see, I believe, a strikingly Cartesian combination of ideas. There is, first, the assumption that any systematic connection between a belief of a particular form and its expression in behaviour is entirely contingent: in its modern guise this doctrine being interpreted—explicitly by Davidson and implicitly by many others—in terms of the idea that a belief needs the addition of a desire (or 'pro-attitude') if it is to lead to action; and so that no linguistic expression of belief can ever, in itself, be an articulation of a reason for action or feeling. Second, it is implicitly assumed that what a person *says* is exempt from this general thesis about the explanation of behaviour: is exempt, indeed, from any of the contingencies on which other features of our behaviour are dependent.

In my next three sections I will take up in turn the three points on which I have just touched: the importance of the idea of *talking* with another, the idea that the connection between a belief of a particular form and its expression in behaviour is entirely contingent, and the idea that what a person *says* is exempt from any of the contingencies on which other features of our behaviour are dependent.

5. Locke offers us a clear statement of the place, and importance, of language in human life:

> Man, though he have great variety of thoughts, and such from which others as well as himself might receive profit and delight; yet they are all within his own breast, invisible and hidden from others, nor can of themselves be made appear. The comfort and advantage of society not being to be had without communication of thoughts, it was necessary that man should find out some external sensible signs, whereof those invisible ideas, which his thoughts are made up of, might be made known to others.[5]

A contemporary version of Locke's view would hold that the importance of language in human life lies in the fact that it provides each of us with an additional source of information: a source of information, not in particular about the thoughts of the other, but about anything of which he, but not I myself, already have knowledge. Perhaps this idea is to be seen in Brandom's proposal that: 'Conversation is the great good for discursive creatures. Extending it increases our access to information, our knowledge, and our understanding'[6]. It is to be seen, less directly but also less ambiguously, in Horwich's suggestion that: 'Lying is wrong because it engenders false belief and thereby does some *harm* to the person lied to. Thus the wrongness of lying is explained by the undesirability of having false beliefs'[7].

Suppose that we think that *the* important thing about language— *the* essential difference between the lives of those who have it and those who don't—is the way in which it provides us with an additional, and very fertile, source of information: a source of information not about the speaker, but about that of which he is speaking. Beings with language can learn, through what others say, about situations to which they have no direct access. If we think of the matter like this we will also think the central constraint on the interpretation of a language is that there is a high degree of harmony between their words and the world: that most of what they say is true. For *that* is what is needed if language is effectively to serve its central function. In this way, this conception of the place of language in our lives dovetails neatly with the demand to leave no room for the sceptical possibilities that are opened by Descartes' picture of the relation between thought and the world.

[5] John Locke, *An Essay Concerning Human Understanding* (1690), A. D. Woozley, (ed.) (Glasgow: Collins, 1964), 259.

[6] Brandom, op. cit. note 3, 644.

[7] Paul Horwich, *Meaning* (Oxford University Press, 1998), 186.

But the significance of what another says is not exclusively of that form. One thing that is missing here is a sense of the way in which conversation is a form of contact with another. What I have in mind here is illustrated, at one level, by the all-pervasive conversational interactions through which we acknowledge those with whom we have passing contact. ('Rain again' she says—as if I hadn't noticed.) It is illustrated at another level by the way in which taking seriously the words of another in a conversation involves expectations for how my life with this person may go on: for example, I get to know *him* through his words only in so far as my attempts to take them up in further conversation are not endlessly frustrated by totally discordant responses from him. With this, the wrongness of lying cannot, I take it, be articulated remotely adequately without a reference to the betrayal of the trust that is involved in such attempts to make contact with another.

I have linked 'making contact with another through conversation' with learning about the other through what she says. While there is, perhaps, an echo of Locke here, we must remember that what is at issue is not learning about, and making contact with, a mind that inhabits a human body, but learning about and making contact with a human being. I only make contact with *her* in a conversation in so far as her words are some indication of what else I can expect from her. Learning about a person through the beliefs that she expresses—for example, through her words 'Smith stole the watch'—involves, among other things: coming to see how certain features of her life—for example, her obvious distrust of Smith—are to be understood, and learning that certain things can be expected from her. If too many of such expectations are disappointed I may begin to take her words lightly; and at the limit, where I learn nothing about her from anything that she says, my relation to what she says will be quite different from that which is normal. Certainly she may, if she is compliant, remain a useful source of information: while a lack of any sense of conversational relevance will be something of an obstacle, I will, like the radical interpreter, be able to feed her questions and make use of her answers. But in such circumstances one of the ways in which language—and, in particular, the linguistic articulation of belief—is important in human life will be lost.

These extremely brief remarks about one aspect of the place that language occupies in human life are, I hope, sufficient to indicate that the difficulties that I raised for Davidson's image of the radical interpreter are not simply 'practical' ones. Our interpretation of a radically new language must be guided and constrained, not solely by a requirement that most of what its speakers say should be true (or well-grounded), but also by the ways in which their words fit in to the surroundings of their lives. It 'must be' if our interpretation is to be faithful to its character as *language*: to the character of what they are doing as *talking* to each other.

But the way in which I have spoken there is dependent on a controversial picture of the relation between belief and its expression in non-linguistic behaviour. I must now say something about that.

6. Despite criticism by a number of philosophers over the past 30 years or so, the assumption that there is always need of a desire, or 'pro-attitude', if someone is to be moved to action by a belief that she holds still has a powerful hold in various areas of philosophy. The assumption is, I suspect, the product of a number of lines of thought—all of them of a distinctly Cartesian tinge.

What *kind* of issue are we dealing with when we ask: is a desire always a necessary part of the motivational package that leads a person to action? The issue is not, I take it, one to be settled by an introspective examination of internal mechanisms. Nor is it to be settled by producing clear cases in which there is no possible gap between someone's having a certain belief and her acting in a certain way. There may well be no such cases. For there is a sense in which it is true that how one's actions are affected by a belief that one has depends on, among other things, what one wants. For example, my recognition that this man is in pain, or is hungry, may fail to lead to any attempt to help because I want to get home in time for the news. And it is not only wants that are relevant here: for example, fear or disgust may stand between my recognition and my stopping to help. And other beliefs may play a role that, in particular cases, needs to be mentioned: for example, my belief that it is almost time for the news; or, in a different case, my belief that this man is dangerous or that someone else will certainly stop to help if I don't. Different again, a desire or a moral principle may play a *positive* role in generating action. My disgust is overcome by my desire to impress the pretty girl who is standing watching, or by my conviction that one ought always to help people in pain or hunger.

Since people and their situations are complex a person's behaviour often fails to be a completely straightforward guide to what she believes. This creates a space in which the belief-desire assumption can flourish. To dislodge it we would need to dismantle in detail the Cartesian imagery that makes it seem inevitable. Consider, for example, the following line of thought:

'A belief is a representation of the way we think the world is' (300): the required direction of fit is that 'the thought content is supposed to match the world' (292). Thus, 'there is no belief to which we might not, in principle, be indifferent' (292). 'Intentional action is goal-directed: it seeks the realization of some state of the world' (291); and so something additional to a belief is needed if there is to be action. A desire is what fits the bill, for a desire is 'a representation of how we would have [the world] be' (300). A desire is, by definition, a state with whose content the world must fit: to have a goal just *is* to have a desire (on a broad understanding of 'desire'); and so a desire is always required in the production of an action.[8]

Consider the second premise of this argument. Is it true that all intentional action is goal-directed? A woman puts flowers on her husband's grave. It is tempting to say: anyone who suggests that the woman must have some goal in doing this has, at the very least, a seriously impoverished view of human nature—of how people may be moved to action. She puts the flowers there because it is her husband's grave, and the action will be seriously misunderstood if it is supposed that she has any goal in view in doing this. In response to this, it might, I suppose, be suggested that in a case such as this her goal is that there be flowers on her husband's grave. Now I take it to be clear that while that is, in a sense, a possible case it is certainly not the only one. More important for my immediate purpose, however, is the fact that the proposal involves the following assumption: the action is not the placing of the flowers on the grave, but something else that has the presence of flowers on the grave as a consequence. A certain set of movements of her body perhaps?

Well, consider another case. A man shakes his fist at the back of the driver who has cut out in front of him at the roundabout, with no intention, or expectation, that she will see his gesture. Again, one might have thought that the man need have no goal in doing so: there is nothing he hopes to achieve by it. (Indeed, being of a timid disposition, he might have refrained from his gesture had he thought it likely that it would have any consequences.) Have those who suggest that all intentional action is goal-directed simply overlooked cases of this kind? Well, assuming that the idea is not that the man's goal in such a case is the satisfaction he will feel as a result

[8] James Lenman, 'Belief, Desire and Motivation: An Essay in Quasi-Hydraulics', *American Philosophical Quarterly*, **33**, No. 3 (July 1996), 291–301. See also Michael Smith, 'The Humean Theory of Motivation', *Mind*, **96,** (1987).

of shaking his fist, the only possible candidate for a goal appears to be the shaking of the fist itself. The Cartesian imagery of 'the self' and 'the world', with my 'body' lying on the side of the world, has not, it seems, been left so very far behind.

Not all intentional action is goal directed. But further, much that is most telling in a person's behaviour is something other than intentional action. The man's shaking of his fist may hover on the borderline between intentional action and the non-intentional expressive behaviour of which I spoke earlier: for example, the oath he utters and the anger to be seen in his face. These—in particular, perhaps, what is to be seen in his face—may be what is most 'telling' in his behaviour in the sense that they are what is most revealing of his thoughts: the prudential and other motivating factors that may stand between belief and intentional action being, generally, less pressing and less forceful in the suppression of expressive behaviour. Further, and, closely connected with that, such expressive behaviour may be most 'telling' in the sense that we may be particularly *moved by* it. A woman may steadfastly deny that she believes her husband did what he is accused of, and her actions may be wholly consistent with that denial; but what her husband periodically sees in her face may tell a very different, and for him much more significant, story.

It is, I think, this second sense in which expression is 'telling' that is primary. We are moved by such expressive behaviour: we see things in a face—for example, resentment or suspicion—that disturb us, or, in other cases, fill us with joy. Perhaps we can imagine beings to whom this kind of expressive behaviour is of little, or no, importance: who are not moved by it. But we are not such beings, and our conception of belief is partially conditioned by this fact. For the significance that another's expressive behaviour has for us is reflected in our readiness to ascribe belief—and to hold on to such ascriptions in the face of countervailing considerations—on the basis of it. And the sense of the claim that various factors may stand between belief and intentional action is, in part, dependent on this: for it is this, in part, that creates a place for the idea that a person may believe—as the woman believes that her husband did what he is accused of—and yet not *act* in ways appropriate to that belief.

7. I want to turn now to an idea that I formulated in this way: what a person *says* is exempt from any of the contingencies on which other features of our behaviour are dependent.

A traditional, one might say 'Cartesian', imagery represents belief as an inner mirroring of a situation in the world. Closely linked with that imagery is the idea that the linguistic articulation of belief is simply an outward manifestation of such inner mirroring: in our words we present a picture of how things are with us—a picture of our beliefs—and so, at one remove, a picture of how things stand in the world. This last idea is taken up, and transformed, in much work in the philosophy of language. The linguistic articulation takes the place of 'inner mirroring' as the *primary* vehicle of belief: it is in what a person is prepared to *say* that her beliefs are to be most directly seen. Further, linguistic articulation is thought of as simply an '*outer* mirroring' of a situation in the world; and so, being a mirroring rather than a doing, as being exempt from any general thesis about the production of actions.

If we think of a person's words—what she says—as the primary mark of what she believes we need to say more about just how this is to be understood. We are, clearly, not to focus exclusively on what the person is saying *now*. For analogous reasons we are not, presumably, to focus on what she does *at some time* say: for we all have many beliefs to which we never give direct verbal expression. And if we put the emphasis on what she is *prepared* to say, the question arises: prepared to say when and to whom? Indeed, might there not be a belief that a person is not prepared to express to anyone in any circumstances? Not to *anyone* in *any* circumstances? Well all right. But then, given the right circumstances, most of us would be prepared to say pretty well anything—whether we believed it or not. So if we take it in this way 'what a person is prepared to say' is hardly going to serve as an adequate criterion of belief.

While it is a central assumption of most contemporary philosophy of language that it should be possible to see in a person's speech behaviour what he means by his words, and so that we must give central place to what people actually *say*, we have never really lost our Cartesian roots. Phrases such as 'assenting to propositions' help to conceal our backsliding. If 'assenting to a proposition' is simply a matter of 'giving an internal nod to a thought'—an internal analogue of the external nods of which Davidson's radical translator makes use—then it is hardly the public criterion we were hoping for. But if it is *saying* things then we must remember, as I will put it, just how much more goes into *saying* something than the simple recognition that it is true. Setting to one side for the moment points relating to conversational relevance and to lies, we must remember, on the one hand, the reluctance that a person may have to talk about a certain issue, and, on the other, the lightness with which things can be said: for example, the way in which we may simply mouth what everyone else says on some matter. The ease with which we forget such points is, I think, a Cartesian legacy: that which speaks is no more a being with a life—a life in which, for example, speaking on some topic may be difficult — than Descartes' thinking thing has a life.

The linguistic expression of belief is subject to contingencies of human life as markedly as is any other expression of belief. Once this is clearly recognized there should be little temptation to construe 'what a person says' as *the* primary mark of belief. With that, verbal expression of belief is not distinguished from other expressions by the fact that it is a *'mirroring'* of a situation while action and feeling are *'responses'* to a situation. But that is not to deny that a person's words have a special place within the range of forms of expression of belief. Verbal expression is marked off from others in the way in which in articulating a belief in words I am contributing to a discussion, and opening up the possibility of, or positively inviting, further discussion. I may be trying to convince another that things stand a certain way. I may be reminding another of something that bears on what she is about to do. I may be letting others know where I stand on some issue. And when I do any of these things I may be asked for my reasons for believing it.

When I tell another what I believe ('I believe he lied to her'), or simply articulate a belief in words ('He lied to her'), I open up the possibility of discussion of the reasonableness of what I believe; and when I inwardly articulate what I believe I open up the possibility of self-conscious reflection. Perhaps my behaviour has, for weeks, been marked by suspicion of, and hostility towards, Smith. But when I am on the point of verbally articulating the belief to myself or to another a question of what I am—in one of the senses of the phrase—prepared to commit myself to arises. In this sense, the verbal articulation of a belief may involve a standing back from my life. The philosophical imagery of the self as an essentially rational being that stands over and against the person's *life* has its roots, in part, in this truth. For all that, the truth becomes distorted in the imagery. In my final two sections I will say something about the form of this distortion and why it is important.

8. I spoke at the start of this paper of the fact that there is, in general, a fair measure of harmony between a person's behaviour, her circumstances, and what she says; and of the place this harmony has in our ascriptions of belief. The tradition in the philosophy of language that I have been considering drops 'behaviour' from this trilogy, and works, I have suggested, with an idealized—one might say tenseless—notion of 'what she says': a notion whose relation to what people actually say at particular times is far from clear[9]. The result is a certain sharpness in the characterisation of our lives: a sharpness that mirrors the sharpness of Descartes' divide between 'mind' and 'body', but which sits uncomfortably with the ways we may in practice carve ascriptions of beliefs out of the jumble of an individual's life.

Consider a simple example. John periodically says, as do all others in his group, 'Flying to New York is safer than crossing the road', or 'This stuff about walking under ladders is superstitious nonsense'. And yet his words are belied by his obvious fear, his skirting round ladders, and so on.

Here is a different kind of case, with a little more detail. While the fact is staring her in the face, Mary never says 'My husband is having an affair'. Is she *prepared* to say it? Well, one question that needs to be asked about this is: prepared to say it when and to whom? (To the radical translator, with his tape recorder, visiting her country from a far off land?) That aside, there may be a quite straightforward, and fairly general, sense in which she is *not* prepared to say it. Indeed, she cannot even bring herself to *think* it: her thoughts veer away from the evidence and from any topic that has potential links with her husband's affair. And yet we can see in her demeanour towards her husband, and, perhaps, in adjustments at other points in her life, a recognition of his infidelity. And we suspect that under certain kinds of pressure she would verbally acknowledge what is going on.

Consider one more example, of a different form again: one in which nobody in their right mind—at least as John and others in his group conceive things—would dream of endorsing the belief in question verbally. John would never dream of asserting that, or defending the claim that, members of other races do not suffer as we do on the death of a child, that the unintelligible noises that they produce are not language in the rich sense in which what passes between us is language, or that what interests them and matters to them is so different from what interests and matters to us that we could never have any form of meaningful human contact with them. And yet, in his attitude towards the suffering of members of this group, in his approaches to them, in his evident surprise when they respond to him in perfect English, and so on we see something that is most naturally read as beliefs of just these forms.

[9] Something akin to this notion appears to feature in everyday locutions of the form 'Would you say that it is going to rain?': an enquiry about his beliefs formulated in terms of 'what he would say'. I would be embarrassed by this were it not so clear, as it seems to me, that this *is* an odd locution.

Just how we will speak of a case such as this will depend on its details: on, perhaps, how inescapably the facts are staring him in the face, the degree of control that we can see in his veering away from the evidence, in the ways in which he veers away from danger areas in conversation, fine details of his behaviour, and in particular, perhaps, in his expressive behaviour, and so on. We have familiar forms of speech for dealing with the indefinite possible complexities of such cases: 'I can't bring myself to believe that he is dead'; or 'It was never really brought home to him before that people are being killed'. Since much of the work of normal speech is done by subtly nuanced expressions, by tone of voice and facial expression, by what is *not* said, and so on, we should not expect it to license, for the philosopher, a neat description of the varied range of cases that can arise. In any case, the task for philosophy here is not, I think, to record how we *do* speak of such cases, but to find a language in which such cases are most helpfully spoken of. And my suspicion is that our ordinary ways of speaking do a much better job here than does its philosophically regimented replacement.

We might, not entirely unfairly, speak of the philosophically regimented conception of language and belief as a 'quiz show' conception. What is at issue is, very roughly: how a person will answer questions if given good reason to answer, and to answer correctly—and, we might add, in 'sanitized' conditions where the question and answer have no place in a discussion, and so are firmly disconnected from his life. In a quiz show (I speak metaphorically here) Mary will assent to the proposition 'My husband is having an affair' and John will assent to the proposition 'These people suffer just as we do'. In quiz show conditions there is a relatively high degree of harmony between what a person says and how things actually are. And a philosophy of language and belief based on the model of such conditions will ensure that there is little room for the sceptical gap that Descartes' imagery opens up. In the way in which it does that, however, it will obscure very real senses in which we are sometimes deeply out of touch with how things actually are.

9. The regimentation of belief and action, and the associated neglect of emotion, that is characteristic of the tradition I have been discussing, does not, I think, provide the most helpful ways of speaking of some of the most important failings in our lives: some of the most important gaps between what people do and feel and what we judge they have reason to do and feel. The point may emerge most clearly through reflection on the kinds of work needed to correct these failings. Suppose that, in the identification of the meanings of a person's words, and so of her beliefs, one gives fundamental place to the requirement that most of what she says is true. This will have as a consequence that the most widespread deficiencies in our lives will be located, not in our beliefs, but in the step from belief to action: in the strengths of our wills or in the character of our desires. Now there are, I take it, procedures that we can follow in order to toughen up our wills: cold baths, grinding three hour sessions at our desk, that kind of thing. There are also procedures that we can follow in order to try to generate in ourselves desires that we lack, or strengthen desires that are too feeble to generate much action: hanging around with people in whom these desires are strong, reading inspirational literature, and so on. But central, and relatively neglected in the philosophical literature, are forms of work that seem better described in other terms.

Reading *The Death of Ivan Illich* it is brought home to me that I too will die some day. The aid agencies flood us with images of the suffering and try to focus our attention on the *particularity* of those who are starving. We are stopped in our tracks by television pictures of the people on whom the bombs are falling. In such cases it sometimes happens that, as we put it, one's eyes are opened to something: one is seeing for the first time what is really going on. One perhaps has nothing to *say* now that one *could* not have said before. For all that, the ascription to me of the belief that, for example, millions are starving will be much richer than it was before in that thoughts of their suffering will have a place in my life that they did not have before. And the point here is not simply that their suffering will be reflected in what I do and feel as it was not before, but also that, while there is a sense in which I *could* have said these things before—could have said, for example, 'Millions are starving'—I may now actually *say* it on suitable occasions.

The philosophical tradition will have it that since we all along knew of these things—as I think we should probably agree we did—we certainly *believed* that the bombs are dropping on people who are being killed by them, that I will die, and so on. But, while it is not, I suspect, helpful to be dogmatic about the precise terms in which such cases are to be described, I do want to suggest that the belief/desire model may be an obstacle to clear thinking here. In particular, that model may go with—it has in fact often gone with—the conviction that the processes involved here are fundamentally non-rational; and while there is, of course, plenty of room for debate about just what is and what is not correctly described as a 'rational' process, that debate will, I believe, be better conducted without the assumption that only what leads to a change in a person's 'beliefs' in the quiz show sense has a chance of being rational.[10]

[10] I am very grateful for comments on earlier drafts of this paper to Lars Hertzberg, Maureen Meehan, Anniken Greve and to participants in seminars at the University of Witwatersrand, Rhodes University, and the University of Cape Town.

Human Minds

DAVID PAPINEAU

1. Introduction

Humans are part of the animal kingdom, but their minds differ from those of other animals. They are capable of many things that lie beyond the intellectual powers of the rest of the animal realm. In this paper, I want to ask what makes human minds distinctive. What accounts for the special powers that set humans aside from other animals?

Unfortunately, I shall not fare particularly well in answering this question. I shall explore some possible answers, but none will prove fully satisfactory. In effect, then, this paper will tell the story of a failure. Still, it is a story worth telling, for it is an interesting failure, I think, and one with significant morals for the study of human minds.

Before proceeding, let me put to one side one familiar answer to my question. Most people, if asked what distinguishes humans from animals, would probably answer—'language'. Now, I certainly do not want to deny that our uniquely human facility with language plays some part in differentiating us intellectually from other animals. But it seems to me that, on its own, 'language' does not add up to a satisfying answer to my question. For we still need to know what humans *do* with language. Does language matter to human cognition because it enhances communication of facts, or because it facilitates social coordination, or because it allows records to be kept, or inferences to be drawn, or what?

Given some such hypothesis about the specific ability supported by language, it may turn out that language was constitutively necessary for that ability, in the sense that humans would not have had any distinctive such ability prior to the emergence of language. (For example, suppose that language was evolutionary significant specifically because it enhanced social coordination. Then one possibility is that no distinctive human powers of social coordination were available prior to the emergence of language.) On the other hand, it is also possible that the relevant ability preceded language, and that language evolved thereafter because it accentuated this ability. (On this scenario, distinctive human powers of social coordination would have come first, with language then being favoured by natural selection because it enhanced those powers.) Or, again, it may have been that the relevant ability *co-evolved* with language, with increased levels of one creating the evolutionary conditions for increased levels of the other, and vice versa.

However, we can ignore these alternatives here. For they all pre-suppose that there is some other ability distinctive to humans, apart from 'language' itself, which explains the evolutionary significance of language. That is, language is important because it enables humans to do something else, be that social coordination, or inference-drawing, or whatever. My focus in this paper will be on this further distinctive ability, rather than the details of its evolutionary relationship with language.

Of course, it is not to be taken for granted that the intellectual contrast between humans and other animals should be explained by reference to the historical evolution of just one distinctive human ability.[1] Maybe the evolution of a number of different abilities has contributed to the contrast (which different abilities could then have been evolutionarily related in various ways). Still, without denying this, I shall here set myself the limited task of identifying at least *one* ability which marks an evolutionary distinction between humans and other animals. We can worry about other similar abilities once we have succeeded in this limited task.

2. Means-End Reasoning

In what follows I shall explore the idea that humans are distinguished from other animals by their powers of means-end reasoning. I shall consider various versions of this hypothesis, but the rough idea will be that animals are not capable of the kind of reasoned selection of means to desired ends that is found in humans.

I first became attracted to this idea as a result of thinking about

[1] Nor is it to be taken for granted that any historically evolved differences between humans and other animals must be entirely genetic in nature. While there are undoubtedly important genetic differences between humans and other animals, the phenotypic intellectual powers that distinguish humans from other animals may well owe as much to non-genetic features of their cultural environment as to their genes. Cf. Deacon, 1997. (Note also that such non-genetic features can be vertically transmitted from parents to children, and thus subject to natural selection, in essentially the same way as genes are. Cf. Avital and Jablonka, 2000, Mameli, 2001, 2002.)

'Evolutionary Psychology'. Those who march under this banner ('Evolutionary Psychologists', with capitals, henceforth) embrace a number of commitments which go beyond the general idea that it is a good thing to bear evolutionary considerations in mind when thinking about human psychology (cf. Barkow, Cosmides and Tooby, 1992, Pinker, 1997). In particular, Evolutionary Psychologists advocate a strongly modular view of the human mind, which they see as a battery of devices each devoted to some specific purpose, such as recognizing faces, selecting mates, detecting social cheats, and so on. The standard metaphor is that of the human mind as a Swiss Army knife, containing a number tools each designed to perform some definite task.

However, this metaphor seems to rule out any account of how the overall selection of action is informed by the processing in the various specialized modules. It is noteworthy that humans seem able to reach decisions, form intentions, and make plans in a way that is influenced by a wide range of information about disparate subject matters. But how is this possible? Evolutionary Psychologists often seem blind to this issue. They often speak about people, and indeed animals, as 'deciding' what to do on the basis of the deliverances of their special-purpose modules (Cosmides and Tooby, 1992, pp. 54, 113). But what system enables the deciding? Evolutionary Psychologists are generally suspicious of Jerry Fodor's 'central system' (Fodor, 1983), some non-modular part of the brain which in higher animals mediates intelligently between the deliverances of sensory input systems and behaviour (Cosmides and Tooby, 1992, pp. 49, 93). And perhaps they are right to reject this specific model for the intelligent guidance of behaviour. But, still, there must be some story to tell about the way human decision-making and planning can be informed by an open-ended range of judgments from disparate input modules.[2]

This line of thought suggests a possible answer to my original question. Maybe some power of integrated decision-making marks a division between humans and other animals. Perhaps other

---

[2] Note that my worry here is different from the complaint that Evolutionary Psychology lacks a mechanism to decide which module to activate in which circumstances. I see no reason why the brain should not be structured so that this problem takes care of itself (*pace* Fodor, 2000). My complaint is more specific: we need some system that will allow information from different modules to be combined in selecting behaviour. Rather than asking for something to control the modules, I'm in effect asking for an extra module, to do means-end reasoning. (Cf. Papineau, 2001, sects. 1 & 5.)

animals, unlike humans, have no way of integrating information from different sources and using it to make well-informed choices. That is, maybe the difference between human and animal cognition is that animals do not have the same intellectual wherewithal to select means to ends.

However, this thought is not easy to focus. It is not hard to see why. After all, nearly all animals have *some* ways of selecting suitable actions, some way of generating behaviour appropriate to their current circumstances on the basis of various kinds of sensory information. So some more precise specification of 'means-end reasoning' is needed, if we are to have any hope of showing that 'means-end reasoning is peculiar to humans. 'Means-end reasoning' can't include *any* ways of gearing behaviour to circumstances, for even sea cucumbers have some of those. Rather, we need to specify a cognitive structure which selects actions in some particular sophisticated matter, and then argue that this specific mechanism is present in humans but not other animals.

In the main body of this paper I shall explore a sequence of hypotheses about such a specifically human cognitive structure. None of these hypotheses stand up. In each case it turns out that there is some well-attested species of animal behaviour that displays 'means-end reasoning' in precisely the specified sense.

So in the end I shall fail to find a satisfactory answer to my original question. Still, this does not necessarily mean that the search will have been fruitless. Much can be learned by exploring hypotheses that eventually turn out to be empirically flawed, and I would say that the path I have taken does much to illuminate the range of cognitive structures available to humans and other animals. But you do not have to take my word for this. Let me fill in the story, and you can judge for yourself whether it is one that is worth telling.

3. Inferential Limitations

My first attempt to identify a distinctive mode of human means-end reasoning involved this hypothesis: non-human animals can't piece together representations of disparate causal facts to infer that some behaviour B is good for some outcome O, unless they or their ancestors have previously experienced Bs leading to Os.

Note that this is not to claim that non-human animals never use *any* representations with the causal content *B will produce O* in selecting behaviour. As I shall explain in a moment, I take there to be a good sense in which even very simple animals do that. Rather the claim is that non-human animals are incapable of combining *different* items of causal information to select *novel behaviour*, where this is defined as behaviour B which is done in pursuit of O even though neither the agent not its ancestors have ever experienced B as leading to O.

Let me elaborate. First let me explain why I take even very simple animals to use causal representations of a sort. This will then bring out why there might be a specific problem with novel behaviour.

In my view, animals use representations of causal facts to guide their behaviour as soon as their cognition is complicated enough to involve *drive* states. By a drive state I mean a state whose purpose is to get the animal to perform behaviours that are good for getting some specific outcome like food, say, water, or sex, or avoiding danger, or so on. I take it that relatively simple animals, such as fish, have such states, in that they will only engage in feeding behaviour, say, when they are hungry. Suppose now that some such animal has some behaviour (B) which it is disposed to perform under a given conditions (C) if a drive directed at some outcome (O) is activated. Moreover, suppose that the animal is innately so disposed because its ancestors who did B in C succeeded thereby in getting O.

In such a case, I say, we should regard their drive as representing the outcome O. And correspondingly we should regard the innate disposition to do B in C given D as representing the causal fact that: behaviour B in condition C will produce outcome O. After all, by hypothesis the biological purposes of the drive state is to generate (behaviour which will lead to) the outcome O. In line with this, the behavioural disposition will serve its biological purpose insofar as it is indeed the case that behaviour B in condition C will produce outcome O.[3]

Some readers may object that this latter information, that B in C will produce O, is at best represented *procedurally*, not *declaratively*. After all, the vehicle of the representation is only a disposition to behaviour, not any sentence-like object in some language of thought. However, I am uneasy about placing any weight here on the distinction between procedural and declarative representation.

[3] In general I understand representation in 'teleosemantic' terms: the representational contents of cognitive states should be analysed in terms of the conditions required for them to serve their biological function. Cf. Millikan, 1984, 1989, Papineau, 1984, 1993. For an explanation of why representational content requires at least specialized drive states, see Papineau, 1998; and for more on the application of teleosemantics to behavioural dispositions, see Papineau, 2001, sects 2 and 3.

After all, dispositions to behaviour are not ethereal traits, but must have some physical basis; there must be physical differences between animals who have such dispositions and those who lack them. Moreover, note that these physical features will enter into a kind of rudimentary practical inference, when they interact with active drives to generate behaviour in a way that is appropriate to their putative representational contents: thus, the drive 'for O', plus a perception 'that C', will interact with the disposition embodying the information 'that B in C will lead to O', to generate the behaviour B. The disposition may not seem particularly sentence-like, but this doesn't stop it here operating in just the way a sentence-like representation would in generating a practical inference appropriate to its content.

So I have no qualms about speaking of representations of causal facts as soon as we have animals with drives and associated innate behavioural dispositions. However, while these causal representations will interact with drives and perceptions of current circumstances in rudimentary practical inferences, they won't necessarily enter into another kind of inference. Simple animals whose causal information is embodied only in innate behavioural dispositions won't be able to piece together separate items of such information to figure out any further links between means and ends.

Let me illustrate. Suppose that some primate is disposed to shake apple trees to dislodge the fruit when it is hungry, and also disposed to throw any handy apples at predators when threatened. This by itself won't be enough to enable it to figure out that it should shake the trees when it is threatened and no apples are to hand, because nothing in the cognitive structure specified will make a threatening predator, as opposed to hunger, a stimulus to shaking trees. It will have the information that 'shaking produces apples' and that 'throwing apples will repel predators', but won't be able to 'chain' these two general claims together to draw the relevant inference.

Of course, if some of its ancestors had genes which disposed them to shake the trees when predators appeared, then these genes would presumably have been selected, assuming those ancestors also had the disposition to throw the apples to repulse the predators. And this would then have instilled a further innate disposition in the primate, to shake the trees when threatened by predators. But the point remains that the two originally posited innate dispositions can be present without this further innate disposition, and then the organism won't be able to figure out the further implication. So here we have a precise sense in which organisms who embody general information about means to ends solely in their innate behavioural dispositions won't be able to perform novel behaviours. They won't perform B in pursuit of O in condition C unless their ancestors achieved O as a result of doing B in C and were genetically shaped accordingly. It's no good being innately disposed to shake the trees for apples, and being innately disposed to throw apples to repel predators, if your ancestors weren't also directly genetically selected shake the trees when threatened by predators.

Nor is the situation substantially altered if we switch from innate behavioural dispositions to those instilled by instrumental learning (that is, 'operant' or 'Skinnerian' conditioning). Here an organism may become disposed to do B in C in pursuit of O, not because B in C led to O in its ancestral past, but because B in C led to O in the individual organism's experience, and this reinforced its disposition to do B when C. (Gross, 1996, p. 161.) Here the cause of the disposition is different—individual rather than ancestral experience—but the resulting structure remains just the same. The information that B in C will yield O will be embodied in the organism's disposition to do B when it has a drive for O and a perception of C. And, given that the information is embodied in this way, the organism won't be able to combine separate items of such information to figure out that some new behaviour is good for some result in some circumstances, when it hasn't itself experienced that behaviour as leading to that result in those circumstances. So, to adapt the above example, an organism that has been conditioned to shake apples trees for fruit when it is hungry, and has also been conditioned to throw apples at predators when threatened, won't automatically shake the trees when threatened by predators, because shaking trees, as opposed to throwing apples, won't have been conditioned to the predator stimulus.

So, just as before, novel behaviour will be beyond the reach of the organism. True, instrumental conditioning can lead you to perform B in pursuit of some result O that none of your *ancestors* obtained from B. But this still requires that you yourself have previously obtained O after performing B. We still have no process that will lead you to perform B in pursuit of O when neither you nor your ancestors have experienced O following B.[4]

Before proceeding, let me make one brief comment about conditioned learning. In what follows I shall refer at various points to

---

[4] Some readers may be wondering whether the phenomenon of 'secondary reinforcement' would produce the requisite novel tree-shaking behaviour. I shall discuss secondary reinforcement in section 5, and its relevance to the tree-shaking example in footnote 5.

instrumental and other kinds of associationist learning. I would like to make it clear that these references carry no implication that associationist learning is more important than genes in constructing cognitive systems in animals or even humans. For all I say in this paper, cognition may be largely hard-wired, and conditioning may do no more than fine-tune pathways laid down by genes. My interest in associationist conditioning here is largely hypothetical: to the extent that it does play a part, does it lead to new kinds of cognitive architecture? And the point I have just made is that it does not, at least as far as the impact of instrumental conditioning on novel behaviour goes.

4. The Power of Classical Association

So there is the initial thesis. Non-human animals are not capable of novel behaviours, that is, not capable of choosing a means to an end in some circumstance when neither they nor their ancestors have previously experienced that means as producing that result in that circumstance.

Unfortunately, the thesis can easily be shown to be false. Animals can embody causal information in what I shall 'classical associations', as well as in dispositions to behaviour, and when these classical associations are combined with behavioural dispositions, then the upshot can well be novel behaviour in the above sense.

By a classical association I mean a disposition to move from a particular judgment S to another particular judgment T. Thus an animal might be disposed to move from *a change in light intensity* to *an edge of an object*, or from *a moving shadow* to *a hawk is overhead*, or from *the sound of a bell* to *food is arriving*.

Such associations can be innate, or can derive from learning. In the latter case, the relevant mode of learning will be classical or 'Pavlovian' conditioning, rather than operant or 'Skinnerian' conditioning. I shall use a familiar example of Pavlovian conditioning to illustrate the way in which classical associations give rise to novel behaviour in the sense specified in the last section. Since pretty much all animals are capable of Pavlovian conditioning, this will show that novel behaviour in this sense is effectively universal in the animal realm.

Pavlovian conditioning does not involve the reinforcement of some behaviour by a reward, as in instrumental conditioning, but rather the association of two stimuli: animals who have experienced stimulus S being followed by stimulus T will come to respond behaviourally to stimulus S in ways they previously responded to stimulus T. (You can think of the association as ensuring that the registration of stimulus S will 'activate' the state which normally registers stimulus T, and thereby will stimulate any behaviour that was previously triggered by stimulus T.) For example, a dog who has experienced the sound of a bell being followed by the nearby presentation of food will come to respond to the bell in ways it previously responded to the sight of food. For example, the bell alone will now make it approach the expected site of the food when hungry, in the way the sight of food itself previously did. (Gross, 1996, p. 157.)

This now immediately gives us an example of a novel behaviour in the relevant sense. Neither the dog nor any of its ancestors need previously have derived any advantage from approaching in response to a bell alone when hungry, yet classical conditioning will bring it about that the dog now does this.

It will be helpful to think about the process in representational terms. Suppose the animal starts out disposed to do B, in circumstances T, given a drive for O. (It is disposed to approach the food, given a drive to eat it.) Then, as argued in the last section, we can view the embodiment of this disposition as representing that *B in T will lead to O*. (Approaching food leads to eating.) Now suppose in addition that classical conditioning leads the dog to associate stimulus S with stimulus T, so that, when it registers S, this activates the state which normally registers T. We can think of the embodiment of this association as representing that *all Ss are Ts*. (Bells are followed by food.) Then we can view the new *behavioural* upshot of the classical conditioning, namely, the disposition to do B in the new circumstances S, given a drive for O (the dog now approaches when the bell sounds, given a drive to eat) as representing the fact that *B in S will lead to O* (*approaching when the bell sounds will lead to eating*). Moreover, we can regard this last claim as the conclusion of an inference from the two already attributed premises that *all Ss are Ts* and that *B in T will lead to O*. The organism puts together these two claims and draws the obvious inference that *B in S will lead to O*. It is thereby led to perform a novel behaviour—doing B in S in pursuit of O—even though neither it nor its ancestors have ever done B in S before (the dog has never previously approached when hungry in response to the sound of a bell).

So this is certainly one sense in which non-human animals can perform novel actions. However, this line of reasoning suggests that there may be another species of novel action which may be beyond them. The 'inference' I have just described allows animals to move

167

from *B in T will lead to O* to *B in S will lead to O*. But such inferences won't ever allow animals to figure out that some behaviour B is good for some result O unless they or their ancestors had previously experienced B as leading to O in *some* circumstances. Classical associations may allow them to transfer this knowledge from one circumstance to another, so to speak, but perhaps the underlying B–O means-end relation always needs. to be grounded in direct individual or ancestral experience of B leading to O.

5. Acquired Desires

But this idea doesn't stand up either. Consider the phenomenon known as *secondary reinforcement*. Standard learning theory tells us that some circumstance P that is not initially rewarding to an animal can come to acquire a positive value as a result of experiences which lead the animals to associate P with something already rewarding. Put it in more familiar terms, the animal comes to desire things it experiences as precursors or means to things it already desires. For example, suppose that an animal habitually passes some landmark on its way to feeding. Then it will come to desire to pass the landmark in itself. Moreover, passing the landmark will come to function as a reward on its own, as will be shown by its ability to reinforce other behaviours, even when it is not followed by feeding. (Of course, continued experience of the landmark not being followed by food will reverse the process, and render the landmark neutral in effect once more.) (Gross, 1996, p. 164.)

Now, secondary reinforcement can bring it about that animals will perform novel behaviour in the strong sense specified at the end of the last section: that is, they will perform some B in pursuit of O even though neither they nor their ancestors have ever experienced O after doing B. (Let me call this 'strongly novel' behaviour henceforth.)

I can usefully illustrate the point by describing an experiment of Anthony Dickinson's (Dickinson and Dawson, 1988, 1989, Heyes and Dickinson, 1990). In the first stage, rats are trained while hungry but not thirsty, in an environment where they gain dry food pellets from pressing a lever, and a sucrose solution from pulling a chain. Both the pellets and the sucrose solution satisfy hunger. If the rats were thirsty, however, only the sucrose solution would satisfy their thirst.

This prompts an obvious question: what will the rats do if they are thirsty? Will they pull the chain which delivers the sucrose solution, rather than press the lever? In fact they won't do this straight off. But provided they are given an opportunity to drink the sucrose solution when they are thirsty, even in circumstances quite removed from the experimental apparatus, they will then differentially pull the chain when they are next placed in the apparatus when thirsty.

This is now strongly novel behaviour. The rats are pulling the chain in order to quench their thirst, even though neither they nor their ancestors have ever quenched their thirst by pulling the chain before.

Dickinson himself takes this experiment to show that rats are capable of genuine cognition, involving the manipulation of some kind of sentence-like representations, and thus are more than simple associationist systems. As he sees it, the rats must have acquired the information that chain-pulling leads to sucrose solution from their original training. Later they learned that sucrose solution quenches thirst. And then they put the two items of information together, to draw the inference that chain-pulling is the thing to do if you are thirsty.

I agree that the rats can usefully be viewed as performing this inference. However, I see no reason to conclude with Dickinson that this elevates the rats beyond associationist systems and into some separate realm of genuine representation and inference, involving the manipulation of sentence-like representations. It is true that the rats must somehow be able to remember, from their original period of training, that the chain-pulling leads specifically to the sucrose solution. Moreover, there was nothing differentially rewarding about the sucrose solution, as opposed to the food pellets, in that original period of training—both sucrose solution and food pellets alike satisfied hunger. This may indeed make it seem that the information that *chain-pulling leads to sucrose solution* must be stored in some non-dispositional sentence-like representation—after all, since the sucrose solution wasn't differentially rewarding, it is not clear how the information that chain-pulling leads to sucrose solution could have become embodied in some specific disposition to chain-pull in pursuit of sucrose solution.

However, recall the possibility of secondary reinforcement. Since the rats, in their original training, experience the sucrose solution as preceding hunger satisfaction, the sucrose solution will have become a secondary reinforcer. In the terms I used earlier, the rats will 'have acquired a desire' for sucrose solution as such. Moreover, when this 'desire' is satisfied it will act as a reinforcer, and so the rats will have become disposed to perform behaviours which in their experience have led to sucrose solution—thus in the case at hand, they will have become disposed by their original training to chain-pull when they are in the experimental apparatus and desire sucrose solution.

Then later, after being given sucrose solution when they are thirsty, they will associate sucrose solution with thirst satisfaction, and consequently be disposed to activate their desire for sucrose solution when they are thirsty. And then they can put this together with the prior disposition, instilled by their original training, to chain-pull when they desire sucrose solution. The overall result, then, is that they will chain-pull when they are thirsty, even though neither they nor their ancestors have ever quenched their thirst by chain-pulling before.[5]

My analysis thus agrees with Dickinson in allowing that the rats are inferring the appropriateness of some behaviour (chain-pulling) to some end (thirst quenching) as a result of embodying the separate items of information that *chain pulling will lead to sucrose solution*, and *sucrose solution quenches thirst*. But I disagree with Dickinson's view that these items of information need to be embodied in some explicit sentence-like manner, open to general logical manipulation, as opposed being embodied in dispositions to behaviour which can be combined in the way sketched above. I am happy to view the rats as performing an inference. But they do this by deriving a complex disposition from the combination of two other dispositions, rather than by manipulating explicit sentence-like representations. Once they are disposed to desire sucrose when thirsty, and disposed to chain-pull when they desire sucrose, then they will derivatively chain-pull when thirsty, and therewith derive the conclusion that chain-pulling is a means to quenching thirst.[6]

---

[5] Consider the earlier example of an animal conditioned to shake apple trees when hungry, and to throw apples when threatened by predators. In section 3 I argued that this alone wouldn't make it shake the trees when threatened. But if its hunger gives it a secondary desire to have apples to hand, the lesson of Dickinson's rats will apply here too: the experiences that conditioned the primate to tree-shake-when-hungry will also dispose it to tree-shake-when-it-desires-to-have-apples-to-hand. And if the appearance of predators also triggers the secondary desire to have apples to hand, the appearance of predators will derivatively trigger tree-shaking.

[6] Given the structural similarity we have observed so far between learned and genetically fixed behaviours, some readers may be wondering whether there is a innate analogue of the process by which dispositions resulting from secondary reinforcement give rise to novel behaviour. We will indeed find such an analogue, provided we are prepared to posit suffi-

6. Observation versus Experience

Dickinson's experiment certainly shows that rats can perform strongly novel actions, that is, that they can do some B in pursuit of some O even though neither they nor their ancestors ever did B in pursuit of O before. But if I am right about the rats embodying the relevant information in dispositions to action, rather than in some sentence-like format, it remains possible that rats are limited in another way. Maybe they are incapable of *learning from observation*, as opposed to learning from experience. Indeed, perhaps this inability differentiates all other animals, and not just rats, from humans.

Let me explain. In the story I have just told, I credited the rats with various items of information to the effect that some action in some situation will lead to some result. Their potential for strongly novel actions then derived from their ability to piece such items of information together. They 'knew' that *chain-pulling leads to sucrose solution*, and that *sucrose solution quenches thirst*, so they were able to 'infer' that chain-pulling is a means to thirst quenching. But note that, in order to acquire the original items of means-end information, the rats needed to have performed the relevant actions themselves, and needed themselves to have experiences the reward of the relevant result. The rats acquired the relevant information because they had experienced their own chain-pulling as leading to their getting sucrose solution, and their own consumption of sucrose solution as quenching their own thirst.

This means that, for all that has been said so far, the rats will have no way of observing some *other animal* performing some B and getting some result O, and on this basis acquiring the information that B leads to O. Still less will they be able to observe inanimate nature 'performing' some action B which leads to O, and thence inferring that B is a means to O.

I can usefully illustrate the point with an anecdote.[7] The trainers of a troop of monkeys on a research station in Puerto Rico

[7] I was told this story by Ned Block, who in turn acquired it from Marc Hauser. It won't matter too much if some of the signal has been lost in the transmission, since I intend the anecdote only to illuminate the logic of my analysis, not to provide empirical backing.

ciently fine-grained *innate desires*. Imagine that a primate is innately disposed to desire apples when threatened by predators, solely because of ancestral events involving predators, and innately disposed to shake trees when it desires apples, solely because of ancestral events involving food deprivation. Then this could lead it to shake the tree when threatened, even though none of its ancestors ever had ever done this before.

occasionally reward the monkeys by putting coconuts in the camp fire; the coconuts then burst open, making the tasty flesh available to the monkeys. However, the monkeys seem unable to learn from this that they can put the coconuts in the fire themselves. Moreover, even when one particular monkey somehow acquired the trick, the other monkeys seemed not to cotton on that they could do it themselves.

Given the points made in this paper so far, this needn't seem so surprising. So far I have considered cases where animals acquire the information that B will lead to O because they (or their ancestors) have themselves performed B and themselves later received O. But the mechanisms behind this will be blind to the observation of *another* animal doing B and getting O. After all, there is nothing rewarding, or otherwise advantageous, to the observer in seeing another animal enjoying outcome O. And even if the observer does get to enjoy the reward—it shares the coconut flesh, say—this still won't do the trick. For this reward won't reinforce the behaviour B—placing coconuts in the fire—since the observer hasn't itself performed this behaviour. The observer didn't place a coconut in the fire prior to the reward—it was just sitting there watching.

It is true that observation of another animal doing B and getting O can give rise to classical conditioning. The sight of the other animal doing B can come to make the observer anticipate O. In the coconut example, the observers may come to respond to the sight of the coconut being put onto the fire with their pre-existing responses to food, such as salivating and approaching. But this will do nothing to get the observers doing B themselves. The classical association will make you salivate and approach when you see another animal putting a coconut in the fire—it won't get you putting the coconut in the fire yourself in the first place.

So here is another possible way in which human intellects may outstrip those of other animals. Perhaps animals are unable to learn about means to ends from observation. Seeing another animal doing B as a means to O won't help them to do B in pursuit of O. Yet humans clearly can learn in this observational way. Indeed humans can draw such lessons from inanimate nature, as well as from animate agents. (If I saw a coconut landing in a fire by chance after falling from a tree, and then bursting from the heat, I would infer that I myself can also burst coconuts by putting them in fires.)

In a moment I shall consider whether this ability to learn from observation does indeed mark a difference between human and animal cognition. But first it will be helpful to make some related points.

7. Mimicry, True Imitation and Empathy

Some readers may be wondering how the issue of learning from observation relates to the topic of animal imitation. There is no doubt that animals often learn behaviour from other conspecifics. One oft-cited example is the rapid spread in the 1940s among British blue tits of the ability to peck open the tops on milk bottles to get at the cream inside. Potato-washing in the sea by Japanese macaques is another frequently mentioned case. Again, patterns of tool-use among both chimpanzees and crows are known to vary between populations within species, suggesting that these behaviours too are copied from conspecifics.

There is no question of engaging with extensive literature on animal imitation in this paper. (For a survey, see Shettleworth, 1998, ch. 10.) Let me content myself by making what I take to be two uncontentious points.

First, while there is no question that patterns of behaviour can spread from some animals to others, as in the examples just mentioned, it is a further issue whether such 'social learning' requires any specific imitative abilities. Thus, one possible explanation for the standard examples is simply that animals tend to follow each other around. Because of this, when animals who are expert in some behaviour go to the sites (milk bottles, sea shores) where they can practice their craft, novices will follow them, and thus be led to those special places where ordinary trial-and-error instrumental learning can instil the relevant behaviour. Without the experts to lead them, they wouldn't be in the right places for their ordinary behavioural experimentation to yield the relevant rewards. Again, another obvious explanation for some examples of 'social learning' is simply that animals can learn from others where certain things are. If I see an expert roll over a log to find grubs, then I will become aware that grubs lie under logs, and thereafter use my pre-existing abilities to remove obstacles to uncover the grubs myself. (Cf. Tomasello, 2000.)

Second, even when there is evidence for specific initiative abilities, these not involve any appreciation of causal links between behaviour and outcome. Let us define *mimicry* as a tendency for an animal to repeat behaviour that it observes in another conspecific. Clearly an animal might be capable of mimicry, even if it is not able to appreciate what the behaviour in question is *good for*. It would then do B simply because it had observed another animal doing B, and not because it appreciated that B would lead to some O. It would be 'parroting', so to speak—it would simply be copying the behaviour, without understanding its significance. There is a large amount of evidence that some animals are capable of mimicry in this sense. But, as just observed, this won't amount to learning from observation in the sense of learning that there is a *connection* between B and some attractive further result O. Mimicry per se may connect your own behaviour with the observation of others performing the same behaviour, but it won't connect your behaviour with any intended outcomes.

Henceforth let me adopt the phrase 'true imitation' for the more sophisticated ability to learn, from observing other animals, that some behaviour B is connected with outcome O. As I observed at the end of the last section, it is clear that humans have this ability, even if other animals do not. So let me offer one speculation about the mechanism behind this ability. (This speculation can be detached from the rest of my argument, but I think it is of some interest in its own right.)

My speculation is that true imitation arises once an 'empathetic faculty' is added to a capacity for parrot-like mimicry. Suppose that, when you observe someone else getting something that you yourself desire, you undergo some vicarious satisfaction as a result of the observation. For example, when you are hungry and see someone else eating, you simulate their hunger satisfaction with a 'faint' version of your own.

Now put this empathetic faculty together with a capacity for mimicry. Take a case where you desire O, and observe someone else doing B and getting O. Your basic tendency to mimicry inclines you to do B. Your empathetic faculty then gives rise to a faint simulation of the satisfaction you would derive from O. This vicarious reward will then reinforce, via normal instrumental conditioning, your tendency to do B when you desire O. The result is thus that your observation of B leading to O leads to your becoming disposed to do B when you desire O. So this gives us a mechanism whereby the observation of some *other* animal getting O from B can give rise to *your* acquiring the information that B leads to O. As before, the information will be embodied in a disposition to do B when you desire O, but now we have an account of how this disposition can be instilled by observation rather than by first-hand experience.[8]

[8] There are obvious affinities between the idea that true imitation derives from the empathetic ability to experience vicarious satisfaction and recent work on 'understanding of mind', particularly simulationist accounts thereof (see Davies and Stone, 1995a and 1995b, Carruthers and Smith, 1996). Tomasello (2000) also suggests that the capacity for true imitation depends on understanding of mind, but for rather different reasons from mine: he

At this point, let me make some brief observations about *imagi-nation* and means-end reasoning. It is a familiar thought that the ability to connect previously unperformed behaviours with intend-ed outcomes might somehow be facilitated by sensory imagina-tion—we figure out that B is a means to O by imagining B being fol-lowed by O. And this use of imagination might seem to offer a more basic and general mechanism for innovatory means-end reasoning than that provided by imitative learning from observation. However, I think that this puts the cart before the horse. As I see it, the power of imagination to inform means-end reasoning depends on imitative learning, rather than vice versa.

Let me explain. I take it that sensory imagination activates some of the same parts of the sensory cortex as would be activated by genuine observations of a similar scenario. When I imagine seeing a red square, this activates some of the same parts of my visual cortex as would be activated if I were really looking at a red square. We might here recall Hume's terminology, according to which sensory imagination is a 'faint replica' of the real thing.

However, if this is the right picture of sensory imagination, then it is unclear how imagining a means-end sequence can be a more basic route to action than actually observing it. If really seeing someone doing B and getting O isn't enough to get you doing it yourself, then 'faintly seeing' an imagined person doing the same seems even less likely to do the trick, for just the same reasons.

Of course, once true imitation does emerge, then we can expect sensory imagination to inform means-end understanding, though not as some separate mechanism, but as a corollary of true imita-tion. The basic mechanism behind true imitation, as I have told the story, is that actual observing a conspecific doing B and getting O can lead, via mimicry and vicarious reinforcement, to you yourself doing B in pursuit of O. However, if sensory imagination is a 'faint version' of actual observation, then we would expect it to produce the same result for similar reasons. In effect, you will be led to imitate the imagined person's pursuit of O by B. Thus, visually imagining someone doing B will lead, via the tendency to mimicry, to a disposition to do B yourself; and then imagining the visualized person receiving O will lead, via empathy, to your own vicarious

---

does not view the widespread absence of true imitation as due to the inability of standard associationist mechanisms to allow observational learning of means-end connections; relatedly, he takes understanding of mind to be important simply because it allows observers to appreciate what their demonstrators *intend*, not because it yields empathy.

satisfaction—and thus you will acquire a disposition to do B in pursuit of O via instrumental conditioning, as before.

8. Japanese Quails

The overall story I have told so far implies one definite prediction. Non-human animals who learn by observing other animals will be 'insensitive to demonstrator reward'. They will be capable of 'mimicking' the behaviour of conspecifics, but will do so with no appreciation of outcomes, and so will not learn differentially depending on whether or not their demonstrator's behaviour leads to some rewarding outcome. According to my latest hypothesis about the distinctive feature of human cognition, only humans can truly imitate, in the sense of copying an action just in case you have observed it leading to some result that you yourself desire.

A wide range of empirical data are consistent with the prediction of animal insensitivity to demonstrator reward. Thus Sara Shettleworth, in her comprehensive text *Cognition, Evolution and Behaviour* (1998) says '…whether or not the observer must also see the demonstrator obtain a reinforcer… is a question that has hardly been tackled' (p. 473), and again '…the role of demonstrator reward has been little studied' (p. 473).

However, a particular series of recent studies by Thomas Zentall and his associates shows clearly that there is at least one animal species that are sensitive to demonstrator reward—Japanese quails. Akins and Zentall (1998) trained demonstrator Japanese quails either to peck at or to step on a treadle. They then allowed other Japanese quails to observe this behaviour. Their findings were that the observer quails copied the demonstrator's behaviour only if they also observed the demonstrator receiving a food reward for the behaviour.

Interestingly, a further study (Dorrance and Zentall, 2001) showed that this effect required the observers to be hungry *when they observed the demonstrator's behaviour*. It wasn't enough that they be hungry when they were later placed in the apparatus and given the opportunity to peck at or step on the treadle. It turned out that even hungry observer quails wouldn't display the relevant behaviour at this later stage, if they hadn't also been hungry at the earlier observational stage.

These experiments clearly indicate that Japanese quail are capable of true imitation of the kind I have hypothesized to be peculiar to humans.

Moreover, the second study by Dorrance and Zentall suggests that quails' imitative powers may hinge on just the kind of empathetic identification that I speculated may be the basic mechanism behind human imitation. This would explain the striking fact that the quails won't imitate unless they are hungry at the time of observation. At first sight, this can seem puzzling: why can't the quails just store the observationally-derived information that pecking at the treadle, say, yields food, and then use this later when they are hungry? Why should they need to be hungry at the time of observation in order to acquire the information? However, if the route from observation to behaviour proceeds. via reinforcement of mimicking tendencies by empathetic reward, as outlined in the last section, then the Dorrance and Zentall finding becomes unpuzzling. The observer quails won't feel any empathetic reward at the sight of another feeding, unless they themselves are hungry.

Of course, other explanations remain possible. Maybe the function of observer hunger is simply to make the observers interested in matters to do with food. Perhaps they don't pay attention to what the demonstrator is up to, if they aren't hungry. If this is right, then perhaps there is some quite different mechanism behind the quails' sophisticated imitative abilities, nothing to do with the empathetic reinforcement model sketched in the last section.

Or, perhaps reinforcement is indeed involved, but not in a way that involves empathy. Consider this possibility. Quails are social creatures, and so in the normal course of events will often have observed others eating while they themselves are feeding. Because of this, the sight of another quail feeding could come to function as a secondary reinforcer—after all, this visual stimulus will characteristically have been experienced as preceding hunger satisfaction. This secondary reinforcer could then combine with basic mimicry to explain the quails' imitative abilities: their observation of the demonstrator will trigger their mimicking tendencies—and then those tendencies will be secondarily reinforced by the sight of the demonstrator eating. Moreover, this story also promises to explain why the learners have to be hungry when observing. If the sight of others feeding derives its status as a secondary reinforcer from experience associating it with hunger satisfaction, then it can be expected to function as a secondary reinforcer only when the observer is hungry.[9]

Let me not continue. The precise mechanism behind the quails'

[9] This possible explanation was suggested to me in conversation by Cecilia Heyes.

abilities is clearly an empirical matter, to be decided by further experimental investigation, not by speculation. (I leave it as an exercise for readers to design experiments to decide between the three mechanisms suggested above.)

In any case, Japanese quail provide a clear counter-example to the hypothesis that only humans are capable of true imitation. True, once we discover the quails' mechanism, it may turn out that their imitative ability is relatively superficial, resting on some idiosyncratic quirk of their psychology, such as secondary reinforcement by observations of others eating, in which case it may be possible to argue that some more powerful species of empathy-involving imitation is peculiar to humans after all. Alternatively, however, it may be that just the same empathy-involving mechanism underlies true imitation in both humans and Japanese quails, and so presumably in many other species too, in which case the distinctive features of human cognition must lie quite elsewhere.

Still, as I said, these are empirical matters, and I do not propose to offer any further hostages to empirical fortune. None of my hypotheses about the special power of human cognition have stood up to the empirical data, and at this stage I have no further replacements to offer. Rather, I would like to conclude by drawing three general morals from my frustrated search for the key to human cognition.

9. General Morals

First Moral: The Significance of Observation. I hope I have at least persuaded readers that the ability to learn from observation is important, whether or not it is anything to do with the distinctive features of human cognition. By 'learning from observation' here I mean specifically the ability to acquire information about potential means-end connections by observing another organism getting the end from the means, as opposed to performing the means and enjoying the end yourself.

In the course of this paper I have showed how standard mechanisms of associationist learning, namely, instrumental, classical and secondary conditioning, can generate various species of novelty, informing organisms that given behaviours will lead to given ends in given circumstances, even when neither the organisms nor their ancestors have experienced those behaviours as leading to those ends in those circumstances. However, all such associationist conclusion must be derived from pieces of information which *are* based on individual or ancestral experience. They can only deal with connections between actions previously performed at first hand and results previously experienced at first hand (even in cases where those specific results haven't previously followed from those specific actions, as with Dickinson's rats). Standard associationist mechanisms therefore offer no way of learning means-end connections from external observation rather than first-hand experience.

So, however the trick is done, the ability to learn about means-end connections from observation rather than experience marks a significant advance in cognition. Of course, there are many other facets to advanced means-end reasoning in humans. I earlier touched on a possible role for *sensory imagination* in making connections between potential means and ends. I also mentioned the ability to learn about potential means-end connections by *observing inanimate nature*, as opposed to observing other organisms. Moreover, once language emerges, the representations of such causal connections will be open to *unlimited logical manipulation*, which will vastly enhance the ability of agents to figure out novel behavioural routes to their ends. They will also be able to formulate *complex plans*, perhaps facilitated by an ability to commit themselves to *fixed intentions in advance*.

However, I think it would be a mistake to think of these developments as eliminating older systems of behavioural control and replacing them with something quite different. In general, evolution doesn't work like that. Rather, each new development must build on pre-existing systems, adding some modification which yields some immediate selective advantage. Given this, we shouldn't expect advanced forms of means-end reasoning to direct behaviour via completely novel mechanisms. Rather, they will feed into prior systems of behavioural control, giving us new ways of adjusting the structures of behavioural dispositions that these older systems worked with.

From this perspective, we can view means-end reasoning as being built up step by step from the kind of basic cognitive architecture produced by innate structures and associationist mechanisms. Each new step provides some extra way of shaping that architecture. And I am inclined to suppose that one absolutely crucial step was the ability to acquire new behavioural dispositions directly from external observation, rather than from first-hand experience. Natural selection and associationist learning can give rise to many powerful and novel behavioural strategies, as I hope I have shown, but they do not lead easily to learning from observation. I may be wrong in my speculations about how this barrier was overcome, and it may

179

have little to do with the distinctive features of human cognition, but I hypothesize that it was a crucial evolutionary development in any case.

Second Moral: The Prevalence of Representation. Much recent thinking about cognition presupposes a sharp dichotomy between computational (propositional, conceptual) cognition, which is presumed to allow general logical operations over sentence-like representations, and mechanistic (associationist, non-conceptual) psychology, which involves no representation and hence no inference as such. This division is upheld by a wide range of theorists, including those who differ on exactly whether they would place the divide (cf. Dickinson and Balleine, 2000, Sterelny, 2000, Fodor, 2000). For example, the division is upheld both by thinkers in the animal learning tradition, most of whom would restrict genuine representation to higher mammals, if not to humans, and also by committed computationalists, most of whom hold that computation and representation is widespread throughout the animal kingdom.

I hope that this paper has done something to show that this sharp dichotomy is misconceived. In earlier sections I showed that we can properly attribute representational contents as soon as organisms are complex enough to have specialized drives which interact with their perceptions and behavioural dispositions. Moreover, many of the interactions between these states can properly be viewed as inferences which appropriately generate further contentful states. So, from the perspective of this paper, representation by no means requires sentence-like vehicles processed as in a digital computer, but will be present as soon as we have the kinds of dispositional architectures produced by associationist learning or analogous processes of natural selection.

At the same time, we should recognize that certain kinds of cognitive architecture, even those that sustain representation, are limited in the range of inferences that they can perform. Thus, my earlier apples-and-predators example showed how an organism can behaviourally embody the information that B will lead to O, and the information that D will lead to B, and yet not be able to infer that D will lead to O. Again, the monkeys-and-coconuts example showed how an organism might represent that B will be followed C in the form of a classical association between perceptions of B and C, and yet not be able to translate this into the practical conclusion that it should itself perform B when it wants C.

Some readers may feel inclined to respond that these inferential limitations only show that we do not yet have genuine representation, since representation by definition involves sentence-like vehicles which are open to a full range of logical manipulations. But I think that this is quite the wrong answer. If this paper has done anything, I hope it has shown how much sophisticated cognition can be performed by architectures which are very different from generalized theorem-provers. I also hope to have shown how some of the initial inferential limitations of such architectures can be overcome by adding further specialized architectures, which will no doubt leave us with further inferential limitations in turn. We will have no chance of understanding this cumulative process if we insist that there is no true representation in the absence of full inferential generality.

Third Moral: The Importance of Evolution. Finally, I hope that this paper has illustrated one uncontroversial way in which evolutionary considerations are important for the understanding of human psychology.

Sceptics about 'Evolutionary Psychology' (with capital letters) often complain that its evolutionary analyses are nothing more than 'Just So Stories'—ungrounded speculations about historical antecedents which differ from Kipling's fables only in not being funny. And there is some substance to this charge, given that the self-styled 'Evolutionary Psychologists' have a quite specific conception of the way in which evolution can illuminate psychology. When Evolutionary Psychologists talk about the evolution of cognitive faculties in the 'EEA' (the 'Environment of Evolutionary Adaptation') they generally have in mind the *differentiation* of human cognition from that of other animals over the last 5 million years or so. Unfortunately, however, there are precious little hard data by which to evaluate theories about the evolutionary pressures responsible for such differentiation. We don't have much more than a few fossilized scraps of tooth and bone to constrain the imaginative reconstruction of stone-age scenarios which might have favoured human intelligence.

But there is a quite different way in which evolutionary consideration can illuminate human psychology. This focuses, not on the last 5 million years, but on what went before. After all, if we knew clearly how animal cognition works, then that would place immense constraints on possible theories of human psychology. Any distinctively human capacities would have to be ones that could plausibly have evolved within the last 5 million years. Equally importantly, they would have to be ones that natural selection could advantageously have added at each stage to what was already there. So, if only we could work out what was already there 5 million years ago, this would tell us a huge amount about the possibilities for human cognition.

This is an obvious enough point, but it is worth emphasizing. It would be a pity if justified doubts about 'Evolution Psychology' made us forget that we evolved fairly recently from other animals, and that this tells us a lot about human minds.

References

Akins, C. and Zentall, T. 1998. 'Imitation in Japanese quail: the role of reinforcement of demonstrator responding', *Psychonomic Bulletin and Review*, 5.

Avital, E. and Jablonka, E. 2000. *Animal Traditions: Behavioural Inheritance in Evolution* (Cambridge: Cambridge University Press).

Barkow, J., Cosmides, L. and Tooby J. 1992. *The Adapted Mind* (Oxford: Oxford University Press).

Carruthers, P. and Smith, P., (eds.) 1996. *Theories of Theories of Mind* (Cambridge: Cambridge University Press).

Cosmides, L. and Tooby, J. 1992. 'The Psychological Foundations of Culture', in Barkow, J., Cosmides, L. and Tooby J., 1992.

Davies, M. and Stone, T., (eds.) 1995a. *Mental Stimulation* (Oxford: Blackwell.)

Davies, M. and Stone, T., (eds.) 1995b. *Folk Psychology* (Oxford: Blackwell).

Deacon, T. 1997. *The Symbolic Species* (London: Allen Lane).

Dickinson, A. and Balleine, B. 2000. 'Causal Cognition and Goal-Directed Action', in Heyes, C. and Huber, L. (eds.) *The Evolution of Cognition* (Cambridge, Mass: MIT Press).

Dickinson A. and Dawson, G. 1988. 'Motivational Control of Instrumental Performance: The Role of Prior Experience of the Reinforcer', *Quarterly Journal of Experimental Psychology*, 40B.

Dickinson A. and Dawson, G. 1989. 'Incentive Learning and the Motivational Control of Instrumental Performance', *Quarterly Journal of Experimental Psychology*, 41B.

Dorrance, B. and Zentall, T. 2001. 'Imitative learning in Japanese quail depends on the motivational state of the observer at the time of observation', *Journal of Comparative Psychology*, 115.

Fodor, J. 1983. *The Modularity of Mind* (Cambridge, Mass: MIT Press).

Fodor, J. 2000. *The Mind Doesn't Work that Way* (Cambridge, Mass: MIT Press).

Gross, R. 1996. *Psychology*. Third Edition. (London: Hodder and Stoughton).

Heyes, C. and Dickinson, A. 1990. 'The Intentionality of Animal Action', *Mind and Language*, 5.

Mameli, G. 2001. 'Mindreading, Mindshaping and Evolution', *Biology and Philosophy* 16.

Mameli, G. 2002. 'Learning, Evolution and the Icing on the Cake', *Biology and Philosophy* 17.

Millikan, R. 1984. *Language, Thought and other Biological Categories* (Cambridge, Mass: MIT Press).

Millikan, R. 1989. 'Biosemantics', *Journal of Philosophy* 86.

Papineau, D. 1984. 'Representation and Explanation', *Philosophy of Science* 51.

Papineau, D. 1993. *Philosophical Naturalism* (Oxford: Blackwell).

Papineau, D. 1998. 'Teleosemantics and Indeterminacy', *Australasian Journal of Philosophy* 76.

Papineau, D. 2001. 'The Evolution of Means-End Reasoning', in Walsh, D. (ed.) *Naturalism Evolution and Mind* (Cambridge: Cambridge University Press).

Pinker, S. 1997. *How the Mind Works* (London: Allen Lane).

Shettleworth, S. 1998. *Cognition, Evolution and Behaviour* (Oxford: Oxford University Press).

Sterelny, K. 2000. *The Evolution of Agency and Other Essays* (Cambridge: Cambridge University Press).

Tomasello, M. 2000. *The Cultural Origins of Human Cognition* (Cambridge, Mass: Harvard University Press).

Non-Personal Minds

STEPHEN R.L. CLARK

Abstract:

Persons are creatures with a range of personal capacities. Most known to us are also people, though nothing in observation or biological theory demands that all and only people are persons, nor even that persons, any more than people, constitute a natural kind. My aim is to consider what *non-personal* minds are like. Darwin's Earthworms are sensitive, passionate and, in their degree, intelligent. They may even construct maps, embedded in the world they perceive around them, so as to be able to construct their tunnels. Other creatures may be able to perceive that world as also accessible to *other* minds, and structure it by locality and temporal relation, without having many personal qualities. Non-personal mind, on both modern materialist and Plotinian grounds, may be the more usual, and the less deluded, sort of mind.

1. Persons, People and the Impersonal

Persons, in the sense I intend, are creatures with a range of 'personal' capacities. They are capable, in appropriate circumstances, of recognizing other individuals and their own reflections, of remembering their very own past and imagining their very own future, of deliberately communicating with others, of thinking about what to do, of holding themselves and others to account for what they do or fail to do, of formulating theories to explain what others do and what happens in the impersonal world. Probably they can also find incongruities amusing, form particular attachments, reconsider their own goals and motives, tell outrageous lies and imagine what the world would be like without them. This is not an exhaustive list, and may or may not be an interconnected one. While I agree that there are indeed such things as persons, I am not convinced that there is such a thing as *being a person*, nor that personal qualities constitute a syndrome, nor that the boundaries of the class are either uniform or distinct. I am not convinced, in short, that *persons* are a natural kind. In case that needs expansion: there may well be red-headed, left-handed ichthyologists who speak Lithuanian— but there is no point treating those overt characters as symptoms of

185

Stephen R. L. Clark

a deeper unity, or seeking to predict their possessors' other features on that basis. Even if almost all ichthyologists who speak Lithuanian are red-heads there is nothing unnatural about a *blonde* Lithuanian ichthyologist. Correspondingly, maybe the characters that all persons known to us may share are only a change aggregate, and there are quasi-persons who share some, not all, of them, without being odd. 'Person' may no more name a natural kind than 'fish' or 'tree' or 'people'[1].

People, in the sense I intend, are human beings. It might indeed be better to refer to them simply as 'human beings', were it not that this latter term has a speciously scientific ring to it. 'People' are what people across the world habitually call the creatures with whom they converse and interbreed. Calling ourselves 'human beings', instead, or members of the species *Homo sapiens sapiens*, has no real advantage. Rather the reverse: it replaces an obviously folk-taxonomical, evaluative term with one that seems, at least in popular speech, to denote a real, scientific category with clear boundaries. Recalling instead that all of us are *people* allows us to consider anyone, anything, that stands in the appropriate relationship to us as just as much 'our kind'. Being people doesn't demand that someone be *like* us, but that we share close ancestors, may share descendants, and are usually able to recognize each other's motives and intentions because we share at least some of them. E.O. Wilson's list of characteristic human characters and activities ('age-grading, athletic sports, bodily adornment, calendar, cleanliness training, ... trade, visiting, weaving and weather control') constitutes—as he acknowledges—'one hodgepodge out of many conceivable'[2]. Such a list no more limits our future than the forms of locomotion known by 1700 exhausted the possibilities. The presence of slaves in every human society till then—always excepting a few hunter-gatherer societies—does not show that we cannot outlaw slavery. That all of us adorn ourselves—which is a far more persuasive character than others that philosophers normally identify—does not prove that our descendants always will. 'Maybe all triangles must have three angles, but not all reptiles must have a three-chambered heart, though in point of fact they might.'[3] My

---

[1] See 'Is Humanity a Natural Kind?' in T. Ingold, (ed.), *What is an Animal?* (London: Unwin Hyman, 1988), pp. 17–34; reprinted in *The Political Animal* (London: Routledge, 1999), pp. 40–58.

[2] E. O. Wilson, *On human nature* (Cambridge, Mass.: Harvard University Press, 1978), p. 22f, after G. P. Murdock.

[3] D. Hull, *Philosophy of biological science* (Englewood Cliffs, New Jersey: Prentice-Hall, 1974), p. 79.

point is not the familiar Aristotelian insistence that human beings, as creatures that characteristically *choose* what to do (individually and corporately), have no one necessary biogram. It is that *no* species has such a biogram, except perhaps in the form of a Platonic Form or metaphysical attractor: in a real sense, there are no species at all (except as presently isolated breeding groups). And there is therefore no good *a priori* reason to think that either 'people' or 'persons' identify a natural kind. Species, in the Darwinian conception, are 'simply progress reports in the history of life'[4]. This was Darwin's really dangerous idea—and one that has not yet been fully absorbed even by those who think that they are Darwinists.

Chimpanzees, bonobo, gorillas and orang utans (that is, the other Great Apes), by this account, are partly persons, but probably not quite people (though there seems no reason in biological principle why there should not be hybrids[5]). Anencephalic infants are people, but perhaps not persons—though they may be more nearly personal than some allow (in that their carers, at any rate, often feel themselves to have a *personal* relationship with their charges[6]). Both concepts, like many other folk-taxonomical concepts, have an ethical dimension, which I have sought to examine on other occasions. My object here is to examine the condition of creatures who are not personal—but who are still 'minds' or 'minded'. That there could be minded creatures that are not people is perhaps uncontroversial. That there are 'non-personal minds', or minded creatures who are not persons, may still be disputed. It is sometimes suggested that nothing can 'have a mind' that does not have the personal capacities I itemized before. This post-Cartesian doctrine is not one that I see any need to spend time refuting[7]. If it were really true that nothing

[4] Niles Eldridge, *Reinventing Darwin: the Great Evolutionary Debate* (London: Weidenfeld & Nicolson, 1995), p. 11.

[5] There is every reason in *ethical* principle: the welfare of such a hybrid would be poor, even if it could talk. It would indeed be hailed, in some quarters, as an ideal experimental subject or convenient slave, and treated with the contempt that we always feel for those we injure unforgivably. See P. Singer & P. Cavalieri, (eds), *The Great Ape Project: Equality beyond humanity* (London: Fourth Estate, 1993).

[6] See Gavin Fairbairn, 'Complexity and the Value of Life', *Journal of Applied Philosophy* **8**, 1991, pp. 211–18.

[7] Peter Carruthers has suggested that although creatures without language could *imaginably* be conscious, they don't *need* to be because 'blindsighted' people could—imaginably—function almost as well as sighted ones, and because drivers sometimes don't remember driving along a familiar route that—apparently—they navigated with their minds elsewhere (*Language, Thought and Consciousness* (Cambridge: Cambridge

could think until it could actually talk, nothing could ever learn to talk at all. If some things can think before they actually talk, there is no reason, it seems to me, why other things might not think and *never* talk, or never even be capable of talking. No doubt the argument could continue, but I intend here to hypothesize that there might be non-personal and non-verbalising minds, and that the really interesting question is simply: what are they like? Rather than offering an immediate abstract definition of what it is to have or be 'a mind' or what it is to 'think', I prefer to examine some particular cases, including mud, earthworms, dogs, philosophers and God.

2. Matter, Mud and Earthworms

Mud, of course, is the oddest candidate for mindedness. Even panpsychists, who reason that the material substance of the world must have something like 'mental' properties if creatures composed of matter have them[8], do not usually attribute mind to any chance aggregate—which is how we ordinarily conceive of mud, mess, dirt and so on. Even eliminative materialists who have somehow convinced themselves that there are no mental properties at all—no qualia, intentions, values or meanings—presumably distinguish mud, worms and brickmakers. But consider Thoreau's marvellous evocation of the forms of mud:

> Few phenomena gave me more delight than to observe the forms which thawing sand and clay assume flowing down the sides of a deep cut on the railroad through which I passed on my way to the village. ...When the frost comes out in the spring, and even in a

[8] See Thomas Nagel, *Mortal Questions* (Cambridge: Cambridge University Press, 1979).

University Press, 1996), pp. 135ff). His only argument that they are *actually* unconscious is that they have, he says, no way of thinking *about* their own experience (ibid., pp. 220ff). He neglects to mention that the distinction between sight and blindsight holds for monkeys too (some of the original research was conducted on a brain-damaged monkey), that drivers can manage familiar routes because they have driven them attentively before, that we don't need to be conscious *that we are angry* to be conscious of the things that anger us, and there are other ways of thinking *about* experience than the verbal. Oddly, he arbitrarily allows that human infants might be subjects of experience because they can discriminate between experiences, 'and this would be enough for those experiences to be conscious ones, and to have a subjective feel' (ibid., p. 222). Non-humans who perform identical discriminations he counts, conveniently, as zombies.

thawing day in the winter, the sand begins to flow down the slopes like lava, sometimes bursting out through the snow and overwhelming it where no sand was to be seen before. Innumerable little streams overlap and interlace with one another, exhibiting a sort of hybrid product, which exhibits halfway the law of currents, and halfway that of vegetation. As it flows it takes the form of sappy leaves or vines, making heaps of pulpy sprays a foot or more in depth, and resembling, as you look down on them, the laciniated, lobed and imbricated thalluses of some lichens; or you are reminded of coral, of leopard's paws or birds' feet, of brains or lungs or bowels and excrements of all kinds. ...You find thus in the very sands an anticipation of the vegetable leaf. No wonder that the earth expresses itself outwardly in leaves, it so labours with the idea inwardly. The atoms have already learned this law, and are pregnant by it.[9]

It may be that Thoreau had a neglected pre-Darwinian theory in mind—that fossils themselves are patterns in the stone, not yet fully embodied in the flesh: hints of the future more than echoes of the past. But the general issue transcends forgotten theories: intelligence, as locating the 'simplest' accommodation of each to all, is pervasive even at the 'lowest', least conscious level of material reality. There is a living order *out there* in nature, and no matter how detailed our inspection we never actually encounter homogeneous and unordered stuff. 'Pure matter', which is to say abstract extension, can never itself be seen beneath the beautiful chains in which it is bound[10]. Insofar as *our* minds can reflect reality, and are right to judge it orderly and beautiful, there is something not unlike intelligence or mind out there. If fashionably materialist thinkers are correct to deny that our minds are transcendentally unified (on which more below[11]), there is so little difference between mind and matter that we may as well agree with animists like Thoreau. The mind of

---

[9] H. D. Thoreau, 'Spring', in *Walden* (Ware: Wordsworth Editions Ltd, 1995), pp. 206f: my thanks to Nancy Marple of Pittsburgh for this reference, located for a discussion on the email list sophia@liverpool.ac.uk.

[10] Plotinus, *Ennead* I.8.15

[11] I should add in passing that I do not myself believe that unity is an illusion or the self a fiction. The very recognition of intelligent order is only possible because it is unified in the perceiving mind, which is not built up out of pre-existent modules, but rather, often enough, broken down into them. But the story may still be an occasionally helpful one. See 'Reason as Daimon': C. Gill, (ed.), *The Person and the Human Mind* (Oxford: Clarendon Press, 1990), pp. 187–206; 'How many Selves make me?': D. Cockburn, (ed.), *Human Beings* (Cambridge: Cambridge

Stephen R. L. Clark

nature isn't *personal* because it lacks, except through the activity of creatures like ourselves, any reflective model of its own activity, and any sense of its own unity. But since such models are—we are told— only convenient fictions, and unity is an illusion, why should that matter?

The mind that is visible as the living order of mud, streaming water, clouds, stars and the rest is presumably very much what Hawking rhetorically identified as 'the mind of God'[12], and need not, so far, be either sentient or unified. One part of it may map another—as mud maps plantlife, or *vice versa*. In seeing any part of the wide world we may be seeing the pattern of the whole, since the very same forms or formulae are active everywhere. That axiom— which is the ground of all induction and extrapolation—was easily explained by our predecessors: the whole intelligible universe is bound up in the divine intellect, and animated only in that all of it is contained there. Without that explanation, the mindedness—that is, the living correspondence between the order of our minds and that of the whole world in all its parts—is simply a bare fact (and one which we cannot demonstrate either by reason or experience).

But even worms are more than mud (even though mud may take on the form of worms), and our ancestors were wrong to think that worms—or any other living thing—sprang up from mud alone[13].

A veterinary officer at a Scottish laboratory who is, under the requirements of the Animals (Scientific Procedures) Act of 1986, responsible for the welfare of the animals kept for use in licensed experiments, has remarked to me that he had on one occasion been asked how best to dispose of worms. Worms, I should add, are not

---

[12] Stephen Hawking. *A Brief History of Time* (London: Space Time Publications, 1988), p. 175. Hawking appears to assume that a knowledge of this 'mind' would explain why everything is as it is, though he also acknowledges that something might be needed to 'breathe fire into the equations' (ibid, p. 174). Plotinus was wiser: even the most accurate and elegant account of what there is cannot serve to explain the fact *that* it is. But that is another story.

[13] Aristotle. *Historia Animalium* 570a16ff; see Ian C. Beavis *Insects and Other Invertebrates in Classical Antiquity* (Exeter: University of Exeter Press, 1988), pp. 1–4.

University Press, 1991), pp. 213–33; 'Minds, Memes and Rhetoric', *Inquiry* **36**, 1993, pp. 3–16; 'Minds, Memes and Multiples', *Philosophy, Psychiatry and Psychology* **3**, 1996, pp. 21–28; 'Plotinus: Body and Mind', *Cambridge Companion to Plotinus*, L.Gerson (ed.), (Cambridge: Cambridge University Press, 1996), pp. 275–91.

protected animals under the rules of A(SP)A[14], but it was important to these particular experimenters, and to that veterinary officer, that their disposal be humane. He concluded that the technique least likely to cause suffering would be first to freeze and then incinerate them. No doubt—as he acknowledged—one important reason for taking such care was to encourage a proper attitude to animals in general. Even if, as might be true, worms *never* suffered even momentary distress when smashed, chopped, drowned, impaled or eaten alive by blackbirds, it was as well to be careful. Animals aren't test-tubes, and it is important to most of us that those we trust to conduct invasive experiments on animals should prefer to treat them as whole living creatures. If it is true, as Aristotle taught, that there is something wonderful and beautiful in even the most trivial or seemingly disgusting creature[15], we ought to treat such creatures with respect, however *they* feel about it. But there is also good reason to suspect that even worms *do* suffer: that is, that they have minds of another sort than mud.

It was easier for our ancestors to recognize that matter is animated into form, since it is literally true of all natural, earthly (or sublunary) matter that living creatures made or at least transformed it. It is as true for us as it was for them that celestial matter is probably of another sort—though we may reasonably admit as well as they that celestial matter is still minded, in the sense I meant before. Charles Darwin, in his final work, on *The Formation of Vegetable Mould*, identified the vital rôle that earthworms play in the creation of the soil. He thought them more than machinery, and unlike his successors he felt no qualms about describing their 'mental qualities':

> We have seen that worms are timid. It may be doubted whether they suffer as much pain when injured as they seem to express by their contortions. Judging by their eagerness for certain kinds of food, they must enjoy the pleasure of eating. Their sexual passion is strong enough to overcome for a time their dread of light. They perhaps have a trace of social feeling, for they are not disturbed by crawling over each other's bodies, and they sometimes lie in contact. ...Although worms are so remarkably deficient in the several sense-organs, this does not necessarily preclude intelligence...; and we have seen that that when their attention is engaged, they neglect impressions to which they would otherwise

[14] The only invertebrate animal to be protected is the common octopus, though there seems no very good reason why other octopuses and squids should not be protected too.

[15] Aristotle, *On the Parts of Animals*, 645a15ff.

have attended; and attention indicates the presence of a mind of some kind. They are also much more easily excited at certain times than at others. ...One of their strongest instincts is the plugging up of the mouths of their burrows with various objects; and very young worms act in this manner. But some degree of intelligence appears... to be exhibited in this work—a result which has surprised me more than anything else in regard to worms.[16]

His evidence for their *intelligence* lay in the way they dragged leaves in to plug their burrows, whether by the tips or bases or middle parts. Neither chance nor instinct, he concluded, could account for the way they adapted their conduct to particular types of leaf, and to prevailing conditions[17]. 'If worms have the power of acquiring some notion, however rude, of the shape of an object and of their burrows, as seems to be the case, they deserve to be called intelligent; for they then act in nearly the same manner as would a man under similar circumstances'[18].

This cannot, he argues, be attributed to 'instinct', ingrained behaviour patterns selected over millions of years for their superior effectiveness. Nor is it the mere adaptation of means to quasi-ends by which water finds the easiest path. Worms vary their techniques for dragging leaves into their burrows, even in the case of leaves 'about which their progenitors knew nothing'.[19] They 'judged with a considerable degree of correctness how best to draw the withered leaves of [a] foreign plant [rhododendron] into their burrows; notwithstanding that they had to depart from their usual habit of avoiding the foot stalk'.[20] Occasionally a batch of worms 'worked in a careless or slovenly manner', but Darwin found an explanation for that in the particular conditions: either the warmth of the air or its dampness meant that 'the worms did not care about plugging up

[16] Charles Darwin, *On Humus and the Earthworm* (London: Faber & Faber, 1945; 1st published 1881), p. 33; see Eileen Crist, 'The inner life of earthworms: Darwin's argument and its implications', Marc Bekoff and Colin Allen, (eds), *The Cognitive Animal* (MIT Press: Cambridge, forthcoming). It was 'common knowledge' in Darwin's day that earthworms were simply pests. The truth is that the upper soil, almost everywhere, is 'composed almost entirely of casts left behind by earthworm feeding', David W. Wolfe *Tales from the Underground: a natural history of subterranean life* (Cambridge Mass.: Perseus Publishing, 2001), p. 10.

[17] Darwin op. cit., pp. 45–58.

[18] ibid., p. 58.

[19] ibid., p. 45 (though Darwin may momentarily have forgotten that 'English' worms had ancestors elsewhere).

[20] ibid., p. 47.

their holes effectively'. In cooler, drier conditions these worms reformed[21].

If this now seems faintly comic, it is largely because of a century's complacent scepticism about 'animal minds'—a scepticism whose honourable roots lie in a careful hesitation to assume too much about creatures radically unlike ourselves, and a distrust of fables[22]. Its *dishonourable* roots lie in a simple desire to think well of ourselves while causing, as it might otherwise seem, enormous distress to other animals. But Darwin was more consistent than his successors: the chief points of Darwinian theory are that we are all related, that species boundaries are historically contingent, and that every contemporary organism is as fully evolved as ourselves. So why should it be ridiculous to empathize with earthworms, even if particular conclusions about their state of mind and character need better evidence than Darwin himself offered?

Again: a sudden light may cause a worm to retreat into its burrow, but the action is not a reflex. When its attention is fully absorbed in leaf-dragging, feeding or hermaphroditic sex, the worm is not affected by the light. 'With the higher animals, when close attention to some object leads to the disregard of the impressions which other objects must be producing on them, we attribute this to their attention being then absorbed; and attention implies the presence of a mind. Every sportsman knows that he can approach animals whilst they are grazing, fighting or courting, much more easily than at other times.'[23] Presence of mind, in short, is shown by its occasional absence. Sceptical critics might respond that this at least could be attributed to 'instinct': different patterns of behaviour are evoked or privileged at different times, amongst the higher animals as well as amongst earthworms. But here it is perhaps the sceptic who has too high an idea of mindfulness: what is attention—even *our* attention—but the exclusion of extraneous stimuli? At the very least, worms aren't simple creatures which respond to chemical or physical stimuli in entirely predictable ways: whatever system it is that sustains their lives it is sophisticated enough to discriminate different forms of leaf, and modify reactions to a sudden light. If we could design a robot with as much sophistication, proponents of AI would be quick to praise its makers.

But even if the system is discriminatory, can we conclude that the earthworm has an 'inner life'? George Romanes responded

[21] ibid., p. 49.

[22] See Bernard Rollin, *The Unheeded Cry* (Oxford: Oxford University Press, 1989).

[23] Darwin op. cit., p. 28.

favourably to Darwin's essay, saying 'that there may be intelligence without self-consciousness'[24]. Might there not also be intelligence without *any* sort of consciousness (as in mud or robots)? *Systems* themselves might be intelligent, without there being anything it is like to *be* them. That, after all, is what we want from robots: we certainly don't want machinery with feelings.

One reply is that earthworms differ from robots in that they are our relations. We know from our own experience what it is like to be an animal, and know by experiment how much we share with worms. We also know how simple and simple-minded any robot, any computer, is compared with the tangled apparatus that constructs both earthworms and ourselves. Every element in our bodies acts discriminatingly, learns from experience and can be diverted: *our* intelligence and inner life rest on that unanalysed, unanalysable, consilience of parts. Robots and computers, though they may one day be almost as complex, have far less claim to be intelligent, and none to have an inner life. Earthworms are more plausible candidates, if we can find a reason to believe. Two particular reasons are sufficient. First, earthworms secrete endorphins. Secondly, their tunnels are constructed to fit their known environments, and—or so it has been suggested—are reconstructed when disturbed: either way, the system of tunnels is experienced as a whole, rather than as a chance record of random motion.

Endorphins are the natural opiates that help to control the neurochemical activity we know as pain. The point that Darwin made—that animals put up with conditions that would otherwise be discomforting when their attention is engaged by work or play—reflects or mimics the neurochemical arrangement. 'Enkephalin and ß-endorphin-like substances have been found in earthworms (Alumets *et al.*, 1979), and injections of nalaxone have been shown to inhibit the worms' touch-induced escape responses (Gesser and Larsson, 1986), suggesting that the opioid substances may play a role in sensory modulation.'[25]

[24] Cited in O. Graff, 'Darwin on Earthworms—the Contemporary Background and What Critics Thought': J. E. Satchell, (ed.), *Earthworm Ecology: From Darwin to Vermiculture* (London: Chapman & Hall, 1983), p. 11.

[25] Jane A. Smith, 'A Question of Pain in Invertebrates': *ILAR News* Vol 33 (1–2), 1991, pp. 25–31, citing J. Alumets, R. Hakanson, F. Sundler, and J. Thorell. 1979. Neural localisation of immunoreactive enkephalin and ß-endorphin in the earthworm. *Nature* **279**, 805–806, B. P. Gesser and L. I. Larsson, 1986. Enkephalins may act as sensory transmitters in earthworms. *Cell Tissue Res.* **246**, 33-37. My thanks to Jane Smith for these references.

If earthworms were not sensitive they would have no profit from endorphins. Of course, it is possible that endorphins were first selected for some quite other function, and only later in the evolutionary story served to blanket pain, long after our ancestors and theirs were parted. But at the moment at least we have no way to identify this imagined other function, and may reasonably conclude that the invention handed down to modern earthworms and to the higher vertebrates (and many others) had much the same function in the long ago. That something is happening neurochemically—it is necessary to add—in no way damages the hypothesis that something is also happening *mentally*. So earthworms may reasonably be held at least to have this much of inner life, that the world appears to them with the colours of pain and pleasure.

Do they do anything more than respond to present appearances? The second claim suggests that they do: namely, that they can, as it were, *hallucinate* a tunnel network that is not physically present, and rule their activity by that remembered world. That they do reconstruct their burrows may be explained, of course, simply in that they make a similar adjustment to the prevailing conditions—itself a sign of Darwinian intelligence. One question might be whether a *new* worm, placed where the old had been, will reproduce the burrows of the old (suggesting that there are physical constraints not unlike those that guide the flow of mud or water), or whether only the first worm will do so (suggesting that it is responding to a memory 'out there' of its own past creation). The latter is at any rate not impossible, and can serve, momentarily, as a guide to understanding. It may also be that the worm leaves physical traces, to be interpreted (or not) by other worms. There is a real and practical distinction between creatures that need only know the present, physical fact, and those who perceive a world unique to every individual, created out of instinct, memory and—sometimes—rational thought. This projected life comes into being when a creature is no longer limited to the present, physical world; alternatively, it is revealed when creatures are deluded. This hallucinated reality does not, or need not, constitute a distinctively *inner* world, as though the worm had to compare the presently sensed reality to a performance in its own Cartesian theatre. That distinction is itself something we learn. It is enough that its experience contains more than the immediate sensa: it lives, like all of us, within a virtual reality whose contact with present fact is intermittent. The worm need have no *blueprint* of a tunnel system: instead it merely tunnels again where it 'perceives' the tunnel still to be. Its memory, whether physically—like its kidneys—or phenomenally, is 'out there'[26]. In grasping the shape of a leaf it perceives more than the immediate sensa. This need be no surprise to us. We too perceive far more than sensa, and often *don't* perceive what is in front of us because we are embedded in a virtual reality created out of hope and memory. Our own hallucinated mindscape (what Jacob von Uexkuell called an *Umwelt*[27], and others have called a *life-world*[28]) is full of ghosts, symbols, remembered pathways and the backsides of ordinary objects. Sometimes those ghosts, those remembered presences, mutate into new shapes. Sometimes images of expected futures also enter. Whether worms have access to such hopes and fears, who knows? At least they have minds of a sort, because they have mindscapes.

3. The Enlightenment and Objectivity

But there is still something slightly comic, or slightly sentimental, about the language Darwin chose to employ: that worms are timid, passionate and occasionally slovenly seems to construct an image of the Worm which owes more to human projection than to careful observation or even rational imagination—like thinking that foxes are sly, lions noble and songbirds fall in love. The Enlightenment Project that sought to divest our perception of the world of misplaced teleology—of the notion, for example, that water 'seeks its own level'—also sought to recognize the *otherness* of other living things. Things aren't as much like 'us' as we first thought. Maybe other animals aren't either. Washburn's level-headed study of 'the animal mind' raised the serious question, 'what is it like to be a wasp?'

> Anger, in our own experience, is largely composed of quickened heart beat, of altered breathing, of muscular tension, of increased blood pressure in the head and face. The circulation of a wasp is fundamentally different from that of any vertebrate. The wasp

[26] See J. Scott Turner, *The Extended Organism: the physiology of animal-built structures* (Cambridge Mass.: Harvard University Press, 2000), especially pp. 99–119.

[27] Jacob von Uexkuell, *Theoretical Biology*, tr. D. L. Mackinnon (London: Kegan Paul, 1926); see also von Uexkuell, 'A stroll through the worlds of animals and men' in C. H. Schiller, (ed.), *Instinctive Behaviour* (New York: International University Press, 1957), 5–80.

[28] M. Schutz, *Collected Papers I: The Problem of Social Reality*, M. Natanson (ed.), (The Hague: Nijhoff, 1971), pp. 205–59.

does not breathe through lungs, it wears its skeleton on the outside, and it has the muscles attached to the inside of the skeleton.
What is anger like in the wasp's consciousness? We can form no
adequate idea of it.[29]

We can add that anger, in our experience, also involves the belief
that we are *wronged* and must seek revenge. Do wasps have such
convictions, or are they as happily free of those delusions as Walt
Whitman thought?

> I think I could turn and live with animals, they are so placid and
> self-contain'd;
> I stand and look at them long and long.
> They do not sweat and whine about their condition;
> They do not lie awake in the dark and weep for their sins;
> They do not make me sick discussing their duty to God;
> Not one is dissatisfied—not one is demented with the mania of
> owning things;
> Not one kneels to another, nor to his kind that lived thousands of
> years ago;
> Not one is respectable or industrious over the whole earth.[30]

This somewhat questionable account is just as much a projection.
Perhaps we should simply acknowledge that there are some things
we do not *know*. Some seek to avoid the pain of ignorance by saying
that what we don't know is not knowledge, that our inability to
prove one thing is a proof of its opposite, that what 'we' no longer
'identify' with may properly be treated as 'mere things'. But even if
it were true that 'the agony of the tail end [of a cut worm] is our
agony, not the worm's'[31] (which it probably isn't), it does not follow
that I can legitimately or sensibly conclude that because I do not
'know' or cannot 'feel in myself' what the worm feels, I somehow do
know and can 'feel in myself' that the worm feels nothing. My not
knowing that it is now raining in Glasgow does not mean that I
know it isn't. 'How knoweth he by the vertue of his understanding
the inward and secretion motions of brutes? By what comparison

---

[29] A. L. Washburn, *The Animal Mind* (New York: Macmillan, 1917, 2nd
edition), pp. 3ff.

[30] W. Whitman, 'Song of Myself' §32: *The Portable Walt Whitman*,
Mark van Doren (ed.), (New York: Viking Press, 1945), pp. 98f.

[31] J. Jaynes, *The Origin of Consciousness in the Breakdown of the BiCameral
Mind* (Boston: Houghton-Miffin, 1976), p. 6. Compare Rorty's assertion
that to say that a pig is in pain is only to include it, for political purposes,
within our moral universe: R. Rorty *Philosophy and the Mirror of Nature*
(Princeton, New Jersey: Princeton University Press, 1979), p. 190.

from them to us doth he conclude the brutishness he ascribeth to them? ...We understand them no more than they us. By the same reason may they as well esteeme us beasts, as we them.'[32] And any chance we have of understanding them depends on abandoning a natural egoism. 'A beetle may or may not be inferior to a man—the matter awaits demonstration; but if he were inferior by ten thousand fathoms, the fact remains that there is probably a beetle view of things of which a man is entirely ignorant. If he wishes to conceive that point of view he will scarcely reach it by persistently revelling in the fact that he is not a beetle.'[33]

That worms are sentient and intelligent, after a fashion, is probable enough, even if we cannot ourselves imagine what it is like to be, specifically, a worm. They are, as I have already implied, quite ordinary animals: they have a claim indeed to be a typical terrestrial animal[34]. It may be admitted that none of them appear— to us—to have very *lively* lives (though how should we know what they do?). What about other creatures, more 'complex' than the median[35]?

That wasps will defend themselves against attack is certain, even if it would be rash to say that we know what they intend. It is enough that we know from the inside what it is like to be an *animal*—and the rhetorical gambit of attributing all mentalistic description to 'anthropomorphism' is a clear case of anthropocen-

---

[32] M. Montaigne, *Collected Essays*, tr. J. Florio (London 1892; 1st published 1603), II.12, p. 144f. See also my 'Understanding Animals', in Michael Tobias & Kate Solisti Mattelon, (eds.) *Kinship with the Animals* (Hillsborough, Oregon: Beyond Words Publishing, 1998), pp. 99–111.

[33] G. K. Chesterton 'A defence of humility', in *The Defendant* (London: Dent, 1922), pp. 134; I owe the reference to Simon Conway Morris.

[34] http://www.earthfoot.org.backyard/earthwrm.html: annelids are at the median point of 'complexity', though 'earthworms themselves are very special because they are super-streamlined, stripped-down, no-nonsense, fairly highly evolved critters'.

[35] Whatever is meant by 'complex': the apparent growth of complexity during evolutionary time suggests, to some, that evolution has a 'direction', and that—as the catholic Darwinist Denys Cochin remarked—Darwin may offer us monkeys for ancestors, but at least promises that we will not have them for children, *L'Evolution et la vie* (Paris 1886), pp. 269f, cited by Harry W. Paul *The Edge of Contingency: French Catholic Reaction to scientific change from Darwin to Duhem* (Gainesville: University Presses of Florida, 1979), p. 67. Darwin really promised nothing of the sort, and any observed increase in complexity over time *may* be no more than an effect of random variation when there is a minimum possible level of complexity: see Stephen Jay Gould *Life's Grandeur* (London: Jonathan Cape, 1996), pp. 167–216.

tricity: it is as sensible to say that it is Anglomorphic to attribute happiness or misery to other people, as though only Anglophones or the English could experience them. A better analysis reveals that people can be miserable or happy simply because they are people— or rather, because they are animals—and so can other creatures. Anglomorphism is indeed an error, but so is Anglocentrism. Chimpanzees—to begin with the most obvious—show the 'full picture of human anger in its three main forms: anger (i.e. aggressive action), sulking, and the temper tantrum'[36]. And of monkeys:

> Anyone [or anyone not in the grip of theory] would surely judge [Harlow's monkeys] as looking severely depressed and regressed (in a clinical sense). The parallel behaviours observed in children and in monkeys exposed to somewhat similar deprivations strongly suggests that the same emotional system, grief or depression, has been activated.[37]

Even if a somewhat different physical structure or process were involved, we need not shrink from labelling it 'depression' any more than we refuse to call a cephalopod's light-receptors 'eyes' merely because they have a different evolutionary ancestry from vertebrate 'eyes'[38]. Similarly, the wings of bird, bat and butterfly.

But though this may seem overwhelmingly plausible in the case of chimpanzees and other 'higher mammals', are we entitled to draw the same conclusion in respect of cephalopods or wasps or earthworms? After all, I did not draw it in the cases of mud, water, stars—all of which follow the easiest route through circumstance in a way that demonstrates a kind of natural intelligence. Systems that maintain themselves in being, or that are transformed by orderly and expectable routes into some other system, are at least akin to mind. Even distant elements of mere matter are connected, it appears, in ways that we might otherwise think limited to the unifying act of mind[39]. What more could matter? The difference, presumably, is the creation of a mindscape on top of the merely physical landscape—as though mud were to vary its behaviour in

[36] D. O. Hebb, *Textbook of Psychology* (Philadelphia: W B Saunders, 1972; 3rd edition), p. 202.

[37] R. Plutchik, *Emotion: A Psychoevolutionary Synthesis* (New York: Harper & Row, 1980), p. 107.

[38] K. Z. Lorenz, *The Foundations of Ethology* (New York: Springer-Verlag, 1981), p. 90.

[39] I refer to the Einstein-Podolsky-Rosen 'entanglements' whereby particles once connected remain weirdly responsive to each other when widely separated.

response to memories or fantasies of larger mudfalls. My object here is to consider the possible *phenomenology* of mind. And I cannot be content with merely neurochemical or functional equivalences. Even if belief is possible without human language—as it must be—we may still not know enough to specify the beliefs, if any, that such creatures have. Plutchik's supposition that a whale is 'paralysed with fright' at the approach of 'killer whales'[40] is a judgement that Buddhist sensibilities might not endorse: maybe the whale gives herself for food? Or maybe something else entirely is going on. Even if it turns out that the genes which now determine much of our usual humanity evolved long before our species (as the Pax-6 gene which every sighted creature possesses evolved long ago[41]), there is no guarantee that those genes have the same effect in all. What *is* it like to be wasp, an ant, a cuttlefish, a crab?

None of these need be persons or even slightly personal, but they still may be minds—and we can, in principle, locate analogies within *our* minds, and try them out in our relationship with them. One of W. B. Yeats' friends meditated on the subject of 'what it is like to be a canary', and concluded that the canary's world contained colour but no outline: doubtless, Yeats remarked sceptically, he had made an error in his contemplative technique.[42] But the story is at least compatible with the deductions of more conventional ethologists—witness male robins who will square up to red rags rather than to models which are, in our eyes, more like robins. Enlightenment objectivity, though a valuable tool, is not the *only* way we can uncover otherness. Contrariwise, it has often been a way of concealing otherness, by the pretence that others are only objects of our gaze, or that there are only ever objects of the sort *we* see for other creatures to respond to. Why may my cat not be playing with me as much as I with her? Why may my cat not be responding to quite another mindscape than my own, without—perhaps—the abiding, minded entities that I see? Ethologists and others have indeed suggested that it is not only canaries that lack experience of outlined entities. 'Earthworms don't have eyes, but they do have light-sensitive cells scattered in their outer skin. These cells don't

---

[40] Plutchik op. cit., p. 105.

[41] First announced by Rebecca Quiring *et al.,* 'Homology of the Eyeless Gene of Drosophila to the Small Eye in Mice and the Aniridia in Humans': *Science* 265.1994, pp. 785–9: the point is that genomes often contain unrealised potentials which can, somehow or other, be turned on. My thanks to Simon Conway Morris for information about Pax-6.

[42] W. B.Yeats *Essays and Introductions* (London: Macmillan, 1961), p. 411.

enable earthworms to see images, or forms, but they do give their skin the capacity to detect light and changes in light intensity.'[43] But even creatures that do have eyes may not use them as we do ourselves. 'Buytendijk considers it doubtful that animals perceive "things" [that is, stable and enduring substances]'[44]—though he supposes that it is obvious that we are *right* to do so, as though *our* mindscape were uniquely what is real. Methodological scepticism (insisting that we should not posit more than we have evidence to prove) sometimes amounts to no more than the conceit that what is immediately present to *us* is the only substance of reality. Sometimes it mutates into an extravagant credulity about things never present to us at all, as long as we can suppose that they are easily obedient to the rules we choose (such as elementary particles or expanding space-times). But maybe William James was right:

> We may, if we like, by our reasonings, unwind things back to that black and jointless continuity of space and moving clouds of swarming atoms which science calls the only real world. But all the while the world we feel and live in will be that which our ancestors and we, by slowly cumulating strokes of choice, have extricated out of this, like sculptors, by simply rejecting certain portions of the given stuff. Other sculptors, other statues from the same stone! Other minds, other worlds from the same monotonous and inexpressive chaos! My world is but one in a million alike embedded, alike real to those who may abstract them. How different must be the worlds in the consciousness of ant, cuttlefish or crab![45]

Our worlds, our mindscapes, are other than that 'real world', and there are other, different worlds within it. So what are the differences that perhaps we can identify? 'Unlike other animals, which live a natural life on the earth as it is given to them, human beings have constructed a world of their own over and above the natural earth.'[46] Arendt's argument was that such a world is vital to

[43] http://www.earthfoot.org/backyard/earthworm.html op. cit. This may rest on the sort of confusion that leads to suggestions that we really see things upside down, or that insects see multiple copies of things through faceted eyes. The pattern of light on light-sensitive tissue is not the same as the experienced *image*.

[44] H. Speigelberg, *Phenomenology in Psychology and Psychiatry* (Evanston, Illinois: Northwestern Universities Press, 1972), p. 290.

[45] William James, *The Principles of Psychology* (New York: Macmillan, 1890), vol. 1, pp. 288f.

[46] M. Canovan, *Hannah Arendt: a reconsideration of her political thought* (Cambridge: Cambridge University Press, 1992), p. 106 after H. Arendt, *The Human Condition* (Chicago: University of Chicago Press, 1958), p. 134.

humanity: if we were instead to let ourselves be absorbed into nature, its 'overwhelming elementary force... will compel [us] to swing relentlessly in the circle of [our] own biological movement'[47]. It could be argued in return that any animal species constructs its own world—as James declared. Most such worlds are sustained by mutual interaction as well as by virtual maps and models, just like ours: the memory is embedded in an outer world for others to encounter. But what we know of those other worlds is at least compatible with the conviction that the *human* world is uniquely symbolical, uniquely narrative. Other creatures may create symbolic markers (urine traces, clawmarks, birdsong), and may re-identify past acquaintances in ways that mimic biographical anecdotes. There is evidence that even sheep (whom we have not bred to be intelligent) can recognize human and other individuals after a lapse of months—or rather, can do something that we interpret as the recognition of such individuals. But people remain, so far as we can tell, unique in the complexity and felt significance of our narratives. Maybe earthworms beguile the winter evenings by recalling past encounters with earthworms, beetles, leaves and birds. Maybe whales sing sagas, and chimpanzees begin to draw conclusions about chimp society from their experience of politics and war. Presumably they are all naturists by birth and education[48]. People, by contrast, are naturally not naturists: the *natural* human being, as Chesterton observed, is the clothed human being[49]—even if the clothes are no more than a pouch and feather, and even if this character is actually no more *essential* than is wearing, specifically, spats. On the one hand, minds move us beyond mere nature. On the other, minds reveal *an unseen nature*. Minds may live in that interface between the invented worlds and an encompassing unseen reality. The world that is more than sense-experience demands more and more of our attention, at the expense of those immediate sensa.

One crucial feature of that unseen reality is that many more minds than one are seen to have a view of it. To have this sort of mind is to be capable of recognizing that others do so too. 'Only

---

[47] Arendt, ibid, p. 137; cited by Canovan, op. cit., p. 107.

[48] Naturism, in its origins, is more than a mere preference for social nakedness: it is the attempt, precisely, to strip off cultural distinctions, to be an animal amongst animals.

[49] G. K. Chesterton, *The Everlasting Man* (London: Hodder & Stoughton, 1925), p. 59. I here acknowledge my debt to R. J. Gill of Keele University, whose doctoral thesis on Chesterton and Arendt drew my attention to the correspondences between these two.

where things can be seen in a variety of aspects without changing their identity, so that those who are gathered around them know they see sameness in utter diversity, can worldly reality truly and reliably appear.'[50] Even creatures with a lively virtual life which fills in all the gaps of immediate sense-experience, even ones that *read* their environment in species-specific and yet more idiosyncratic ways, may not be fully mindful. The point about minds is that they reach out to a reality beyond their own experience, and in recognizing that reality is *other* than their own perspective are aware of manifold perspectives (or contrariwise: by noticing that there are manifold perspectives are aware of that unseen reality beyond all views). As Plotinus taught us: the Intellect through which all things that are take shape, and are understood, may be likened to 'a living richly varied sphere, or... a thing all faces, shining with living faces, or as all the pure souls running together into the same place... and universal Intellect seated on their summits so that the region is illuminated by intellectual light'[51]. Or as Lamberton paraphrases Plotinus: 'As long as we continue to focus our attention outside ourselves we are like a creature with many faces surrounding a single brain, each face unaware of the others, and of his identity with them. Were one able to be spun around, either by his own effort or through the good fortune of being yanked by Athena herself, he will find himself face to face with the good, with himself, with the universe'[52]. Whereas, we may for the sake of argument presume, earthworms have no access to anything beyond their worlds, other mindful creatures, knowing that there are many outlooks and perspectives *on the world*, are thereby required to form a concept of that single world.

We have chosen to class animals, mountains, islands, rivers as 'mere nature'. As older story treated them as alive and vocal, and ourselves as witnesses or servants of those (perhaps) projected

---

[50] H. Arendt, 'Philosophy and Politics' J. Kohn (ed.), *Social Research* 57/1, 1990, pp. 80, 87: cited by Canovan, op. cit., p. 113.

[51] Plotinus, *Ennead* VI.7.15, 26ff. Compare Hopkins: 'there is an infinity of possible strains of action and choice for each possible self in [the infinity of possible] worlds and the sum of these strains would be also like a pomegranate in the round, which God sees whole but of which we see at best only one cleave [or exposed face]. Rather we see the world as one cleave and the life of each person as one vein or strain of colour in it': G. M. Hopkins, *Sermons and Other Devotional Writings*, C. Devlin (ed.), (Oxford: Oxford University Press, 1959), p. 151.

[52] R. Lamberton, *Homer the Theologian* (Berkeley: University of California Press, 1986), p. 94.

powers[53]. The Enlightenment demanded that we step further back, or send nature back, and in so doing chose to ignore even the signs of sentience and purpose that we could have acknowledged without denying the uniquely human. This distancing of reality from the manifold releases us to notice that there are many views and many pathways round reality. Without that careful discipline it is only what *we* see that is real: a 'we' that is what Arendt (probably falsely) thought that sheep would be—namely, unanimous[54]. The Enlightenment gives us the opportunity to realize Wittgenstein's error: 'the spirit of the snake, of the lion' is emphatically *not* our spirit[55], but we might never have discovered what it was if we had not first sought to exclude our own.

4. Another Sort of Mind

So maybe non-human minds, so far, have mindscapes lacking either things or persons. Such creatures sculpt new worlds from James' inexpressive chaos, but do not necessarily encounter *things* at all, still less things which have themselves an outlook on the world. Maybe cats, as it sometimes seems, have simply no room in their mindscapes for more than familiar occasions, and do not realize that their furry toys—or rather the elements of their playfulness—are independently living things. Maybe Montaigne's cat *did* play with him, but not with any recognition that he actually existed, or was himself at play. Some will conclude that this means that such creatures have no minds (and also transform this mere *possibility*, somehow, into their own default conception). But humanism of this sort continues to ignore the fact that species are not natural kinds. Maybe *our* mindfulness—the mindfulness of anyone likely to be listening to this paper—has all the properties that Arendt (and Chesterton and Aristotle long before) identified as ours. But this does not mean that there are things, called 'minds', that *we* have and others known to us do not, any more than our manual skills imply that nothing else has hands. In thinking away those attributes that—maybe—are located only within our species, our currently isolated

---

[53] Michael Clarke, 'Gods and Mountains in Greek Myth and Poetry' in Alan B. Lloyd, (ed.), *What is a God?: studies in the nature of Greek Divinity* (London/Swansea: Duckworth/Classical Press of Wales, 1997), pp. 65–80.

[54] Canovan, op. cit., p. 111, after Arendt, *Human Condition* op. cit., p. 7. I doubt if sheep-farmers agree.

[55] L. von Wittgenstein, *Notebooks: 1914–1916* (Oxford: Blackwell, 1961): 20 October 1916.

and relatively homogenous gene-pool, we should not conclude that *other* creatures have no analogous powers. Even if opposable thumbs and upright gait are diagnostic of 'humanity', there are other creatures who can as easily survey and even manipulate their world. And even those who can't may still have limbs both like and unlike ours, and may be able to do things that we never could. Minds may be much the same. What we don't know may still be knowledge.

And maybe such minds are less unified than we commonly suppose our own to be. To return to the earthworm:

> The nervous system of the earthworm is 'segmented' just like the rest of the body. The 'brain' is located above the pharynx and is connected to the first ventral ganglion. The brain is important for movement: if the brain of the earthworm is removed, the earthworm will move continuously. If the first ventral ganglion is removed, the earthworm will stop eating and will not dig. Each segmented ganglion gets sensory information from only a local region of its body and controls muscles only in this local region.[56]

In this the earthworm resembles other invertebrates—but also of course other vertebrates, including the human: we are not ourselves wholly in conscious control of all our own activities (even the most obvious mentalistic ones), and are not equally conscious of all the 'sensory information' in every region. Nonetheless, it may serve as a thought experiment to imagine what it might be like to be something a little more obviously like a colony, in which our various mini-selves have to agree on what to do.

So what is it like to think away our favourite attributes, and what other attributes do other mindful creatures have? The world we experience is full of colours, scents, feelings, nuances, phantoms, memories, values, meanings, of a personal or species-specific or animal sort. The qualities we notice, that are real to us, are picked out by our evolutionary or personal history from an unobserved expanse of presently (maybe permanently) hidden qualities. Our very identification of things as the *same* things as we have perceived before is structured by our biology, our culture and our personal life. Why should our world be 'truer' than the lived worlds of the sheep tick, bee or armadillo? Why should we think 'the real world' is composed of just the sort of things that hominids with our particular history find significant? Past experience creates a worldscape, for earthworms as well as people. We see more than reflected

---

[56] From http://faculty.washington.edu/chudler/invert.html

light, hear more than a tape recorder can preserve, even smell, taste and feel far more than any present physical contacts can explain. It takes considerable effort, and sometimes long training, to be able to report exactly what we strictly *sense*. What we ordinarily perceive is a whole worldscape, full of memories and meanings, which may be wholly obscure to creatures of another kind, or time, or class. We even perceive *absences*.

So (leaving invertebrates aside[57]) what is it like—say—to be a dog? We can be fairly confident that dogs and earthworms differ. I have no evidence, for example, that earthworms develop hierarchies, let alone ones in which the lesser worm would seek to appease the greater by feigning infantile behaviour. Any worm (or any worm of the right sort) will do as well (though we may, so far, simply have missed the signs). Dogs, like many other social animals, distinguish one dog from another, and recall each other's character and standing. This need not be true of every mammal nor even every social animal. Rats, by contrast, seem to be much less individualistic, approaching any properly-scented rat without distinction. Conversely, worker ants apparently operate an hierarchical system that we would not have expected of creatures that seem to us to be interchangeable units.

A dog, it is now orthodox to insist, may possibly expect its master, but cannot expect its master to be back *tomorrow*. The claim is one of those that are repeated from one textbook to another, with little attempt to verify or explain it. Is it that *we* could not distinguish anything in the dog's behaviour that would lead us to conclude that its master was expected tomorrow or the next day or on the Greek Kalends? Has anyone actually tried to do so? Or is it that there could be no way to identify 'tomorrow' without a grammar or vocabulary? How then would anyone ever have invented such a grammar or vocabulary? No one without words can have 'invented' them. Lucretius, recording Epicurean opinion:

> To think that someone in those days assigned names to things, and that is how men learnt their first words, is crazy. Why should he have been able to indicate all things with sounds, and to utter the various noises of the tongue, yet others be supposed not to

[57] Strictly, 'invertebrates' is a term as useless as 'non-molluscs': vertebrates constitute one phylum out of many, and are special to us only because we are vertebrates. In other possible histories, some other phylum grew the kind of minds we have; or at any rate, we have no good reason to doubt it (*pace* Stephen Jay Gould, *Wonderful Life* (New York: Norton, 1990); cf. 'Does the Burgess Shale have Moral Implications?' *Inquiry* **36** 1993, 357–80; and Simon Conway Morris, *The Crucible of Creation: the Burgess Shale and the Rise of Animals* (Oxford: OUP, 1998)).

have had that ability at the same time? Besides, if others had not already used sounds to each other, how did he get the preconception of their usefulness implanted in him? How did he get the initial capacity to know and see with his mind what he wanted to do?[58].

There is actually an easy solution to the question of tomorrow: the existence of mindscapes, including pathways and landmarks, means that any minded entity is surrounded not only by signs for whatever is physically present, but also by paths stretching away into both past and future. The dog is conscious of its master's presence far down the track: it can, in fact, expect its master's return 'tomorrow' or at any moment that it is capable of visioning. 'Tomorrow' is a place as much as the house next door, and the dog's master is located there. Some creatures may envisage themselves advancing through the house of time; others only find that distant times draw closer. Which would be true of dogs we do not know. Language, in either case, comes later.

Dogs recognize other individuals and seek to advance themselves within the literal pack or human household. They form attachments, fall into routines, manage their masters and follow verbal instructions when it suits them. 'Only someone in the grip of a philosophical theory would deny that small babies can literally be said to want milk and that dogs want to be let out or believe that their master is at the door'[59], even though the baby has no conception of milk as such, and dogs no grasp of the indefinitely many logical implications of the proposition that so and so is at the door. They come very close to having strictly *personal* relationships. Indeed, the only secure way of insisting that they can't be persons is to emphasize that 'being a person' is a folk-taxonomic, socio-legal concept: they aren't persons solely because we will not think them persons. If they were to take on human shape they wouldn't be easily distinguished from many people whom we currently insist are persons because we wish them to have the rights of persons. Or is it rather that if we thought them persons we would be bound to think them defective, or even disgusting? At any rate this may be the thought behind Frans de Waal's odd insistence[60] that it would be

---

[58] Lucretius, *De Rerum Natura* 5. 1040ff, in A. Long & D. Sedley *The Hellenistic Philosophers* (Cambridge: Cambridge University Press, 1987), 19B: I, pp. 97f; see 'The Evolution of Language: Truth and Lies': *Philosophy* **70** 2000, pp. 401–21.

[59] J. R. Searle, *Intentionality* (Cambridge: Cambridge University Press, 1983), p.5.

[60] F. de Waal, *Good Natured: the origins of right and wrong in humans and other animals* (Cambridge, Mass.: Harvard University Press, 1996), p. 215.

'condescending' to grant apes any of the rights we demand for people, or aim to prevent or punish their kidnapping, humiliation, imprisonment without trial, torture, mutilation or murder: presumably he supposes that apes regarded as persons would be thought defective when they should instead be reckoned glorious apes. Doubting that there are, strictly, *persons*, I prefer to judge that they have the sort of personal characteristics that make such acts (as kidnapping, humiliation, imprisonment, torture, mutilation, murder) injurious, and precisely *because* they are glorious deserve to be protected or avenged.

But maybe there is some reason, at least in the case of dogs, to adopt another convention: to suppose that they are mindful, but not personal, because they have no sense of their own dignity, and do not care to dress. Would they be persons if they were somehow endowed, as fable and occasional science fiction hopes, with speech? Or would such speech reflect a non-personal mentality? To what extent—despite the obvious truth that they can identify old acquaintance and follow verbal instruction—do they have the sort of minds we think we do? And what sort is that? Personal beings act and think in the context of their very own characters and histories, and are inclined to hold, at least capable of holding, themselves and others to account. They believe that in each of them there is a Self that owns its thoughts and actions. Among the furniture of their mindscapes is an Ego. But not even all people act and think like that—and oddly enough some modern philosophers seem to think that those who do are really in error. If the personal being who once wrote and now is uttering these words is what 'Dennett', for example, reckons, then all that makes it personal is the error of supposing that there is such a single self that can be held responsible for what was written and is now said. So minds or mindscapes lacking that delusion must be possible, and may be better.

So to recap. There are minds that make no distinction between what is and what appears to them. Earthworms—let us suppose—respond intelligently and maybe imaginatively to the world presented to them, without ever supposing that they live within a reality much larger and more mysterious than they know. Even chimpanzees, it has been argued, usually conceive the world of their experience to be the only world: they assume, that is, that everything *they* know is immediately apparent to an absent experimentalist—the experimentalist, they assume, will know which box a treat has been hidden in just because *they* know[61]. Actually, the experiment is

[61] This is not to say that they aren't personal: similar experiments catch out human infants and people classed as autistic.

flawed, and somewhat implausible. No sensible chimpanzee will doubt that the experimentalists know perfectly well what is going on (as in fact they do). In the wild, it is evident that chimpanzees can calculate their own actions on the basis of their educated guesses about what others will think of what they do. But we can more plausibly suspect that other creatures do not have this gift, and that the world presented to them (including the hallucinated framework) is, for them, Reality. Another way of approaching the same issue is to note that *some* creatures can recognize misinformation: they adjust their responses to avoid the errors that they were previously led into, and may themselves purvey misinformation to mislead their neighbours[62].

Persons, people, dogs, earthworms, mud and molecules are all orderly accommodations ruled by the principle of least effort. Such order, such *intelligence*, is implicit in the unseen world and in the lesser worlds spun out from particular accommodations. Materialists and animists alike suggest that the separate self of personhood is as much an illusion as the separate *species* of everyday humanism. Being a person is like being royal: a collective hallucination having little to do with anyone's ordinary attributes. Non-personal mindfulness is the commoner and maybe the better state. Maybe Simone Weil was right in her diagnosis: 'If the "I", in the personal sense, fades away in proportion and in so far as man imitates God, how could it be sufficient to conceive of a personal God? The image of a personal God is a hindrance to such an imitation.'[63] So though I have followed precedent in seeming to rank mud, earthworm, dog, chimpanzee and fully human being, as though the later is invariably the better (and the human always later), it is open to us to consider our own standing. Mindfulness is as present in the non-personal as in ourselves, and what makes us *persons* is a distraction. Platonizing philosophers have often identified their core self with Intellect, and concluded that, insofar as we think *rightly*, we think the same—*and are the same*. Persons (that is, creatures that think of themselves as isolated subjects and 'captains of their soul') may be in error, and those who think and feel 'unself-consciously', and in accord with truth, may not be persons. But that is another story.

[62] See Colin Allen & Marc Bekoff, *Species of Mind: The Philosophy and Biology of Cognitive Ethology* (Cambridge, Mass.: MIT Press, 1997), pp. 148–51.

[63] Simone Weil, *Notebooks*, tr. A. Wills (London: Routledge & Kegan Paul, 1956), vol. 1, p. 241.

Personal Agency

E. J. LOWE

Why does the problem of free will seem so intractable? I surmise that in large measure it does so because the free will debate, at least in its modern form, is conducted in terms of a mistaken approach to causality in general. At the heart of this approach is the assumption that all causation is fundamentally event causation. Of course, it is well-known that some philosophers of action want to invoke in addition an irreducible notion of agent causation, applicable only in the sphere of intelligent agency.[1] But such a view is generally dismissed as incompatible with the naturalism that has now become orthodoxy amongst mainstream analytical philosophers of mind. What I want to argue is that substances, not events, are the primary relata of causal relations and that agent causation should properly be conceived of as a species of substance causation. I shall try to show that by thus reconceiving the nature of causation and of agency, the problem of free will can be made more tractable. I shall also argue for a contention that may seem even less plausible at first sight, namely, that such a view of agency is perfectly compatible with a volitionist theory of action.

1. Event causation and substance causation

First, let us focus on the distinction between event causation and substance causation—the latter term being, of course, one that is little in use at present. What is at issue here is a question concerning the relata of causation, that is, a question as to what ontological category or categories the items related by causal relations should be conceived to belong. I speak of 'causal relations' in the plural here advisedly, because I think it is tendentious to assume that there is such a thing as 'the' causal relation, although this assumption is very widespread amongst contemporary analytical metaphysicians. The obvious and most appropriate way to begin to approach the question just raised is through a consideration of the syntax of causal statements in natural language—which is not to say, of

[1] See, for example, Richard Taylor, *Action and Purpose* (Englewood Cliffs, NJ: Prentice-Hall, 1966), pp. 111–12.

course, that metaphysical questions have a purely linguistic resolution, only that syntax can be a guide to metaphysical presuppositions. We see, then, that some causal statements in everyday language undoubtedly have an event-causal formulation. These are statements such as 'The explosion caused the collapse of the bridge', where the transitive verb *to cause* has as its grammatical subject a noun-phrase denoting a particular event and as its grammatical object a noun-phrase denoting another particular event. However, we also have what might be called 'mixed' causal statements, such as 'The bomb caused the collapse of the bridge', in which the grammatical subject of the verb *to cause* is a noun-phrase denoting a particular persisting object or individual *substance* (to use the traditional vocabulary of metaphysics) while its grammatical object is a noun-phrase which once again denotes a particular event.

Now, faced with such mixed causal statements, the devotee of event causation—that is to say, the metaphysician who holds that all causation is really or ultimately a matter of one event's causing another—is likely to say something of the following sort. Such a mixed causal statement, he will say, is really just an abbreviation for some more complex statement of event causation which involves quantification over events. He will say, for instance, that what is really meant by the statement 'The bomb caused the collapse of the bridge' is something like this: 'There was some event, *e*, such that *e* involved the bomb and *e* caused the collapse of the bridge'.[2] To make this suggestion work, something must be said, of course, about what it means for a persisting object or individual substance, such as a bomb, to be 'involved' in an event—and this may not be altogether easy. That is to say, it may not be easy to spell out a suitable sense of the word 'involve' which does not in some manner compromise the proposal now under scrutiny—for instance, by rendering it implicitly circular. After all, the notion of 'involvement' which will need to be invoked cannot be something as thin as merely to imply, in the case in hand, a *spatiotemporal overlap* between the bomb and the event that is putatively the cause of the collapse of the bridge. That would allow the event in question to be something like a surge of flood-water, which swept over the bomb and caused the collapse of the bridge, while the bomb sat inertly in its fixed position on the river-bed. Obviously, what the proposer has in mind is that it is some such event as *the explosion* of the bomb that caused

---

[2] See further my *A Survey of Metaphysics* (Oxford: Oxford University Press, 2002), p. 197.

the collapse of the bridge when we say truly, but by way of abbreviation, that *the bomb* caused the collapse of the bridge. So the relevant notion of 'involvement' must be one that would allow us to say that the bomb is *involved* in the explosion in a way in which it is *not* involved in the surge of flood-water. But there, for the time being, I shall leave the issue of involvement and turn to other matters.

2. The primacy of substance causation

What we have just been looking at is a proposal to reduce all talk of substances as causes to talk of events as causes, in line with the following sort of schema:

(1) Substance s caused event e_2 just in case there was some event, e_1, such that e_1 involved s and e_1 caused e_2.

However, one could readily acknowledge that (1) expresses a conceptual truth without agreeing that all causation is 'really' causation by events, rather than by substances. Indeed, it is perfectly possible to argue that (1) is a conceptual truth precisely because it is *substances* that are in the most fundamental sense 'causes'. And in support of the latter claim one may urge that it is, after all, *substances*, not events, that possess causal powers and liabilities. Familiar examples of these causal powers and liabilities are the natural physical dispositions of material objects, such as magnetism and solubility. Substances *manifest* these powers when they interact causally—for example, when an electromagnet attracts a piece of iron or when the water in a glass dissolves a lump of sugar.

What is it for the water to dissolve the sugar? It is, precisely, for the water to *cause* the sugar to dissolve. The verb *to dissolve*, like so many others in everyday language, has both a transitive and causal sense and an intransitive and non-causal sense, which are intimately related. For x to dissolve$_T$ y is for x to cause y to dissolve$_I$, just as for x to move$_T$ y is for x to cause y to move$_I$. Dissolving$_T$ and moving$_T$ are species of *causation*, no less. And the entities that engage in these species of causation are quite evidently individual *substances*, that is, particular persisting objects of various kinds.

Note, however, that nothing that I have just said implies that we can straightforwardly *analyse* a species of substance causation, such as dissolving$_T$, in terms of a generic notion of substance causation together with a specific non-causal notion, such as dissolving$_I$. Indeed, it is well-known that such a suggestion faces difficulties at least in some cases: that, for instance, it is hard to maintain that *to kill* just means *to cause to die*. In this case, there are plausible counter-examples. For example, if Jones forces Smith at gunpoint to kill Brown, then it would seem that Jones may be held causally responsible for Brown's death, even though it was Smith and not Jones who killed Brown. However, I have no desire to defend the analytical claim in question. Indeed, I would prefer to represent the direction of semantic explanation as running, if anything, the opposite way: from a multiplicity of quite specific notions of substance causation, bearing various overlapping family resemblances to one another, to an abstract generic notion of substance causation, conceived of as being the common residue of these more specific notions.[3] This is one reason why I expressed a reluctance to speak of 'the' causal relation, as though there is really just one such relation, in which anything describable as a 'cause' may be said to stand to anything describable as an 'effect'. As I see it, dissolving$_T$, moving$_T$, attracting$_T$ and the rest are simply all distinct, but in some ways similar and in other ways dissimilar, species of causal relation: they are not all analysable in terms of some single and independently intelligible notion of causation of a generic character. That there is no such independently intelligible generic notion of causation would explain, of course, why it is that philosophers have so signally failed to provide a satisfactory analysis of what it means to say that one thing (whether it be a substance or an event) was a 'cause' of, or 'caused', another.

3. The reduction of event causation to substance causation

If we say, now, that it is *substances* that are in the most fundamental sense 'causes', what should we say about statements of event causation, such as 'The explosion of the bomb caused the collapse of the bridge'? What we can say may be captured in the following schema,[4] which need not be seen as a rival to (1), inasmuch as both may be seen as capturing conceptual truths:

(2) Event e_1 caused event e_2 just in case there was some substance, s_1, and some substance, s_2, and some manner of acting, F, and some manner of acting, G, such that e_1 consisted in s_1's Fing and e_2 consisted in s_2's Ging and s_1, by Fing, caused s_2 to G.

---

[3] See again my *A Survey of Metaphysics*, pp. 212–13.
[4] This proposal is an elaboration of one set out in my *A Survey of Metaphysics*, p. 209.

Thus, for example, it is correct, according to (2), to assert 'The explosion of the bomb caused the collapse of the bridge', because (we suppose) it was the bomb that, by exploding, caused the bridge to collapse. (I should perhaps remark that, in order to keep matters as simple as possible, I have stated (2) in a way which accommodates only causation by single substances, not causation by a plurality of substances acting in concert. But nothing of importance is compromised by this simplification.)

Indeed, the truth of (2) can be used to explain the truth of (1), if we say, as we plausibly can, that for a substance to be 'involved' in an event, in the sense required by (1), is just for that event to consist in that substance's acting in a certain manner.[5] (Again, I simplify, for ease of exposition, by considering only events that 'involve' a single substance.) This is to say, for example, that the explosion 'involved' the bomb precisely inasmuch as that event consisted in the bomb's exploding—whereas, by contrast, the surge of flood-water did not consist in the bomb's doing anything and so did not in this sense 'involve' the bomb. For then (1) reduces to this:

(1*) Substance s caused event e_2 just in case there was some event, e_1, and some manner of acting, F, such that e_1 consisted in s's Fing and e_1 caused e_2.

But if (2) is correct, then it obviously goes a long way towards explaining the truth of (1*), because 'e_1 caused e_2', according to (2), is true just in case the following is true: 'There was some substance, s_1, and some manner of acting, F, such that e_1 consisted in s_1's Fing and s_1, by Fing, caused e_2'. We see, thus, that, on the assumption that (2) is true, (1*) is equivalent to the following (see the Appendix for a proof):

(1**) Substance s caused event e_2 just in case there was some event, e_1, and some manner of acting, F, such that e_1 consisted in s's Fing and s, by Fing, caused e_2.

Now, (1**) is plausibly true, because it is plausible to say that whenever a substance causes an event, it does so by acting in a certain manner and that its acting in such a manner constitutes an event. So, the implication is that (1) is true simply because it is equivalent to a plausible principle of substance causation, (1**), and that, rather than its truth being indicative of the reducibility of substance causation to event causation, it is indicative of the very reverse of this.

---

[5] For a defence of a view of the nature of events consistent with the present proposal, see my *A Survey of Metaphysics*, ch. 14.

E. J. Lowe

4. Agent causation and basic actions

However, (1**), while plausible, is not incontrovertible and, indeed, will be rejected by some advocates of agent causation. The philosophers I have in mind are those who would contend that, for instance, when I raise my arm—cause my arm to rise—as a so-called 'basic' action, there is nothing I do *by doing which* I cause my arm to rise.[6] For my own part, I am inclined to disagree with these philosophers, because I am sympathetic to a volitionist theory of action.[7] I am inclined to believe, thus, that even when I raise my arm in the most 'direct' way possible—not, for instance, by pulling on a rope attached to it—I still cause my arm to rise by doing something, namely, by *willing* to raise my arm. So, in short, I am prepared to allow that schema (1) is true, being prepared to explain this by appealing to the truth of (1**) and, ultimately, to the truth of schema (2). At the same time, however, I am prepared to allow that it is at least intelligible to suppose that (2) is true but (1) is not. That is to say, it is conceivable that all event causation may be explicable in terms of substance causation and yet that some statements of substance causation do not imply corresponding statements of event causation.

5. Personal agency and volitionism

I hope it will now begin to be clear in what sense I can both be an advocate of agent causation and espouse volitionism. A person is an individual substance, in the broad metaphysical sense of that term, in which it denotes a persisting object of some kind. In my own opinion, 'person' denotes a basic kind of persisting object and is not what is sometimes called a 'phase sortal', denoting a status that an object of a more basic kind can take on during some part or phase of its existence.[8] Those who think that all persons are *animals*, that is, biological organisms, take the latter view, for by their way of thinking no human organism comes into existence as a person: it is not a person during its early embryonic stages and very often not a person during the final stages of its existence, just before biological

[6] For the notion of a 'basic' action, see Arthur C. Danto, *Analytical Philosophy of Action* (Cambridge: Cambridge University Press, 1973), p. 28.

[7] I defend such a theory in my *Subjects of Experience* (Cambridge: Cambridge University Press, 1996), ch. 5.

[8] See further my *Subjects of Experience*, ch. 2.

death ensues. As I say, I disagree with this view, because I consider that persons have persistence conditions which differ from those of any biological organism. However, this dispute is not immediately relevant to the present matter in hand, the nature of personal agency, since all that I need to insist on for the time being is that every person is a substance of *some* kind, even if persons do not constitute a basic kind in their own right. This then allows me to adopt a theory of personal agency which is a causal theory, while at the same time maintaining that all causation is fundamentally substance causation.

On this view, persons are agents inasmuch as they are substance-causes of certain events. Which events, though? What we should *not* say, in my opinion, is that persons are causes of their *actions*. Rather, we should say that a person's actions almost exclusively *consist in* that person's causing certain events, events which we may call 'action-results'. The distinction between action and action-result may be illustrated by the distinction between the action of raising one's arm and the event of arm-rising which occurs as a result of that action. In English, we do not have a transitive verb 'to rise', but instead use the distinct verb 'to raise'. Raising one's arm is a matter of causing one's arm to rise, however, just as dissolving$_T$ some sugar is a matter of causing the sugar to dissolve$_I$. Notice, however, that I said only that a person's actions *almost exclusively* consist in that person's causing certain events, to wit, action-results. The most important exception is the action of *willing* itself, for willing does not *consist in* causing an event of an appropriate kind, in the way in which arm-raising, for example, consists in causing a rising of an arm.[9] According to volitionism (or, at least, my version of it), acts of will, or 'volitions', are indeed causes, in the event-causation sense, of all the action-results of our voluntary actions. But this doesn't imply that to will is to cause something to happen. And, indeed, of course, it is perfectly possible to will to no effect: possible, for example, to will to raise one's arm and yet for one's arm not to rise as a result.

I have just said that acts or will, or volitions, are causes, in the *event-causation* sense, of action-results, where voluntary actions are concerned. There is no conflict here with my advocacy of the primacy of substance causation. An act of will consists in some agent's—some person's—willing something. And, in line with schema (2), whenever such an act causes an event, such as the rising of an arm, it does so simply because the act consists in some

[9] Compare Carl Ginet, *On Action* (Cambridge: Cambridge University Press, 1990), p. 11.

person's willing something—for instance, to raise an arm—and that person, by so willing, causes the event in question to occur. Thus, one can consistently be a substance-causalist and espouse a volitionist theory of action. Volitions *are* causes—not of actions, but of action-results—but only insofar as they consist in persons' exercising their power of will and by so doing causing certain events. Talk here of the 'power of will' is to be taken literally, not in the popular sense of 'will-power', but to mean quite simply that the will is a *power* or natural *capacity* of agents, which can be exercised or manifested from time to time.[10] Just as an electromagnet exercises or manifests its power to attract ferrous metals when it draws a piece of iron towards it, so a human agent exercises or manifests his or her power or capacity of will whenever he or she wills to do something.

6. Causal powers and the nature of the will

However, there are also important differences between the will, conceived thus as a species of power, and a natural causal power such as magnetism or a natural causal liability such as solubility. What they have in common is that they are all species of *potentiality*, in the sense in which the potential is to be contrasted with the *actual*.[11] Something which has a power or potential to act in a manner *F* typically need not always be exercising that power by acting in that manner, but, typically, it will at least be *naturally possible* for it to act in that manner. I say 'typically' because we can easily think of relevant exceptions. For instance, every massive body has a gravitational power to attract others, but it is *always* exercising that power: gravity can't be 'switched off'. On the other hand, sometimes circumstances may render it naturally impossible for an object to manifest one of its powers or liabilities. Think, for example, of a fragile glass that is prevented from being shattered by a protective shield which, however, cannot be removed without vaporizing the glass: it is naturally impossible for this glass to be shattered and yet it can still be correct to say that it is fragile.

Now, what is distinctive of *causal* powers and liabilities is that they are powers to affect or be affected by objects in certain ways. (In an older terminology, the distinction here between powers and liabilities is often registered as a distinction between 'active' and

[10] This, of course, was Locke's view: for discussion, see my *Locke on Human Understanding* (London: Routledge, 1995), ch. 6.

[11] The *locus classicus* for this contrast is, of course, Aristotle, *Metaphysics*, book θ.

'passive' powers, but I shall avoid this way of talking because I think it can be misleading.) A causal power is a power to cause some object to act in a certain way, for instance, a power to cause sugar to dissolve. And a causal liability is a power to be caused by some object to act in a certain way, for instance, a power to be caused to dissolve by water. The will, however, is not a causal power, inasmuch as its exercise does not *consist in* the causing of some relevant kind of effect, even though its exercise does normally have an effect of a predictable kind, namely, an *action-result* appropriate to the kind of action that the agent wills to perform—as it might be, an arm-rising, in a case in which the agent wills to raise an arm. Nor, clearly, is the will a causal *liability*, like solubility. The exercise or manifestation of an agent's will does not consist in the agent's being caused to will, in the way that the manifestation of a lump of sugar's solubility consists in the sugar's being caused to dissolve by some suitable solvent. This is not to deny that acts of will may in principle be caused, only to deny that the power that is the will just is a liability to be caused to act in a certain way.

Because the will is a power, but is neither a causal power nor a causal liability, I shall call it a *spontaneous* power. There are other such powers in nature, such radium's spontaneous power to undergo radioactive decay, its atoms splitting into various fission products. Of course, it is possible to cause a radium atom to split up in such a way, by bombarding it with high-energy particles. But current scientific orthodoxy has it that radium can also decay 'spontaneously' and that when it does so there is simply *no* prior event which can properly be said to be the cause of the event of splitting: the latter, it is maintained, is a genuinely uncaused event. It is not even the case that such a splitting event, in such a case, has a non-deterministic or probabilistic cause: that is to say, it is not even the case that, whenever such a splitting event occurs 'spontaneously', there is always some prior event whose occurrence raises the probability (or 'chance') of the splitting event's occurrence, albeit only to a probability that still falls short of unity. Now, of course, it may seem tendentious in the extreme to describe the will as a 'spontaneous' power, given that the spontaneous radioactivity of radium is taken to be a typical example of such a power. For it may seem that we do not in like manner have any compelling reason to suppose that acts of the will are generally, or indeed ever, uncaused by prior events. However, we shall see in due course that there may indeed be good reason to suppose precisely this.

E. J. Lowe

7. Classic agent-causalism versus volitionism

Before we pursue this issue, let us turn to another and strategically prior issue: the question of whether it is sensible even to attempt to combine an agent-causation approach to action with volitionism, given that our ultimate objective is to make headway with the problem of free will. For, classically, agent-causation theories are opposed to volitionism and exploit this opposition in attempting to solve the problem of free will. What the classic agent-causation theorist may say about an episode of supposedly free action is something like this. Consider a case in which an agent, *a*, raises his arm 'freely' and as a so-called 'basic' action, or in the most 'direct' way possible (not, thus, by pulling on a rope attached to the arm, or some such thing). In such a case, the classic agent-causalist will say, *a* causes his arm to rise but *not* 'by' doing anything else whatever—and so, in particular, not by 'willing'.

The classic agent-causalist may well have positive reasons for doubting the existence of acts of will, but he also has the following strategic reason for denying their existence: it allows him to say that there really is *nothing at all* by doing which *a* causes his arm to rise in the sort of case under discussion. This in turn allows him to contend that in such a case a fact of agent-causation does not imply any corresponding fact of event-causation. As a consequence, he is in a position to block any attempt to reduce agent-causation to event-causation, along the lines suggested by schema (1). He may contend that *a*'s causing the event of arm-rising, in such a case, is a primitive causal fact which obtains at least to some extent independently of any facts of event causation that may also obtain. He may also urge that, inasmuch as *a*'s action of arm-raising *consists in* his thus irreducibly causing the event of arm-rising, his action itself is not properly categorised as being an *event*: rather, it is an irreducible *causing of an event by an agent*. But then, if the action is not an event, it is not something which is apt to be assigned a cause, on pain of committing a category mistake.[12] Hence, if we seek an explanation for the action, it cannot be right to seek a *causal* explanation for it, but at most a rational explanation in terms of the agent's reasons for so acting. Moreover, now there is no room to agree with

---

[12] See further my *A Survey of Metaphysics*, pp. 202–5. But even if it is allowed that agent *a*'s causing event *e does* itself qualify as an event, there are reasons for denying that such an event may be supposed to be caused: see Timothy O'Connor, *Persons and Causes: The Metaphysics of Free Will* (New York: Oxford University Press, 2000), pp. 52–5.

the Davidsonian contention that reasons *are* causes insofar as they explain actions.[13]

By contrast, it may seem that volitionism faces a much more difficult task in explaining how supposedly free action could escape the causal net of events, for the volitionist is in no position to dispute the correctness of schema (1). The volitionist believes that it is always *by willing* that we cause action-results, such as arm-risings, to occur when we act freely and that, indeed, our willings or volitions are causes of those events, in the event-causation sense of 'cause'. Precisely because, as we have seen, willings are not *causings*, they may qualify as *events* and thus as causes and effects of other events. So, to acknowledge that whenever we act freely we exercise our will and that our willings or volitions are events is to invite the question of whether our volitions are the effects, deterministic or probabilistic, of prior causes. The volitionist cannot, like the classic agent-causalist, hope to sidestep the question of prior causes simply by urging that actions are in the wrong ontological category to qualify as entities apt to be assigned and therefore explained in terms of causes. For volitions themselves seem to be at once actions and events—and to be events that are constitutively involved in all episodes of supposedly free action.

8. In defence of volitionism

I concede that the classic agent-causalist has a temporary strategic advantage over the volitionist for the foregoing reason, but consider that it is an advantage which is of little value in the longer run. This is partly because the classic agent-causalist's contention, in contravention of schema (1), that a substance *s* can cause an event *e* even though it is not *by acting in any manner* that *s* causes *e*, while perhaps being intelligible, appears both utterly improbable and unsupported by anything in our own experience of voluntary agency.

It is true enough that when I raise my arm 'directly', or in the most 'direct' way possible, there is no other *bodily movement* that I perform by performing which I cause my arm to rise—or, at least, no such bodily movement that I perform *intentionally*, by performing which I cause my arm to rise (for, after all, it may be said that I move certain muscles in my shoulder, albeit not intentionally, and

---

[13] See Donald Davidson, 'Actions, Reasons, and Causes', in his *Essays on Actions and Events* (Oxford: Clarendon Press, 1980).

by so doing cause my arm to rise). That, I suggest, is all that we are entitled to understand by performing a bodily movement 'directly', or in the most 'direct' way possible—namely, performing it without doing so by intentionally performing any other bodily movement.[14] It is altogether tendentious of the classic agent-causalist simply to define a 'basic' or 'direct' bodily action as one which is performed without doing so by doing *anything else whatever*.

I would moreover contend—I know somewhat controversially—that the phenomenology of voluntary action in fact supports volitionism, in that we are at least sometimes consciously aware of our willings as such. The most obvious examples of this arise in cases of sudden and unexpected paralysis, when we knowingly exercise our will but completely fail to effect any bodily movement. In such cases, we are aware of acting, but know also that our action cannot consist in our causing any bodily event. This is not to say that our action might not *be* a bodily event: it will be one if any of various forms of physicalism is true. However, the truth or falsity of physicalism is not at present my concern, although I think that there is in fact good reason to suppose that volitions cannot be identical with neural or cerebral events of any kind.

The classic agent-causalist may be well equipped, then, to duck the question of prior causes which is at the heart of the problem of free will, but can do so only at the expense of espousing a doctrine which is at once metaphysically and psychologically implausible. The volitionist, it seems, must acknowledge that volitions, even if they are actions, are also events and as such entities of the right category to be assigned causes and to be subject to causal explanation. So it may seem that all the work I have been doing to accommodate volitionism within a substance-causal view is not going to pay dividends as far as the problem of free will is concerned. I disagree. Although I am prepared to acknowledge that volitions are events, it is more important that they are actions and still more important that all causation, if I am right, is fundamentally substance causation, that is, causation by substances exercising their powers upon other substances. According to this way of thinking, all talk of event causation is mere shadow-talk—legitimate enough for purposes of abbreviation, but not revelatory of the real causal machinery that operates at the level of substances and their powers. Furthermore, as we saw earlier, the ontology of powers allows scope for various fine-grained distinctions between kinds of powers, which we may hope to exploit in attempting to make headway with the problem of free will.

[14] See further my *Subjects of Experience*, pp. 150–2.

9. The will and its freedom

An important point to emphasise here is that one can endorse both schema (1) and schema (2), while also making the following claims. First, that schema (2) is genuinely reductive, in the metaphysical sense, in that it tells us what event causation *consists in*, whereas schema (1) is simply a conceptual truth which is explicable in terms of the truth of schema (2) together with the principle (rejected by the classic agent-causalist) that substances always cause by acting in some manner. Second, that not every event—that is, not every case of a substance's acting in some specific manner—is *caused*. By 'caused' here I mean, of course, caused by a substance acting in some manner, which I hold to be the fundamental sense in which anything is ever caused. Given my substance-causalism, to say that some event may be uncaused is just to say that, sometimes, a substance may act in a certain manner even though it is not the case that any substance, itself included, *causes* it to act in that manner (which, of course, it could only do *by acting in some manner*, if I am right). Such an event will be an exercise of a 'spontaneous' power of the substance concerned, to use the terminology introduced earlier. And we have seen that there plausibly are such spontaneous powers in the natural world, such as the spontaneous radioactivity of radium atoms. Consequently, there is nothing unintelligible in the idea that the will itself may be a spontaneous power in this sense. Indeed, it is very natural to suppose that the will is such a power, because we have already seen that it appears to be neither a causal power nor a causal liability. Certainly, the will seems to be quite unlike such natural causal powers and liabilities as magnetism and solubility.

It is a characteristic of such natural causal powers and liabilities that the objects possessing them have, as we say, no *choice* as to whether or not to exercise or manifest them: when a piece of iron is placed near to a magnet, the magnet cannot refrain from attracting it, nor can a lump of sugar refrain from being dissolved when it is placed in water. It is equally true, however, of the spontaneous power of radium to undergo radioactive decay that a radium atom has no choice as to whether or not to manifest that power on any given occasion. But what do we mean when we talk thus of 'choice'? We mean, I would say, precisely an exercise of the power of will. Willing precisely is *choosing* a course of action, normally in preference to some other course of action: choosing, say, to raise one's arm rather than to leave it down. So our very conception of the will is as a power the conditions of whose exercise are quite different from those governing the exercise of other natural powers, whether causal or spontaneous. We conceive of it neither as a power whose exercise is characteristically determined by the causal influence of other objects, nor as one whose manifestations are merely the outcome of chance. Rather, we conceive of it as being a power that is chararacteristically exercised in the light of reason. We conceive of it, that is to say, as being a *rational* power.[15]

A power's being a spontaneous power is clearly not a sufficient condition of its being a rational power, as the example of radium's radioactivity shows. But it is a necessary condition, I would urge, because a power whose nature is such that its exercise or manifestation is characteristically determined, or even merely made more probable, by the causal influence of objects acting upon the possessor of the power cannot, for that very reason, qualify as a rational power. For a substance to act in a certain way because it was *caused* to act in that way, whether by another substance or even by itself acting upon itself, is not for that substance to act rationally, or genuinely 'in the light' of any reasons it may have for so acting. By so acting, a substance may act in a way that is *in accordance with* certain of its reasons for acting, if it has any, but it cannot be acting *for* any of those reasons, given that it was caused to act in that way.[16] To act for a reason is to act in a way that is responsive to the cogency of certain considerations in favour of one's so acting—and this is incompatible with one's being *caused* to act in that way, because causal processes bring about their effects with complete indifference to the question of whether those effects have cogent considerations in their favour.

To act in the light of one's reasons for acting in this or that way, one must, then, be able to *choose* so to act, where choice is understood as being the exercise of a rational power.[17] However, this doesn't mean that when one so acts there must always be an alternative course of action open to one, other than in the minimal sense that one must be able to *refrain* from choosing to act in a certain way. It

---

[15] The notion of a 'rational' power is, once again, Aristotelian in origin: see *Metaphysics*, book θ.

[16] See further my *An Introduction to the Philosophy of Mind* (Cambridge: Cambridge University Press, 2000), pp. 252–62. For a similar view, see John R. Searle, *Rationality in Action* (Cambridge, MA: MIT Press, 2001), pp. 12–17 and ch. 3.

[17] There is no implication here that one must be able to *choose to choose*, or *will to will*, much less that the conception of choice now being defended falls foul of a vicious infinite regress. For discussion, see my *Locke on Human Understanding*, pp. 133–4.

may well be that, in certain circumstances, whatever I choose to do, a certain action-result will eventuate. For example, my hand may be strapped into a device which allows me either to move my finger down, thereby depressing a button and exploding a bomb, or else to leave my finger where it is, in which case I shall prevent a lever from falling, as a consequence of which again the bomb will explode. In this case, whatever I do and however I exercise my power of choice, I shall cause the bomb to explode. Of course, I am presented with alternative courses of action as far as the movement of my finger is concerned, but even this feature of the example may be eliminated by envisaging some device which is directly activated by my mental act of choice, rather than via an intervening bodily movement. In that case, it is beyond my control to make any difference to the course of events affected by my will. Whether I choose to act or choose to refrain from acting, my choice—my volition or act of will—will have the same effect. But in respect of the act of choice itself, I suggest, I am and must be presented with a genuine alternative: to choose to act in a certain way or to refrain from choosing so to act.

Choice being the exercise of a rational power, it cannot coherently be supposed to be determined by prior causes: and nothing that we know about physical nature or the human mind, I suggest, demonstrates that one could not be in possession of such a rational power. Indeed, I would go further and say that one cannot rationally believe that one is *not* in possession of such a power, for this would be to undermine one's own claim to be a rational agent and thus a rational being—and to deny oneself the title of a rational being is to deprive oneself of any right to appeal to reason in support of any of one's beliefs. Consequently, it is incoherent to suppose that one might encounter either evidence of an empirical or scientific nature, or arguments of a metaphysical character, which would rationally compel one to judge that one is not in possession of a rational power of choice, such as I conceive the human will to be.[18]

---

[18] The present paper has been an attempt to draw together, reconcile and develop further views about the philosophy of action expressed in the four books of mine cited earlier: *Locke on Human Understanding*, ch. 6, *Subjects of Experience*, ch. 5, *An Introduction to the Philosophy of Mind*, ch. 9 and *A Survey of Metaphysics*, ch. 11. I am grateful for comments received when the paper was delivered in the Royal Institute of Philosophy's 'Minds and Persons' lecture series. I am also grateful to Randolph Clarke for his comments and for alerting me to an error in an earlier version.

E. J. Lowe

Appendix

Here is a formal proof that (1*) is equivalent to (1**), given certain further assumptions that will be made explicit. Let us write (1*) more formally as follows:

(1*) s caused $e_2 \leftrightarrow (\exists e_1)(\exists F)(e_1 = s$'s F'ing & e_1 caused e_2)

Then let it be assumed that schema (2) embraces the following schema as a special case:

(2*) e_1 caused $e_2 \leftrightarrow (\exists t)(\exists G)(e_1 = t$'s G'ing & t by G'ing caused e_2)

Substituting the righthand side of (2*) for 'e_1 caused e_2' in (1*), we get:

(1*+) s caused $e_2 \leftrightarrow (\exists e_1)(\exists F)(e_1 = s$'s F'ing & $(\exists t)(\exists G)(e_1 = t$'s G'ing & t by G'ing caused e_2))

Now let us make the following further assumption:

(3) $(\forall t)(\forall G)(t$'s G'ing $= s$'s F'ing $\rightarrow t = s$ & $G = F$)

and consider the righthand side of (1*+), namely:

(4) $(\exists e_1)(\exists F)(e_1 = s$'s F'ing & $(\exists t)(\exists G)(e_1 = t$'s G'ing & t by G'ing caused e_2))

(4) may be rewritten as

(5) $(\exists e_1)(\exists F)(\exists t)(\exists G)(e_1 = s$'s F'ing & $e_1 = t$'s G'ing & t by G'ing caused e_2)

Now, '$e_1 = s$'s F'ing & $e_1 = t$'s G'ing' in (5) entails, by the laws of identity, 't's G'ing $= s$'s F'ing', which, given assumption (3), entails '$t = s$ & $G = F$'. It follows that, by Leibniz's law, (5) entails

(6) $(\exists e_1)(\exists F)(e_1 = s$'s F'ing & s by F'ing caused e_2)

which in turn entails, and is therefore equivalent to, (5). Hence, (6) is equivalent to and so may be substituted for the righthand side of (1*+), to yield as a statement equivalent to (1*+) and hence equivalent to (1*)

(1**) s caused $e_2 \leftrightarrow (\exists e_1)(\exists F)(e_1 = s$'s F'ing & s by F'ing caused e_2)

Q.E.D.

The key assumption in the proof is principle (3) which, however, seems relatively uncontroversial. Informally expressed, this is the principle that if a substance t's acting in a manner G is identical with a substance s's acting in a manner F, then t is identical with s and G is identical with F.

Mental Substances[1]

TIM CRANE

1. Do minds exist?

Philosophers of mind typically conduct their discussions in terms of mental events, mental processes, mental properties, mental states —but rarely in terms of minds themselves. Sometimes this neglect is explicitly acknowledged. Donald Davidson, for example, writes that 'there are no such things as minds, but people have mental properties, which is to say that certain psychological predicates are true of them. These properties are constantly changing, and such changes are mental events'.[2] Hilary Putnam agrees, though for somewhat different reasons:

> The view I have long defended is that the mind is not a *thing*, talk of our minds is talk of *world-involving capabilities that we have and activities that we engage in*. As Dewey succinctly put it, 'Mind is primarily a verb. It denotes all the ways in which we deal consciously and expressly with the situation in which we find ourselves. Unfortunately, an influential manner of thinking has changed modes of action into an underlying substance that performs the activities in question. It has treated mind as an independent entity *which* attends, purposes, cares and remembers'. But the traditional view, by treating mental states as states of the 'underlying substance', makes them properties of something 'inside', and, if one is a materialist philosopher, that means properties of our *brains*. So the next problem naturally seems to be: '*Which* neurological properties of our brains do these mental properties "reduce" to?' For how could our *brains* have properties

[1] This paper is intended as a preliminary attempt to bring together issues in the mainstream of the philosophy of mind and the personal identity debate. I am grateful to audiences at the University of Nottingham, the Australian National University, University College London and at the Royal Institute of Philosophy for generous and constructive criticism. I would like also to thank Robert Black, Martin Davies, Stephen Everson, Katalin Farkas, Mike Martin, Hugh Mellor, Peter Menzies, Michael Smith and Daniel Stoljar for especially helpful discussion.

[2] Donald Davidson, 'Davidson, Donald' in *A Companion in the Philosophy of Mind* Samuel Guttenplan (ed.) (Oxford: Blackwell 1995) 231.

that *aren't* neurological? And this is how materialist philosophers saw the problem until the advent of such new alternatives in the philosophy of mind and philosophy of language as Functionalism and Semantic Externalism.[3]

What is the idea behind this denial that the mind is a thing? Putnam's own reasoning here seems somewhat incomplete. The traditional view he is rejecting moves from saying that mental states are states of an 'underlying substance'; to saying that they are 'inside' the subject, and from there to the idea that mental states must be states of the brain if one is a materialist. But what is the connection between a *thing* and being an 'underlying substance'? And why does that mean that the states must be 'inside'—and what does 'inside' mean here, in any case? Philosophers do frequently argue that mental states are brain states without (or so it seems) making the prior explicit assumption that mental states must be states of an underlying substance.[4] So what role does the idea that *the mind is a thing* play in this dialectic?

The situation is not helped by the fact that there is something initially unsatisfactory about the positive suggestion Putnam is offering. Putnam says that talk about the mind is really talk about 'world-involving capabilities that we have and activities that we engage in', and he quotes Dewey's view that the mind refers to 'all the ways in which we deal consciously and expressly with the situation in which we find ourselves' and Dewey's rejection of the view that a mind is 'an independent entity *which* attends, purposes, cares and remembers'. But, on the face of it, there is a conflict between the idea that mental talk is talk of *our* activities, and the idea that there is *nothing* which attends, purposes, cares and remembers. Do Dewey and Putnam really mean that there is nothing—no entity, in the broadest sense—which is doing the attending, caring and remembering? Surely not. Their rejection is a rejection of the idea that it is an entity *of a certain kind* which attends, purposes and so on. But what kind? The candidates for being these entities, which are doing these things, can hardly be properties, processes or events. The obvious answer—suggested by Putnam and Dewey's talk of 'our' activities—is that it is people (or persons) who are

[3] Hilary Putnam, *The Threefold Cord: Mind, Body and World* (New York, Columbia UP 1999) 169–70; the quotations from Dewey is from J. Dewey, *Art as Experience* in *John Dewey: The Later Works, 1925–1953*, vol. 10, 1934 (Carbondale, Ill.' Southern Illinois UP, 1991) 268.

[4] See, e.g., David Lewis, 'An argument for the Identity Theory' in Lewis, *Philosophical Papers* Volume I (Oxford: Oxford University Press 1985), where no such assumption is explicitly made.

participating in these activities. But people are good candidates for being *things*, at least in the sense of being particular objects, the bearers of properties. And what is supposed to be so problematic about the idea that people are things?

One possible source of a problem here is not the idea that a person remembers, attends and so on, but that a *mind* does. The suspicion might be directed against the idea that there are mental *things*, which we call minds. This might explain Dewey's denial that 'there is nothing *independent*' which does these things, if 'independent' is meant to have the connotations it has in traditional discussions of substance: on one dominant tradition, substance is that which exists independently, or capable of independent existence.[5] Here, then, is a link to the idea of substance. But there is still not an obvious objection contained in this link: for there is an obvious sense in which the persons who are the subjects of these mental activities are 'independent' of one another (though this may not be the sense in which Dewey uses the term).

The question I wish to address, then, is this. Given the implausibility of denying that when there is mental activity there is something which is the subject of this activity, why is it that philosophers have found themselves denying that what thinks (remembers etc.) is a mental thing? One reason has emerged: a suspicion of the idea of a *thinking thing* or mental substance in the Cartesian sense.[6] Suspicion of this idea might come from two distinct sources: first, a suspicion of the role that the idea of mental substance has played in framing the mind-body problem, and in traditional controversial theories of the mind-body relation (notably Cartesian dualism). And second, it might come from suspicion of the idea of substance in general.

My aim in the rest of this paper is to argue that these suspicions are not well-founded: the mind-body problem (in the sense in which

[5] For recent defences of this idea of substance see Gary Hoffman and Joshua Rosenkrantz, *Substance: its Nature and Existence* (London: Routledge 1996), and E. J. Lowe, *The Possibility of Metaphysics* (Oxford: Clarendon Press 1998). Some of these claims are discussed in section 3 below.

[6] Thus Jaegwon Kim writes: 'The idea of minds as souls or spirits, as *entities* or *objects* of a special kind, has never gained a foothold in a serious scientific study of the mind and has also gradually disappeared from philosophical discussions of mentality... There has been a near consensus among philosophers that the concept of mind as a mental substance gives rise to too many difficulties and puzzles without compensating explanatory gains.' *Philosophy of Mind* (Boulder: Westview 1996) 3.

it is debated today) does not essentially rest on, or even derive from, the idea of a mental substance. On this matter, I think, Putnam is partly right: it is true that mental substances or subjects are sometimes rejected by materialists because they are supposed to be the main source of the mind-body problem. But these materialist philosophers are, nonetheless, wrong; insofar as we have a mind-body problem today, it is not primarily the result of the idea of mental substance.[7] Therefore rejecting the idea of mental substance does not help us solve the mind-body problem.

However, the idea of a mental substance might be objectionable on other grounds—for example, if the idea of substance itself is objectionable. So the second theme of this paper is the idea of substance. Though frequently attacked, this is one of the most pervasive, resilient and fertile ideas in metaphysics. I will outline some general elements of a concept of substance, and say something about what an acceptable notion of mental substance might be. My ultimate aim would be to defend the thesis that *persons* are, in a certain sense, mental substances, but I can only gesture at what this might mean here.

2. The mind-body problem: a traditional view

Presentations of the mind-body problem tend to start with something like the following line of thought. Descartes argued that minds were substances distinct from bodies. Bodies are made of matter or material substance, characterized by its characteristic attribute *extension*, and the existence of matter was ultimately independent of the existence of minds. A mind is a mental substance, and it is characterized by its characteristic attribute, *thought*. Minds and bodies interact, but this interaction is seen to be deeply problematic because mental and material substances are so completely different in character. Mental substances are thought to be at best causally problematic, and at worst unintelligible. Now the Cartesian view is often presented as having some intuitive appeal, even though it is unacceptable, and the mind-body problem is therefore posed by the question of how to articulate an adequate alternative to the Cartesian view, given that we must reject its commitment to two substances.

One idea which we must dismiss at this stage is that the unintelligibility of mental substance comes from the idea that on the

[7] For agreement on this point, see David Rosenthal 'Identity theories' in Samuel Guttenplan (ed.) op. cit., 348.

Cartesian view, minds are 'made of' mental substance, just as bodies are made of matter.[8] This reading of 'mental substance' trades on the ordinary language use of 'substance' as meaning *stuff*—this is the mass noun use of 'substance', as in 'tar is a thick black sticky substance'. There is nothing wrong with using the word 'substance' in this way, of course. But with the word understood in this way, a *mental* substance is certainly something very strange: rather like a ghost, made of some mysterious 'ectoplasm'. And this cannot be what Descartes meant by mental (or thinking) substance, since on Descartes's view the mind is not made of anything at all. The mind is a simple substance, it has no parts (though it has faculties or capacities), it is fundamentally and essentially indivisible. The term *substance* is being used by Descartes in a technical, traditional philosophical sense. A substance in Descartes's sense is what exists most fundamentally, an idea which is partly spelled out in terms of the idea of independent existence (see section 3 below for further discussion). So an important aspect of this definition is that there is as many *individual* substances as there are things capable of independent existence: the Cartesian view is that each individual mind is an individual mental substance, not that minds are 'made of mental substance'.

This idea that things are 'made of' substance is more applicable to Cartesian material substance, since it is true on the Cartesian view that everyday objects are just bits of matter (or material substance). But this idea of substance is still connected with the idea of a particular thing capable of independent existence: the material world is one substance. Human bodies are not substances, they are just portions of the matter of the material world itself, which is the only material substance.

Another construal of substance which we must reject is that which construes it as a 'featureless substrata', underlying all matter, or, applied to a particular object, a 'bare particular' with no properties as such. G. E. M. Anscombe has pointed out clearly the fundamental confusion in this view: in attempting to answer the question 'what is substance?' we start off saying that it is the bearer of

---

[8] This view is still quite common in contemporary philosophy. For example, when discussing dualism, Frank Jackson says that 'ectoplasm is to be understood as the kind of stuff incompatible with the physicalists' view of what kinds there are—perhaps the stuff out of which thoughts are made according to Descartes.' *From Metaphysics to Ethics* (Oxford: Oxford University Press, 1998), 15. For a useful corrective, see E. J. Lowe, *The Possibility of Metaphysics* (Oxford: Clarendon Press, 1998) 201.

properties, but end up saying that 'in itself' it has no properties at all.[9] But surely if we define substances as *essentially* the bearers of properties, then we have already said enough to rule out the idea that substance can be featureless or without properties: for it follows from this definition that there can be no substance without any properties at all.

These qualifications made, how is the idea of mental substance connected to the mind-body problem? As mentioned above, there are two dominant lines of connection: first, that mental substance is unintelligible, and second, that causal interaction is problematic. These days, the focus is on the second, for the following reason. Assuming (as is fairly standard) a fairly liberal approach to metaphysical and logical possibility, many philosophers argue that there is nothing in principle impossible with the idea of Cartesian mental substance, or even that there is nothing in principle impossible in the idea that there are disembodied beings.[10] Rather, the resistance to Cartesianism is based on the idea that *our* world is not like this. There may be possible worlds which contain Cartesian substances, but our world is not one of them. The reason for this is that we know enough about the physical world to know that physical things only come about through physical causes, and that since mental things do have physical effects, they must themselves be physical. This is the argument for physicalism from the causal closure (or causal 'completeness') of the physical world.[11]

This part of the mind-body problem, then, is a problem about causation: how does the mind have effects in the physical world, given that physical effects seem to be brought about by purely physical causes? And the obvious answer to this is that the mind is a physical thing: the brain. The other part of the mind-body problem concerns the explanation of consciousness: if the mind is a physical thing, how can consciousness be explained? I therefore see the contemporary mind-body problem as a dilemma: if the mind is not physical, then how can it have effects in the physical world; but if it is physical, how can we explain consciousness?[12]

[9] 'Substance' in her *Collected Philosophical Papers Volume II: Metaphysics and the Philosophy of Mind* (Oxford: Blackwell, 1981).

[10] For example: 'Since there seems no reason to deny the intelligibility of souls, we affirm their logical possibility', Hoffman and Rosenkrantz, op. cit. 6.

[11] See David Papineau, *Thinking about Consciousness* (Oxford: Oxford University Press, 2002) and Barry Loewer, 'From physics to physicalism' in *Physicalism and its Discontents,* Barry Loewer and Carl Gillet (eds.) (Cambridge: Cambridge University Press 2001).

[12] For more on this conception of the mind-body problem, see my *Elements of Mind* (Oxford: Oxford University Press, 2001), §19.

Does this formulation of today's mind-body problem in any way presuppose that the problem be formulated in terms of Cartesian dualism? I don't think so. One way to see why is to consider how little is achieved—in attacking either horn of the dilemma—by accepting or denying Cartesian dualism. On the second horn (the explanation of consciousness): it has long been recognized that it is hardly an answer to the question of how a physical thing can be conscious to say that consciousness inheres in an entirely non-physical thing (even if that thing is something whose essential attribute is consciousness). If the original puzzle was supposed to be with our understanding of how a physical thing can be conscious, no progress is made by saying that consciousness is a property of a mental substance. But maybe the *first* horn of the dilemma is generated by the distinctive nature of mental substance? Jerry Fodor certainly thinks so:

> The chief drawback of dualism is its failure to account adequately for mental causation. If the mind is non-physical, it has no position in physical space. How then, can a mental cause give rise to a behavioural effect that has a position in space? To put it another way, how can the non-physical give rise to the physical without violating the laws of conservation of mass, of energy and of momentum?[13]

The objection here is certainly to Cartesian substance dualism (hence the reference to 'no position in physical space'). And it does seem to be a decisive objection to the idea of causal interaction between mind and body that one is in space and one is not. For how can something cause something else if it has no location? What would explain why it brought about effects at one location rather than another? So perhaps the first horn of the mind-body problem is generated by the assumption of Cartesian mental substances.

If this were true, then denying mental substance would remove the problem. But it clearly doesn't; the problem remains exactly as it was. Suppose one denied that there are any mental substances in the Cartesian sense. If one does not deny mental events and properties, then the causal part of the mind-body problem would remain, since events and properties (and not substances) are normally considered to be the relata of causation. The problem arose because of a conflict between mental causation and the causal closure (or 'completeness') of the physical world. If there are no mental substances, but nonetheless mental causes of some kind

[13] Jerry Fodor, 'The mind-body problem' in *The Mind-Body Problem,* T. Szubka and R. Warner (eds.) (Oxford: Blackwell, 1994), 25.

(events, properties or facts) then this conflict still arises. A dualist about mental properties or events would have just as much need to respond to the argument as a dualist about mental substance does. Most presentations of the argument see it as an argument against dualism without acknowledging that the essential feature of the dualism in question is that it is a dualism of *causes*, rather than a dualism of substances. And if substances are not causes (as most participants in the debate agree[14]) then the moral is clear: the idea of substance plays no role in causal problem which is the first horn of the mind-body dilemma.[15]

One might respond that although the idea of mental substance is not the main generator of the mind-body problem, nonetheless it does not make the problem more tractable. After all, it can hardly help understand how the mind makes the body move by saying that its properties are properties of an immaterial substance, or that mental events are events in which things happen to immaterial substances. This is plausible; but the question I now want to address is whether it is the idea of *mental* substance *as such* which adds this extra difficulty, or whether it is the Cartesian idea of a non-extended (and therefore non-spatial) substance. We first need to ask whether it is the idea of substance which is at fault here, or is it something else? In the next section I shall outline some reasons for believing in substance; in the final section I shall provide some support for the idea that there are mental substances.

3. Substances and non-substances

Some philosophers do think, largely on grounds independent of the mind-body problem, that the idea of substance is one which has had

[14] A notable exception is E. J. Lowe. See his 'Event causation and agent causation', *Grazer Philosophische Studien* forthcoming.

[15] It might be objected that fundamental to substance dualism is the idea that the world does not have one kind of explanation, but that fundamentally different styles of explanation are required for mental and physical substances and their effects. Monists (e.g. physicalists) may then argue that the same form of explanation (e.g. subsumption under physical law) applies to mental and physical things, and this is because they are fundamentally the same kind of substance. This does link the rejection of substance dualism to the current debate in an interesting way, and requires further discussion. My basic response is that the driving idea here is the idea of a single kind of explanation, an idea I was expressing in terms of the causal closure of the physical world. I am indebted here to discussions with Mike Martin.

its day.[16] Of course, I cannot hope to embark on a full-scale defence of the idea of substance here. All I can do within the confines of this paper is to try and outline some main elements of an adequate idea of substance, and try to indicate some of the sources of resistance to it. In §2 I dismissed two inadequate yet common ways of thinking of substance. The first was the idea that substance is merely *stuff*, the second is the idea that a substance is a *bare particular*. These ideas are not part of the best conception of substance; so what is that conception?

What we are interested in here are *individual substances*, what Aristotle called *primary substances*, of which the paradigmatic examples are human beings and animals. (I will not say much about kinds of substance, what Aristotle called *secondary substances*, nor about substance in the sense of stuff.) Individual substances are particulars—unrepeatable individuals, in modern ontological thinking. But not all particulars are substances. Events, on the best understanding of them, are particulars, but they are not substances.[17] Since all particulars are the bearers of properties, being a bearer of properties does not suffice for being a substance. What distinguishes events from particular objects, on the traditional understanding which seems to me essentially correct, is that events have temporal parts or stages and objects do not. In C. D. Broad's terminology, this is the distinction between *continuants* as opposed to an *occurrents*.[18] As David Wiggins puts it:

> An event takes time, and will admit the question 'How long did it last?' only in the sense 'How long did it take?'. An event does not persist in the way a continuant does—that is *through* time, gaining and losing new parts. A continuant has spatial parts. To find the whole continuant you have only to explore its boundaries at a time. An event has temporal parts. To find the whole event you must trace it through the historical beginning to the historical end. An event does not have spatial parts in any way that is to be compared with (or understood by reference to) the way in which it has *temporal* parts.[19]

[16] See, for example, Peter Simons, 'Farewell to substance: a differentiated leave-taking' *Ratio* New Series 11 (1998), 253–252; also in *Form and Matter. Themes in Contemporary Metaphysics,* D. S. Oderberg (ed.) (Oxford: Blackwell, 1998), 22–39.

[17] See Donald Davidson, 'Events as particulars' in Davidson, *Essays on Actions and Events* (Oxford: Oxford University Press 1980).

[18] C. D. Broad, *An Examination of McTaggart's Philosophy* (Cambridge: Cambridge University Press, 1933,) 138.

[19] David Wiggins, *Sameness and Substance Renewed* (Cambridge: Cambridge University Press, 2001), 31, note 13.

Tim Crane

But the idea of a particular, a bearer of properties which does not have temporal parts, does not yet amount to the idea of a substance. For on the face of it, a pile of stones in a field seems a perfectly good continuant: it is a particular, it has properties, it (arguably) persists through change by remaining the same pile of stones even when one or two stones are removed from it. Likewise, the ball of dust in the corner of my room is a continuant—the same ball of dust can remain in the corner, even as it grows by the accumulation of more dust. But no-one who believes in individual substances would count things like balls of dust and piles of stones as substances. On what grounds, then, should we distinguish substances from other non-substantial continuants?

In the broadly Aristotelian tradition to which the idea of individual substance belongs, an account of individual substances substance involves at least the following three ideas: (i) substances have independent existence; (ii) substances are the bearers of properties or attributes, the subjects of predication which are not themselves predicated of anything else; (iii) substances persist through change. These ideas can be related in the following way: substances are the bearers of attributes; therefore attributes have dependent existence, since they depend on their instantiation in substances; but substances do not depend for their existence on the existence of attributes, since a substance can survive the loss of an attribute and remain the same substance. In other words, a substance has existence in a more fundamental way than an attribute, since it can persist through change—i.e. survive the loss of an attribute—in a way that its attributes cannot survive the destruction of a substance.

There is a lot to be said for this line of thought. But as a way of making the distinction between substance and attribute, it is ultimately unconvincing. For if we have rejected 'bare particulars', then we do not allow that a substance can exist independently of some attribute or other: every substance must have some attribute. But then by parity of reasoning we can say that if we reject uninstantiated universals (as modern Aristotelians do) then we do not allow that an attribute can exist independently of some substance or other. And just as we say that a particular undergoes change by gaining and losing properties, and thus persists through change, we can equally say that an attribute undergoes change when it changes its instantiation among the various particulars that there are.[20]

[20] This presupposes that attributes are universals in D. M. Armstrong's sense, rather than tropes or 'abstract particulars': see *Universals and Scientific Realism* (Cambridge: Cambridge University Press, 1978) especially volume I. For further discussion of the kind of issue discussed in

Neither the idea of substances being the bearers of properties, nor the idea of substances persisting through change, enables us to capture a sense in which substances have independent existence and attributes do not, and thus to distinguish substances from other particles.

Can the idea of independent existence be employed in some other way to define the idea of substance? 17th century discussions assumed so. Descartes claimed that a substance must be capable of existing independently of all other things: 'by *substance* we can understand nothing other than a thing which exists in such a way as to depend on no other thing for its existence'.[21] He acknowledged that since everything's existence depends on God, therefore God is the only substance in the strict sense (the conclusion famously drawn by Spinoza). But let us follow Descartes in our investigation into empirical substances and put God to one side. What, given this, should we make of this 'independence criterion' of substance?

The important question is, 'independent from what?'. Suppose we take Descartes's lead and say that a substance, properly so-called, is something which is capable of existing independently from all other things. Ignoring independence from attributes for the reasons just given, we should express this as: *independent of all other particulars*. Thus we allow that, if A is a substance, there is a possible world where A is (tenselessly) the only object. Note the consequences of there being such a 'lonely world'. If it is really possible, then essentialist theses like the necessity of origin cannot be true.[22] For if A is a person, then according to the necessity of origin thesis, A's parents are essential to A's existence. So A cannot exist

[21] R. Descartes, *Principles of Philosophy* I.51 in *The Philosophical Writings of Descartes* trans. & eds. J. Cottingham *et al.* (Cambridge: Cambridge University Press, 1985), vol. I, 210.

[22] For the necessity of origin, see Saul Kripke, *Naming and Necessity* Oxford Blackwell, 1980, Lecture 3. E. J. Lowe willingly accepts this consequence of the independence criterion in *The Possibility of Metaphysics* op. cit., 152, but usefully distinguishes between saying that A might have not been born—i.e. might have come into existence without parents, or might have always been in existence—and saying that given that A was born, A might have had different parents. He admits only the possibility of the first of these.

this paragraph, see E. J. Lowe, *The Possibility of Metaphysics* chapter 6, especially 141–2, and G. Hoffman and J. Rosenkrantz, 'The independence criterion of substance', *Philosophy and Phenomenological Research* **51** (1991) 835–52.

(tenselessly) in a lonely world. This conclusion seems too strong to be derivable from the definition of substance alone. Why should the mere *definition* of what it is to be a substance rule out these essentialist claims? This is particularly unsatisfactory since many defenders of substance have wanted to defend a form of essentialism too.[23]

Perhaps it could be responded that what matters is not independence from all other things, but independence from all things which are not essential (or otherwise necessarily connected) to the thing in question. But this is going around in a very small circle: we are asking how to tell whether A is a substance, and told that A must be capable of existing apart from certain other things. Which other things? Answer: all those things which are *inessential* to A; in other words, all those things which A is capable of existing without. Suppose that it is true that for any A, there are things which A is incapable of existing without and things which it is capable of existing without. Then to say that A's being a substance consists in it being capable of independent existence from those things it can exist independently of is to say almost nothing at all.

One idea behind the 'independent existence' criterion of substance is that the existence of certain things (say, artefacts) is dependent on a creator, whereas some kinds of thing (say, organisms) do not need a creator to come into existence. So artefacts have a dependent existence where organisms do not. But without wanting to deny the importance of the distinction between organisms and artefacts, the idea of an organism's dependence on its genesis is too closely analogous to an artefact's dependence on its creator for us to be able to use this distinction to distinguish organisms as substances.

The idea of independent existence has not got us very far in distinguishing substances from other continuants. A clue that the criterion was not satisfactory was that it failed adequately to distinguish particulars from their properties or attributes. Then we saw that the idea of 'independence of all other particulars' does not allow a doctrine of substance to be compatible with some forms of essentialism; and 'independence of inessential particulars' is a vacuous criterion, which applies to everything. Everything is capable of existing independently of those things of which it is capable of existing independently.

So let us abandon the independent criterion of substance, then. The two other Aristotelian ideas were that a substance is the bearer

---

[23] See Wiggins, *Sameness and Substance Renewed* chapter 4.

of properties (the subject of predication that is not predicated of anything else) and that a substance persists through change. But neither will these ideas help distinguish substances from other particulars and continuants. For (i) all particulars, including events, are bearers of properties; and (ii) all continuants (as I am using the term) persist through change. These ideas on their own will not help us to distinguish substances from other continuants. This is not to say that these ideas could not be used as part of the whole story of what characterizes substances according to some other conception. But none of these ideas is sufficient.

Rather than abandon the hunt for substance, let us instead focus on the *point* of calling some particulars 'substances'. Here it is useful to consider an important aspect of Leibniz's criticism of Descartes's conception of material substance.[24] Descartes believed that the material world is one substance, and that what we think of as particular objects within the material world are really just modes of that substance. This has the consequence that for Descartes (unlike Aristotle) a particular dog, for example, is not a substance. Nor is a human body. Leibniz objected that on this Cartesian view, there is no real way of distinguishing between mere aggregates— entities which are unities only because we group them together as such—and the substances which make them up. Consider a flock of birds. We can identify the flock as a continuant—it doesn't have temporal parts, for instance—and we can think of it as the *same flock* even when some birds leave and others join it. But there is a clear sense in which the flock does not have the kind of unity which each individual bird has. The flock is a collection, an assemblage, what Leibniz called an *ens per aggregationem*. Leibniz argued that such aggregates must themselves be made up things which are not aggregates, otherwise matter would have to be infinitely divisible. And if it were infinitely divisible, then it would be impossible to solve the 'problem of the continuum': i.e. how an infinite number of infinitely small parts can combine to form something of a certain size. This is why Leibniz concluded that there must be simple substances, since there are complexes.[25] Simple substances are monads.

Without wishing to follow Leibniz down this route towards monads, we should take seriously his insight that the Cartesian view of

---

[24] See, for example, the criticism in Leibniz's *Discourse on Metaphysics* §12. All page and other references to Leibniz's works in this paper are to the translation in *G. W. Leibniz Philosophy Texts* R. Woolhouse and R. Francks (eds.) (Oxford: Oxford University Press, 1998).

[25] See *Monadology* §1–3, and 'Principles of Nature and Grace, Based on Reason', §1.

matter has no way of accounting for the distinction between those entities which have a unity in themselves, and those whose unity is the result of mere aggregation. For the unity of certain aggregates, like a pile of stones, is in a certain sense arbitrary, and in a certain sense dependent on our conception of it. There is a sense in which the pile is not a *real unity*, what Leibniz called an *unum per se*. In a letter to Arnauld, Leibniz illustrates this point with the example of bringing together a pair of diamonds:

> the composite which is made up of the diamond of the Grand Duke and that of the Great Mogul can be called a pair of diamonds, but that is only a being of reason; if they were brought together, that would be a being of imagination or perception, a phenomenon, that is, because contact, share motion, co-operating in a single design do not change anything in substantial unity.[26]

I propose that the idea of a *unum per se* is what we intend when we say that something is a substance. The notion of a particular I introduced above is a very minimal notion, which can be true of anything which is the bearer of properties and not instantiated by anything (i.e. not a universal). If there is no distinction in nature worth making between particulars like individual birds and particulars like flocks of birds, then there is no point in talking about substances at all. The point of talking in terms of substance, then, is to distinguish those entities which are real unities from those which are only unities because of a relatively arbitrary or interest-relative stipulation on our part, or because of mere aggregation. To understand the unity of a substance is to understand the principle of its unity, the principle which explains why the substance hangs together as it does. Let me illustrate these ideas with two examples, one from early modern philosophy and the other more contemporary.

The first example is from Leibniz's own theory of substances. Anything which is divisible into parts will itself be only an aggregate. So if bodies are divisible into parts, then bodies cannot be substances themselves. This is why, although he began by criticizing the Cartesian conception of material substance on the grounds that it could not account for the way in which animal bodies were real unities, Leibniz ends up denying that bodies are substances at all, 'strictly speaking'. As he wrote to Arnauld: 'a body is an aggregation of substances, and not strictly speaking a substance. It must therefore be that there are substances in bodies everywhere, substances which are indivisible, ingenerable, and incorruptible'.[27]

[26] Leibniz, letter to Arnauld, 30 April 1687.
[27] Leibniz, letter to Arnauld, 23 March 1690.

From the perspective of position I am trying to arrive at in this paper, Leibniz's position has the (to my mind) unfortunate consequence of denying the original motivation behind the search for a conception of substance: the intuitive need to distinguish between those continuants which have the unity which, say, an animal has, and the mere aggregative unity which a pile of stones or a flock of birds has. If we want to preserve this intuition, then we should reject Leibniz's requirement that substances are 'indivisible, ingenerable and incorruptible'.

Another, equally radical, approach has been proposed recently by Peter van Inwagen.[28] Van Inwagen does not put forward his theory of material objects explicitly as an theory of substance. Rather, he puts forward his theory as an answer to what he calls the 'Special Composition Question': roughly, what is it for the parts of a material object to constitute that object? His answer is that they do so when and only when the activity of these parts 'constitute a life'.[29] ('Life' here is independently understood in a fairly rich biological sense according to which only organisms have lives.) It follows from van Inwagen's account that the only material objects which there are are organisms, and their elementary parts ('simples').[30] There are no artefacts, for example, nor are there things like the moon, stars, stones, fields, countries and so on, and even non-elementary parts of bodies like heads and hearts. Although not expressed as an account of substance, it is easy to think of it in these terms. Van Inwagen sometimes expresses his view in terms of what makes something a unity:

What is the ground of my unity? That is, what binds the simples that compose me into a single being? It seems to me to be plausible to say that what binds them together is that their activities constitute a life, a homeodynamic storm of simples, a self-maintaining, well-individual event.[31]

The question is here applied to himself, but the answer applies to all things. The theory of material objects which van Inwagen puts forward counts as objects only what I have been calling genuine unities, and what makes something a unity is that the activity of its parts constitutes a life. So his theory does not only deny that things like flocks of birds and piles of stone are 'real unities'; it denies that

---

[28] See especially *Material Beings* (Ithaca: Cornell University Press, 1990).
[29] Op. cit. section 9, especially 81–3.
[30] On the reasons why there are simples, see op. cit., 99.
[31] Op. cit., 121.

Tim Crane

they exist at all. Leibniz differs: 'I do not say that there is nothing substantial or nothing but what is apparent in things which have no true unity, because I allow them always as much reality or substantiality as there is true unity in what enters into their composition'.[32] Where Leibniz allows that there are composites, even if they are not substances or true unities, van Inwagen holds that the only composites are organisms and their only parts their simple parts.

I mention these two examples of theories of substances not because I agree with either of them, and nor because I intend to dispute them here. I mention them as examples of theories which take seriously the idea that certain objects (or in van Inwagen's case, the *only* objects) have a kind of unity, which is explained in terms of some fundamental principle. In Leibniz, the unity of a substance is explained partly by its simplicity (indivisibility, incorruptibility); in van Inwagen, it is explained in terms of the idea of a life.

Generalizing from these cases, we can draw the following picture. Either substances are simple, or they are composite. If they are simple, then no story needs to be told about what binds them together. This is Leibniz's approach. If they are composite, then—whether or not there are any *other* composite things—some account needs to be given of how their parts combine to make a real unity. This account will either appeal to some independently understood non-substance notion (like van Inwagen's notion of a *life*) or to some principle which explains why substances have the unities they do.

So if we believe in composites, and we believe in the distinction between kinds of composites which I have been trying to defend here, then we need to uncover some principle of unity which explains the manifest unity of a substance. An analogy here with philosophical discussions of natural kinds may be helpful. A natural kind like gold may be considered a large particular, scattered over the whole of the world wherever there is gold. The natural kind *gold*—which is what I talk about here in using the mass noun 'gold'—should therefore be distinguished both from individual pieces of gold, and from the *property of being gold*, which is not a particular but a universal (if there are such things). Gold has certain superficial qualities, some of them literally on its surface (like its colour) and others dispositional characteristics (like its malleability). These qualities are explained by the underlying nature of gold (for example, its atomic number). Something cannot be gold unless it has that underlying nature, and something could still be gold even if its underlying nature resulted in different macroscopic or

---

[32] Leibniz, letter to Arnauld, 30 April 1687.

superficial properties (because, e.g., of changes in surrounding context or other laws of nature). Given the surrounding context and laws of nature, the underlying structure explains the superficial properties of gold.

Without commitment to any essentialist doctrines about the essence of species, we might say that an individual substance might have its unity explained by its underlying nature, in an analogous way to the way a natural kind has its superficial properties explained by its underlying nature. An individual animal is a unity because it has a genetic structure, embodied in every cell in its body, which explains in part why it appears the way it does and why it grows and develops in the way it does. The flock of birds or the ball of dust has not such underlying structure which explains why it is one way rather than the other. The explanations of the 'merely phenomenal' unity these things have will be in terms of things extrinsic to the thing themselves. The idea in the abstract was well-expressed by Leibniz when he said that 'each one of these substances contains in its nature the law of the continuation of the series of its operations... all its actions come from its own depths'.[33]

Thinking about substance in this way involves returning to some ideas from the history of metaphysics which go beyond today's common conception of what a particular is. If we only have the idea of a particular to work with, then we will not be able to make the distinctions which Leibniz and others wanted to make by using the idea of substance. What we are trying to do, of course, is not to save Leibniz's conception of substance, or Descartes's, or Aristotle's, but rather to dig into these conceptions and try and find out whether there is any *point* to the classification of entities in terms of (anything like) these conceptions, and anything worth preserving, consistent with what we presently know, in these older ideas. I hope I have said enough to show that there is an independently specifiable point to the idea of substance, so that a belief in substance is not something entirely innocuous, nor something absurdly anachronistic. Rather, a belief in substance, in this sense, is a non-trivial doctrine, something worth asserting, and something worth denying.

Who might deny it? I envisage the rejection of substance as coming from (at least) two sources: first, it might be rejected that the things I am calling substances are really continuants, on the grounds that the distinctions between continuant and occurrent is empty and unnecessary. In other words, they might oppose the idea

[33] Leibniz, letter to Arnauld, 23 March 1690.

of a continuant with a *four-dimensionalist* ontology of entities with spatial and temporal parts.[34] Or second, it might be rejected on the grounds that the idea that there are any non-*ad hoc* principles of unity is unmotivated, and is undetermined by a systematic application of mereology in metaphysics, the formal calculus of parts and wholes, to particulars. We should distinguish between mereology, understood as the formal calculus of parts and wholes, and a metaphysical application of this calculus, a theory which allows the 'composition' of entities out of other entities in a way which does not respect any other principle of unity, other and 'mereological composition'. So an ontology of substance is opposed to (at least) the following two kinds of theory: four-dimensionalism, and a metaphysics of unrestricted mereological composition.[35] A defender of substance has to reject outright these two kinds of theory.

4. What might mental substances be?

To summarize: the fundamental motivation behind a belief in substance is the idea that there are kinds of particular entity in the world whose existence and unity is not simply a consequence of stipulation, postulation or theory-building. Their unity is rather explained in terms of some underlying natural principle which is responsible for their organization, activity and boundaries.

Given this way of understanding substance, then what might mental substances be? The general answer is simple: a mental substance is a continuant whose underlying natural principle—what explains its identity as the kind of thing it is, what explains its persistence through time, its being the same thing over time, and what explains its organization—is mental. Cartesian souls are certainly such mental substances. Their nature is explained in terms of their possessing the essential mental attribute of thought, and their persistence similarly consists in the continued existence of something with modes of this attribute; Cartesian souls are what have thoughts, what persist through changes in thoughts, and what survive the death of the bodies to which they are contingently related.

Perhaps it is this kind of conception of mental substance which

[34] The *locus classicus* of this kind of view is W. V. Quine's 'Identity, ostension and hypostasis', in Quine, *From a Logical Point of View* (Cambridge, Mass.: MIT Press, 1953).

[35] David Lewis's metaphysical system is perhaps the best and most sophisticated example of the combination of these two theories. But the theories are independent of each other.

Putnam has in mind when he rejects the idea that the mind is a thing: the mind has to be the 'underlying substance' which thinks and remembers. The materialist alternative to this, according to Putnam, is to say that the mind is the brain, and that mental states are states of this material substance, the brain. But from what we have said about substance so far, it is not clear that this is what a believer in mental substance *has* to say; and nor is it obvious that a materialist or naturalist philosopher has to say that the underlying substance, or subject of mental predications, is the brain. The notion of substance with the central features which I sketched in the previous section does not imply that the only way something could be a mental substance is either by being a Cartesian soul or by being a brain. A substance, according to that conception, is an enduring particular whose unity is explained by its nature. As I noted, organisms are perhaps the best examples of substances in this sense. But applied to the mental case, it is clear that nothing about this conception of substance requires a materialist to believe that the *brain*, rather than the whole creature, to be the bearer of mental properties. I did employ the analogy with underlying and superficial properties of natural kinds to illustrate the idea of its unity being explained by its nature. But this doesn't mean that the substance is 'hidden', 'inner' or 'underlying' in any problematic sense. (Remember, of course, that we have rejected in §2 the confused conception of substance as something essentially without properties which is essentially the bearer of properties.)

So Cartesian souls are not the only conceivable kind of mental substance. Mental substances must be the bearers of mental properties, but the bearers of mental properties may also be the bearers of other kinds of properties. For why should it not be that there can be substances whose organizing principle is mental, but which have some special relationship to a body, something whose organizing principle is bodily? It is consistent with the idea that there are substances which have a mental organizing principle that they also have bodily features, capacities and a kind of bodily unity too. The result of thinking in these terms would resemble what Descartes called the *substantial union* of mind and body in *Meditation VI*:

> Nature also teaches me by these feelings of pain, hunger, thirst, etc., that I am not lodged in my body, like a pilot in his ship, but, besides, that I am joined to it very closely and indeed so compounded and intermingled with my body, that I form, as it were, a single whole with it. For, if this were not so, when my body is hurt, I would not on that account feel pain, I who am only a

thinking thing, but I should perceive the wound by understanding alone, just as a pilot sees with his eyes if any damage occurs to his ship; and when my body needs to drink or eat, I would know this simply without being warned of it by the confused feelings of hunger or thirst. For in truth all these feelings of hunger, thirst, pain etc., are nothing other than certain confused ways of thinking, which arise from and depend on the union and, as it were, the mingling of the mind and the body.[36]

It is an important question in the understanding of Descartes's philosophy to see how this phenomenological insight can be made consistent with his official metaphysics of two substances. But this historical question is not my concern here. What I want to emphasize in this context is the idea of something substantial which involves a 'mingling' of mind and body.

The idea of such a substantial union is strikingly similar to P. F. Strawson's discussion of persons in chapter 3 of *Individuals*.[37] Strawson argued there that we have a primitive concept of a person as something of which mental and bodily predications are made. Persons in Strawson's sense are substances, since persons are continuants and they also have a natural unity. Might it be, then, that a person is a mental substance? What this would mean, according to the present understanding of substance, is that the principle of unity of a person is mental. That is, what would explain the unity of a person at a time is the way the person's mental life is unified, around a single point of view; and what would explain the identity of a person over time are the fundamental connections between the elements of a person's mental life. This is not a reduction of the idea of a person to the idea of a sequence of mental states or events, for there is no way of identifying the mental states and events in question independently of the person whose mental states they are. (This is part of what Strawson means by saying that the concept of the person is primitive.) But the point is that identifying something as a person is identifying something whose nature is essentially mental, something which could not survive the utter absence of all mental organization.

It is also part of Strawson's proposal that persons have bodily properties. And this must be right: for it is undeniable that the bodily organization of a person contributes to its unity. However, this plunges us immediately into the personal identity debate, where it seems possible to separate out the mental and the bodily aspects of

---

[36] Meditation VI, in *The Philosophical Writings of Descartes* volume II.
[37] P. F. Strawson, *Individuals* (London: Methuen, 1959).

persons, and create situations where the same mental unity can remain even though the bodily unity does not. While I cannot hope to resolve this debate here, it is important to distinguish two questions. One is the question of what makes anything a person at all. The Strawsonian answer proposed here is that a person is something with mental and bodily properties. The other question is what makes a person the same particular person over time. Here we have to confront the question of whether a person could be the same even if it changes its body in the various ways described in the personal identity debate. I have no answer to this (much-discussed) second question here, but I would like to conclude by briefly considering the issue of disembodied persons.

In his discussion of persons, Strawson allowed that 'within our actual conceptual scheme, each of us can quite intelligibly conceive of his or her individual survival of bodily death'.[38] Conceding that what is conceivable is possible, this seems to allow the real possibility of the person existing without their body. Commenting on this view of Strawson's, Paul Snowdon remarks that:

> Strawson's even-handedness is revealed when he allows that just as a person's body can outlive the person's consciousness, a possibility that is not seriously in question, so a person's consciousness can outlive his or her body. This claim is questionable because it seems to be inconsistent with materialism.[39]

Snowdon is surely right that Strawson's view is inconsistent with materialism. But for those philosophers (like myself) who are not concerned to defend materialism, Strawson's concession to non-materialist views is not especially worrying. More worrying would be the suggestion that Strawson's acknowledgement of the possibility of survival after bodily death threatens the idea that persons are substances with a mental and a bodily nature. But what would support this threat? One traditional answer is the 'independent existence' account of substance. For if a person's mental nature could exist entirely independently of its actual body, then by the independent existence criterion, the mental nature would be a substance, and the person's body is only contingently connected to the person.[40] But we have rejected this account of substance; it cannot, for

[38] Strawson, op. cit., p. 115.
[39] Paul Snowdon, 'Persons and personal identity' in *Essays for David Wiggins: Identity, Truth & Value*, S. Lovibond and S. Williams (eds.) (Oxford: Blackwell, 1996) 44.
[40] This is the consequence drawn by E. J. Lowe, *The Possibility of Metaphysics*, op. cit., 172.

reasons unrelated to the issue of disembodied existence, provide us with an adequate way of distinguishing substances from other entities. So if persons are substances, the possibility of disembodied existence does not show that a person could exist without their body; all it shows is that *something* mental could exist without a body. But it takes further assumptions to show that this 'something' is a person. So if a person is a mental substance which also has a bodily nature, then the fact that a mental life without a bodily nature is possible does not itself show that persons can be disembodied; it just shows that a mental life could exist without a body. And if we reject the independence criterion of substance, then we do not have a reason to think that a mental substance can exist without its body.

How does this relate to the idea with which we started, that the mind is not a thing? In a sense, our reflections have led us to a similar conclusion to Putnam's: the *mind* is not a mental substance. If anything is a mental substance, the person is. Persons are not minds; for persons have bodies and minds do not. Having a mind is having certain mental capacities: the capacities for thought, sensation, imagination, perception, will, appetite and action. These capacities are distinctive of the kinds of substances which persons are, substances which also have a bodily nature. This is the fundamental reason to call persons mental substances. And if this way of understanding the idea that persons are mental substances is at all appealing, then we must address the personal identity debate from this perspective.

Mind and Illusion

FRANK JACKSON

Much of the contemporary debate in the philosophy of mind is concerned with the clash between certain strongly held intuitions and what science tells us about the mind and its relation to the world. What science tells us about the mind points strongly towards some version or other of physicalism. The intuitions, in one way or another, suggest that there is something seriously incomplete about any purely physical story about the mind.

For our purposes here, we can be vague about the detail and think broadly of physicalism as the view that the mind is a purely physical part of a purely physical world. Exactly how to delineate the physical will not be crucial: anything of a kind that plays a central role in physics, chemistry, biology, neuroscience and the like, along with the *a priori* associated functional and relational properties count as far as we are concerned.

Most contemporary philosophers given a choice between going with science and going with intuitions, go with science. Although I once dissented from the majority, I have capitulated and now see the interesting issue as being where the arguments from the intuitions against physicalism—the arguments that seem so compelling—go wrong.[1] For some time, I have thought that the case for physicalism is sufficiently strong that we can be confident that the arguments from the intuitions go wrong somewhere, but where is somewhere?

This paper offers an answer to that question for the knowledge argument against physicalism. I start with a reminder about the argument. I then consider one very popular way of dismissing it and explain why I am unmoved by it. The discussion of this way delivers a constraint that any satisfying physicalist reply to the knowledge argument should meet. The rest of the paper gives the answer I favour to where the knowledge argument goes wrong. This

[1] Over the years I have received a large number of papers, letters and emails seeking to convince me of the error of my old ways. Much of what I say below was absorbed from, or was a response in one form or another to, this material but I am now unsure who deserves credit for exactly what. More recently I am indebted to discussions of various presentations of 'Representation and Experience' in *Representation in Mind: New Approaches to Mental Representation,* H. Clapin, P. Slezack and P. Staines (eds) (Wesport: Praeger, to appear 2002).

answer rests on a representationalist account of sensory experience and, as the title of the paper indicates, I say, among other things, that there is a pervasive illusion that conspires to lead us astray when we think about what it is like to have a colour experience.

The knowledge argument[2]

The epistemic intuition that founds the knowledge argument is that you cannot deduce from purely physical information about us and our world, all there is to know about the nature of our world because you cannot deduce how things look to us, especially in regard to colour. More general versions of the argument make the same claim for all the mental states with a phenomenology—the states for which there is something it is like to be in them—as it is so often put, and sometimes for consciousness. But we will be almost entirely concerned with colour experiences. We will say nothing about consciousness *per se*; our concern is with the phenomenology of visual experience, and not our consciousness of it or of mental states in general.

The familiar story about Mary is a way to make vivid and appealing the claim about lack of deducibility. To rehearse it ever so briefly: A brilliant scientist, Mary, is confined in a black and white room without windows. She herself is painted white all over and dressed in black. All her information about the world and its workings comes from black and white sources like books without coloured pictures and black and white television. She is, despite these artificial restrictions, extraordinarily knowledgeable about the physical nature of our world, including the neurophysiology of human beings and sentient creatures in general, and how their neurophysiology underpins their interactions with their surroundings. Can she in principle deduce from all this physical information, what it is like to see, say, red?

There is a strong intuition that she cannot. This intuition is reinforced by reflecting on what would happen should she be released from her room. Assuming that there is nothing wrong with her colour vision despite its lack of exercise during her incarceration, she would learn what it is like to see red, and it is plausible that this

---

[2] See, e.g., Frank Jackson, 'Epiphenomenal Qualia', *Philosophical Quarterly* 32 (1982), 127–36. The argument has a long history in one form or another. For an outline version drawn to my attention recently, see J. W. Dunne, *An Experiment with Time* (London: Faber and Faber, 1927), 13–14.

would be learning something about the nature of our world, including especially the nature of the colour experiences subjects enjoy. From this it would follow that she did not know beforehand all there was to know about our world.

Moreover, there is a marked contrast with our epistemic relation to properties like solidity, elasticity, boiling, valency and the like. If I give you enough information about the behaviour of a substance's molecules and how they govern the substance's interactions with its environment, you will be able to work out whether it is a liquid, a solid or a gas. If I tell you about the forces that hold water molecules together and the way increases in the velocity of those molecules as a result of heating can lead to these molecules reaching escape velocity, you will learn about boiling.[3] Likewise for valency and elasticity. But the deduction of what it is like to see red from purely physical information seems a totally different matter.

There are two challenges to physicalism here. One is to explain why there should be a marked apparent difference between the case of seeing red and the case of being liquid or boiling. After all, the phenomena are *alike* in being purely physical ones according to physicalism. The second, more direct challenge is to explain how it can be that Mary's knowledge of our world's nature is, it seems, deficient, despite the fact that she knows all there is to know according to physicalism.

I now turn to the very popular response to the knowledge argument that seems to me to fail but which gives us a constraint on any acceptable physicalist response.

The response that draws on *a posteriori* necessity

This response[4] on behalf of physicalism to the knowledge argument starts from the point that being necessitated does not imply being *a priori* derivable. This suggests that although physicalists are committed to the experiential being necessitated by a rich enough physical account of our world—otherwise it would take more than the

---

[3] This claim is common enough but it has been disputed on the basis of a Twin Earth argument. See Ned Block and Robert Stalnaker, 'Conceptual Analysis, Dualism and the Explanatory Gap', *Philosophical Review* 108 (1999), 1–46. For a response, see David J. Chalmers and Frank Jackson, 'Conceptual Analysis and Reductive Explanation', *Philosophical Review* 110 (2001), 315–61.

[4] See, e. g., Block and Stalnaker, op. cit., but this is but one example among many.

physical nature of our world to secure its experiential nature, contrary to physicalism—they are not committed to the experiential being *a priori* derivable from the physical. But the epistemic intuition that lies behind the knowledge argument is, when all is said and done, that Mary cannot carry out an *a priori* derivation from the physical information imagined to be at her disposal to the phenomenology of colour vision. Physicalists should respond to the knowledge argument by adopting a version of physicalism according to which the experiential is necessitated by the physical but is not *a priori* derivable from the physical.

I have two reasons for rejecting this reply. The first I have given a number of times. It draws on the two-dimensional account of the necessary *a posteriori*. I will not repeat it here.[5] My second reason can be introduced by reflecting on the famous reduction of the thermodynamic theory of gases to the kinetic theory via statistical mechanics.

Our belief that gases have temperature and pressure is grounded in their behaviour. Moreover, we know that their behaviour is fully explained by the various features recognized and named in the kinetic theory of gases. There is no need to postulate any extra features of gases in order to explain their behaviour. This makes it very hard to hold that no matter how much information we have framed in the terms of the kinetic theory and in terms of the functional roles played by the properties picked out by the terms of that theory, and no matter how confident we are that the kinetic theory and its future developments provide a complete picture in the relevant respects of the essential nature of gases, the passage from this information to whether or not gases are hot and have pressure is *a posteriori*. What relevant information are we waiting on? We know that all we will get is more of the same. Scepticism about gases having temperature and pressure threatens if we insist that we cannot go *a priori* from the molecular account of gases and the concomitant functional roles to gases having temperature and pressure.

This point is implicit in the well-known schematic account of why it is right to identify temperature in gases with mean molecular kinetic energy:

Temperature in gases is that which does so and so (*a priori* premise about the concept of temperature)

[5] See, e. g., Frank Jackson, Critical Notice of Susan Hurley, *Natural Reasons, Australasian Journal of Philosophy* 70 (1992), 475–87, and *From Metaphysics to Ethics: A Defence of Conceptual Analysis* (Oxford: Clarendon Press, 1998).

That which does so and so is mean molecular kinetic energy
(empirical premise)
Therefore, temperature in gases is mean molecular kinetic
energy.

The need for the first, *a priori* premise is sometimes challenged.[6]
But unless something like the first premise is *a priori*, eliminativism
about temperature and pressure in gases is inevitable. The right
conclusion from the discoveries of the kinetic theory of gases could
only be that gases are not hot on the ground that what we needed
temperature to explain (their feeling hot and behaving thus and so)
is fully explained by their mean molecular kinetic energy. *Mutatis
mutandis* for pressure.

It is sometimes objected to this argument that identities need no
explanation. I doubt this doctrine.[7] But the issue is by the way.
Identities certainly need justification, and the problem is that we
have a choice between

(A) Temperature is not a property of gases although there is
plenty of molecular kinetic energy, and the mean value of that
does all the explaining of gas behaviour once assigned to
having such and such a temperature.

(B) Having such and such a temperature in gases is one and the
same property as having so and so a mean molecular kinetic
energy, and 'they' do all the needed explaining of gas
behaviour.

Without the first, *a priori* premise above, we have no reason to
favour (B) over (A).

The considerations that tell us that we had better be able to move
a priori from the molecular account of gases to the temperature
account can be generalized to the question of all of our empirical
beliefs about what our world is like. Physicalists hold (have to hold)
that the evidence we have for any of our claims about what our

---

[6] Most recently by Block and Stalnaker, 'Conceptual Analysis, Dualism
and the Explanatory Gap', op. cit. For a fuller development of the reply in
the text, see Frank Jackson, 'From H_2O to Water: the Relevance to *A
Priori* Passage', *Real Metaphysics*, papers for D. H. Mellor, Hallvard
Lillehammer, *et al.* (eds.) (London: Routledge, 2002). Many once held,
and some still hold, that the first premise, suitably fleshed out, is necessarily true as well as *a priori*. Nothing here turns on this issue. Incidentally,
I am following the philosopher's lazy practice of simplifying the science.

[7] See David J. Chalmers and Frank Jackson, 'Conceptual Analysis and
Reductive Explanation', op. cit.

world is like—that England fought two World Wars, that horses eat grass, that Carter was a one-term President of the United States, and so on—is determined without remainder by our world's physical nature. How then can we be justified in holding that we have evidence for what our world is like that outruns what might be inferred in principle from its physical nature alone? It might be objected that this rhetorical question assumes an unduly 'causal cum best explanation' view of the relation of evidence to empirical hypothesis. What about simplicity and all that? But physicalists hold that considerations of simplicity, good methodology, and all the rest, favour physicalism. That is why they are physicalists (and rightly so, in my view).

It is this wider consideration that explains my puzzlement over why many hold that the claim that physicalism is committed to the *a priori* deducibility of the way the world is in all empirical respects from the physical nature of the world is an extreme one.[8] Think of the famous 'Russell hypothesis'. According to it, the world came into existence five minutes ago containing each and every putative 'trace' that might suggest that it has existed since the big bang. As a result, we cannot here and now point to features that distinguish the correct view that our world has existed since the big bang from the Russell hypothesis. What entitles us to reject the Russell hypothesis is that it violates the principles of good theory construction by being *excessively ad hoc*. Now consider the *bare physicalism hypothesis*: the hypothesis that the world is exactly as is required to make the physical account of it true in each and every detail but nothing more is true of this world in the sense that nothing that fails to follow *a priori* from the physical account is true of it. This hypothesis is not *ad hoc* and has all the explanatory power and simplicity we can reasonably demand. Ergo, we physicalists can have no reason to go beyond the bare physicalist picture.

It might (will) be objected that bare physicalism is *a posteriori* impossible, that there are empirical truths about our world, including truths about experiences, that are necessitated by the bare physical account but which do not follow *a priori* from that account. But that would be to miss the point. The point is that we could not know this. Bare physicalism is a conceptual possibility; the argument is that we have no reason not to allow that it is also a metaphysical possibility. Or, to make the point with a word, recall that many call conceptual possibility *epistemic* possibility. Or, to make the point

[8] See, for example, Alex Byrne, 'Cosmic Hermeneutics', *Philosophical Perspectives*, 13 (1999), 347–83.

with an example, those who hold that the existence of God is *a posteriori* necessary (or *a posteriori* necessitated by agreed features of our world) are not thereby excused from having to provide reasons for believing in God.

To avoid misunderstanding, I should emphasize that when I talk of being able to move *a priori* from the physical account to, say, Carter being a one-term President, I do not mean being able to move literally. I mean that there exists an *a priori* entailment. We cannot derive the gravitational centre of the universe from the mass and location of all its parts because, first, we do not and could not know the mass and location of all its parts, and, secondly, the calculation would be way beyond our powers. All the same, the location of the centre of gravity does follow *a priori* from the physical account of our world, and we know that it does.

This gives us the following constraint on any physicalist solution to the challenge of the epistemic intuition: it should allow us to see how the passage from the physical to the nature of colour experience might possibly be, somehow or other, *a priori*.

I now come to the positive part of the paper; the part where I explain why physicalists are entitled to reject the epistemic intuition. As heralded, my argument will involve the claim that we are under an illusion about the nature of colour experience, an illusion that fuels the epistemic intuition.[9]

Mistaking intensional properties for instantiated properties

I start with the diaphanousness of experience: G. E. Moore's thesis that the qualitative character of experience is the character of the putative object of experience.[10] The redness of sensings of red is the putative redness of what is seen; when vision is blurred, what is seen appears to be blurred; the location quality of a sound is the putative location of the sound; the experience of movement is the experience of something putatively moving; and so on. Hume observes that the self's experiences always get in the way of experiencing the self.[11] Equally, the putative properties of what is experienced always get in the way of accessing the qualities of experience. I am going to take

[9] In my view, the illusion also fuels the modal intuitions encapsulated in the zombie, absent *qualia*, inverted *qualia* etc. arguments, but I do not argue that here (though it may be clear how the argument would go).

[10] G. E. Moore, 'The Refutation of Idealism', *Philosophical Studies* (London: Routledge and Kegan Paul, 1922), 1–30.

[11] David Hume, *Treatise of Human Nature*, bk. I, pt. IV, sec. VI.

diaphanousness for granted. The case for it is widely accepted[12] and it is especially appealing in the case of our topic, colour experience. Indeed, reservations about it are typically confined to certain bodily sensations where attitudes, pro or con, arguably contribute to the felt quality. The degree to which we dislike a pain is arguably part of its feel.

There are two very different ways to think of the lesson of diaphanousness, corresponding to two very different ways of thinking of the object that putatively has the qualities. On one, Moore's, the object really is an object. It is the object of the act-object theory of experience or the sense datum theory of sensing: experiences are composed of an act of awareness directed to an object or sense datum which bears the qualities. And the lesson of diaphanousness is that these qualities determine the qualitative nature of the experience. On the other way of thinking, Harman's, op. cit., for example, the object is an intensional object. That is to say, 'it' is not an object at all, and our use of verbal constructions that belong in the syntactic category of names is a convenient, if metaphysically misleading, way of talking about how things are being represented to be. We talk of being directly aware of a square shape in our visual fields but there is no square shape to which we stand in the relation of direct awareness; rather, our visual experience represents that there is something square before us. What makes it right to use the word 'square' in describing our experience is not a relation to something which has the property the word stands for but the fact that the way the experience represents things as being can only be correct if there is something square in existence. The squareness of an experience is an intensional property, not an instantiated one. The same goes *mutatis mutandis* for all the properties we ascribe to what is presented in experience, the properties we have in mind when we talk of the qualities of experience and to which the argument from diaphanousness applies.[13] When we use words like 'square', 'two feet away' and 'red' to characterize our experiences, we pick out intensional properties not instantiated ones.

I think, with the current majority, that the second is the right way

[12] See, e. g., Gilbert Harman, 'The Intrinsic Quality of Experience', *Philosophical Perspectives* 4 (1990), 31–52.

[13] These properties include the usual suspects like extension, colour and shape but I see no reason not to include, e.g., being a hydrometer. We can see something *as* a hydrometer. The difference between, *e.g.*, being extended and being a hydrometer is that you cannot see something without seeing it as extended whereas you can see something without seeing it as a hydrometer.

to think of the lesson of diaphanousness. My reason is that perceptual experience *represents*. My experience as of a round, red object in front of me represents that there is a round, red object in front of me. I may or may not accept that things are as they are being represented to be, but I take it as axiomatic that each and every sensory experience represents that things are thus and so.

This implies that the first way of thinking of the lesson of the argument from diaphanousness, the way that leads to the sense datum theory, must be rejected. We one-time sense datum theorists thought that the requirement that there be something red and round, say, of which the subject is directly aware, automatically captures, or part way captures, the key representational notion.[14] This is a mistake. It is true that I can represent how I am representing something to be by using the actual way something is. For example, I might represent to you the colour I remember X to be by holding up an actual sample of the colour. Here I would be using the actual colour of one thing, the sample, to represent how my memory represents the colour of something else to be; a colour which X may or may not have. In that sense, we have a model for understanding the sense datum theory. But, and this is the crucial point, the fact that I am using an actual sample of the colour cuts no representational ice *per se*. I could be using the sample to indicate the one colour I do *not* think X has. Or I could be following the convention of holding up a sample with the colour *complementary* to that I remember X as having. In the same way, standing in a certain direct-awareness relationship to a mental item with such and such properties says nothing, represents nothing *per se*, about how the world is. The act-object cum sense datum theory leaves out the most important feature of experience: its essentially representational nature. In order to capture the representational nature of perception, what makes it true that words like 'red' and 'square' apply to our experiences has to be understood on the intensional model.

It might be objected that this argument from the fact that perception represents leaves open the possibility that some but not all of the properties of experience are intensional. Why not hold that experiences have both a representational aspect and a non-representational aspect?[15] In a sense they do. It may be a fact about an experience that it is occurring in Alaska or in the Middle Ages, and neither of these properties is an intensional property of the experience.

[14] See, e. g., Frank Jackson, *Perception* (Cambridge: Cambridge University Press, 1977).

[15] For a recent view of this kind, see John Foster, *The Nature of Perception* (Oxford: Oxford University Press, 2000), part three.

But the issue for us is whether the aspects that constitute the phenomenal nature of an experience outrun its representational nature, and there are good reasons to deny this.

First, whenever there is a difference in phenomenal character, there is a difference in how things are being represented to be. This follows from diaphanousness. Any change in phenomenal character means a change in the putative character of what is being experienced, and a change in the putative character of what is being experienced *is* a change in how things are being represented to be. Make an experience of red a bit brighter and you make it the case that your experience represents that some object's redness is that bit brighter. But if phenomenal character outran representational character, it would be possible to change the former and leave the latter unchanged.

There have, of course, been attempts to describe cases where phenomenal character differs without a difference in representational content and an important exercise is the critical review of all the cases that might be thought to show the possibility of phenomenal variation without difference in representational content. I am not going to conduct this review, because I think the job has been well done by other supporters of representationalism.[16]

Secondly, there is a marked contrast between, on the one hand, the way representational devices like maps and sentences represent, and, on the other, the way perceptual experience represents. There is a gap between vehicle of representation and what is represented in the first case that does not exist in the second. In the case of maps and sentences, we can distinguish the features that do the representing—the gap between the isobars on a weather map, the concatenation of the letters 'c', 'a' and 't' in that order in a sentence,

---

[16] E. g., recently by Michael Tye, *Consciousness, Color, and Content* (Cambridge, Mass.: M.I.T. Press, 2000); see also Alex Byrne, 'Intentionalism Defended', *Philosophical Review* 110 (2001), 199–240. I should, perhaps, footnote what I think should be said about one example. The very same shape may have a different visual appearance depending on its putative orientation with respect to oneself. This in itself is no problem for representationalism, as orientation is part of how things are represented to be. However, as Christopher Peacocke points out, e. g., in 'Scenarios, Concepts and Perception' in Tim Crane (ed.) *The Contents of Experience* (Cambridge: Cambridge University Press, 1992), 105–135, seeing something as a regular diamond and as a square on its side need differ neither in putative shape nor orientation, and yet differ experientially. However, when this happens, one figure is being represented to be symmetrical about a line through its corners and the other about a line parallel to its sides.

the green colouring on parts of a map, *etc.*—from what they represent: a pressure gradient, a cat, areas of high rainfall, *etc.* We can, for example, describe the gap between the isobars without any reference to what it represents. But, in the case of perceptual experience, we cannot. When I have a visual experience of a roundish, red object in front of me, *that* is what it represents. My very description of the vehicle of representation delivers how it represents things to be. I may or may not accept that things are the way they are being represented to be, but there is just the one way that things are being represented to be, and that way is part and parcel of the quality of the experience. Ergo, we have to understand the qualities of experience in terms of intensional properties.[17]

A major issue for the intensionalist account is how to distinguish sensory representational states from more purely cognitive representational ones like belief. But rather than break the flow of the argument, I postpone my discussion of it. In the next few sections we take the intensionalist picture as a given and note how it allows physicalists to explain away the epistemic intuition.

Explaining away the epistemic intuition

We start by noting how the intensional account undermines the picture of experience that goes with the phrase 'what it is like'.

There is a redness about sensing red (a yellowness about sensing yellow, and so on). We naturally think of the redness as a property we are acquainted with when we sense red and as the property Mary finds out about on her release. We may want to distinguish redness as a property of objects from redness as a property of an area of our visual field, perhaps using 'red*' for the latter. Either way, what it is like is, on the picture, a matter of having redness or redness*, knowing what it is like is knowing about redness or redness*, and the knowledge argument is an argument to the conclusion that Mary does not know about redness or redness*—that is, about the property we are, according to the picture, acquainted with when we sense red.

---

[17] How things are being represented to be need not be determinate. My experience may represent that something is a roundish shape without representing that it is any particular shape—the experience represents that there is some precise shape it has but there is no precise shape that the experience represents it to have. Indeed, it is arguable that all experience has some degree or other of indeterminacy about it. The same goes for maps and most sentences, of course.

Intensionalism tells us that there is no such property. To suppose otherwise is to mistake an intensional property for an instantiated one. Of course, when I sense red and you sense red, there is something in common between us which we English speakers report with descriptions that include the word 'red'. But what is in common is not the property tagged with the word 'red' but, first, how things have to be for our experiences to represent correctly, and, second, our both being in states that represent things as being that way.

Intensionalism means that no amount of tub-thumping assertion by dualists (including by me in the past) that the *redness* of seeing red cannot be accommodated in the austere physicalist picture carries any weight. That striking feature is a feature of how things are being represented to be, and if, as claimed by the tub thumpers, it is transparently a feature that has no place in the physicalist picture, what follows is that physicalists should deny that anything has that striking feature. And this is no argument against physicalism. Physicalists can allow that people are sometimes in states that represent that things have a non-physical property. Examples are people who believe that there are fairies. What physicalists must deny is that such properties are instantiated.

Moreover, the representationalist-cum-intensionalist approach can explain the origin of the dualist conviction that redness is non-physical. It is vital for our survival that we are able to pick out recurring patterns. Recognizing your best friend or a hungry tiger requires spotting a commonality. Sometimes these patterns are salient ones. Square tables have an obvious commonality. Sometimes they are not. An example is the commonality that unites an acceptable pronunciation of a given word in English. The lack of salience is why it is hard to develop speech to text computer programs, though the fact that it is nevertheless possible, that we always knew it was possible in principle and now know that it is possible in practice, reminds us that it is a folk view that there is a commonality. In many cases, the commonality's importance lies in highly relational facts about it. If the theory that colour vision evolved as an aid to the detection of food is correct, a series of highly unobvious optical commonalities between edible things and differences from their forest backgrounds are the patterns colour vision evolved to detect. Now, highly unobvious commonalities like these normally get detected only after a great deal of collecting and bringing together of information. Colour experience is, therefore, a quite unusually 'quick' way of acquiring highly unobvious relational and functional information. It is, in this regard, like the way we acquire information about intrinsic properties: one look at an object tells us that it is more or less round. In consequence, colour experience presents to us as if it were the acquisition of information about highly salient, more or less intrinsic features of our surroundings. But there are no physical features fitting this characterization; in consequence, colour experience presents itself to us as if it were information about certain non-physical features. Indeed, we may want to go so far as to say that sensing red *misrepresents* how things are. If this is right, we should say that nothing is red, for nothing would be as our experience of red represents things as being; we should be eliminativists about red and about colour in general. A more moderate position is that though our experience of colour contains a substantial degree of misrepresentation—the misrepresentation that leads dualists astray—there are complex physical properties 'out there' which stand in relations near enough to those captured by the colour solid for us to be able to identify them with the various colours.

Meeting the constraint

We argued that the physicalist response to the epistemic intuition should allow us to see how the nature of colour experience might possibly follow *a priori* from the physical account of what our world is like. The representationalist account of sensory experience meets this constraint.

Seeing red is being in a certain kind of representational state on this account. The project of finding an analysis of representation is not an easy one—to put it mildly. But it is a standard item on the philosophical agenda and the answers that have been, or are likely to be, canvassed are all answers that would allow the fact of representation to follow *a priori* from the physical account of what our world is like. They are accounts that talk of co-variation, causal connections of various kinds, selectional histories, and the like, and accounts made from these kinds of ingredients are ones that might be determined *a priori* by the purely physical.

We will need also an account of how sensing red represents things as being—the content. This would involve, *inter alia,* making up our mind on whether or not the content of sensing red was such as to imply, given physicalism, eliminativism about redness. Again, this will not be easy—if it were, it would have been done long ago—but there is no reason to think it would be an account that would make being in a state that has that representational content something that could not be derived *a priori* from the physicalist picture of

Frank Jackson

what our world is like. I know only too well the residual feeling that somehow the *redness* could not be got out of the physical picture alone, but that is nothing more than a hangover from the conflation of instantiated property with intensional property. That 'redness' is not a feature one is acquainted with, but instead is a matter of how things are being represented to be.

What happens to Mary on her release?

The epistemic intuition is that it is impossible to deduce what it is like to sense red from the physical account of our world. In particular, Mary in her room will not be able to do it. I have argued that if what it is like means all the properties of seeing red, it is possible in principle to deduce them all. That follows from representationalism, and the appearance to the contrary arises from the conflation of intensional properties with instantiated ones. But this leaves open what to say of a positive kind about what would happen to Mary on her release. The negative points that she would not learn about a feature of our world she could not know of while incarcerated, and that tub thumping convictions to the contrary carry no weight, do not tell us the positive side of the story.

What to say about the relevant change in Mary turns, it seems to me, on what to say about an old, hard issue for representationalist approaches to experience. It is the issue we postponed earlier of how to find the feel in the representationalist picture.

Sensing and believing

I can believe that there is, here and now, a round, red object in front of me without having the relevant visual experience. Perhaps my eyes are shut but I remember, or perhaps I am being told, that there is such an object here and now in front of me. Or perhaps the thought that there is such an object in front of me has simply 'come into my mind', and I have boldly gone along with it. Or perhaps I am one of the blind sighted: it seems like guessing but my success rate shows that I am drawing on a subliminal representational state.

It can be very tempting at this point to try for a mixed theory. Sensory experiences have a representational component and a sensory one. The difference between belief *per se* and sensory experience lies in a sensory addition. But we saw the problems for this earlier. For example, if this is the right view to take, it should

264

be possible to vary the sensory part alone, but for every sensory difference, there is a representational difference. Moreover, it is hard to make sense of a non-representational, sensory core. Any experience with some 'colour or shape feel' is putatively of something coloured and shaped somewhere, and thereby represents something about that location.[18] Once there is some phenomenal experiential nature, there is thereby some representation.

Conceptual versus nonconceptual content—a wrong turn

Many representationalists tackle the problem of finding the 'feel' via a distinction between conceptual and nonconceptual content. The claim is that belief has conceptual content, whereas experience has nonconceptual content.[19] I think that there are problems for this style of response.

The view that beliefs have conceptual content whereas experiences have nonconceptual content can be understood in two different ways.[20] It can be thought of as the view that beliefs and experiences have content in different senses of 'content'; that they have different kinds of content in the strong sense in which *that there are electrons* and *that there are protons* do *not* automatically count as different kinds of content. I think this is the wrong way for representationalists to go.[21] Belief is the representational state *par excellence*. This means that to hold that experience has content in some sense in which belief does not is to deny rather than affirm representationalism about experience. There needs to be an univocal sense of 'content' at work when we discuss representationalism; a sense on which content is how things are being represented to be,

[18] I am indebted here to a discussion with Ned Block but he will not approve of my conclusion.

[19] See, e. g., Michael Tye, *Consciousness, Color, and Content* (Cambridge, Mass.: M.I.T. Press, 2000) and *Ten Problems of Consciousness* (Cambridge, Mass.: M.I.T. Press, 1995). Tye's suggestion is *not* that the whole story about where the feel comes from lies in sensory states having nonconceptual content. But it is a key part of the story.

[20] As has been widely recognized, most recently in Richard G. Heck Jr., 'Nonconceptual Content and the Space of Reasons', *Philosophical Review* 109 (2000), 483–523; see also Tim Crane, 'The Nonconceptual Content of Experience' in Tim Crane, (ed.), *The Contents of Experience*, op. cit., 136–157.

[21] I think it is the way Tye wants to go but I am unsure. But let me say that here, and in the immediately following, I draw on helpful if unresolved discussions with him.

and on which both beliefs and experiences have (representational) content.

Of course, many say that the content of belief (and thought more generally) is a structured entity containing concepts.[22] But this should not, it seems to me, be interpreted so as to run counter to what we have just said. When I believe that things are as my experience represents them to be, what I believe is precisely that things are as my experience says that they are, not something else.[23] Alex Byrne says 'that the content of perception ... may outrun the representational capacity of thought ... is surely the default assumption'.[24] But we can *think* that things are *exactly* as our experience represents them to be. What is outrun is our capacity to capture the content in words, but that is another question. As it happens, my current experience correctly represents that there is something rectangular before me. I also believe that there is. What makes my experience correct and my belief true is the very same configuration of matter in front of me, and that configuration contains no concepts. Maybe, in addition, my belief implies that I stand in some special relation to concepts, but that would be a reason to acknowledge an additional content to the representational one that belief and experience both possess. And you might, or might not, hold that sensory states possess that kind of content also. But giving belief a possibly extra kind of content is not going to help us with our problem. Our problem is that both belief and experience represent that things are thus and so but only experience has feel—or anyway feel to the relevant degree. We are looking for something extra, so to speak, for experience, not a possible extra for belief.

The second way of understanding the view that belief has conceptual content whereas experience has non-conceptual content is as a claim about what it takes to have a belief with (representational) content versus what it takes to have an experience with (representational) content.[25] The kinds of content are the same but

[22] For recent example, Richard G. Heck Jr., 'Nonconceptual Content and the Space of Reasons', op. cit. He is affirming it as an agreed view.

[23] I am here agreeing with Tim Crane, 'The Nonconceptual Content of Experience' op. cit., p. 140, but he would not, I think, agree with the use I make of the point on which we agree.

[24] Alex Byrne, 'Consciousness and Higher-Order Thoughts', *Philosophical Studies* 86 (1997), 103–129, see p. 117.

[25] Some argue that the two understandings are connected as follows: the reason for holding that belief contents are special in containing, in some sense, the relevant concepts is that having a belief is special in requiring that one has the relevant concepts.

what it takes for the states to have them differs. Experience represents in a way that is independent, or largely independent, of subjects' mastery of concepts, whereas belief does not. For example, it is observed that we can perceptually discriminate many more colours than we have names for or can remember. It is then inferred that I might have a perceptual state that represents that something is, say, red_{17}, without having the concept of red_{17}. But I could not believe that something is red_{17} without having the concept of red_{17}.

I doubt the claim that perceptual representation is nonconceptual in the explained sense. To perceptually represent that things are thus and so essentially involves discrimination and categorization, and that is to place things under concepts.[26] Of course, I agree that when I experience red_{17}, I need not have the term 'red_{17}' in my linguistic repertoire; I need not be representing that the colour before me is correctly tagged 'red_{17}'; it need not be the case that before I had the experience, I had the concept of red_{17}; and my ability to remember and identify the precise shade may be very short-lived. But none of these points imply that I do not have the concept of red_{17} at the time I experience it.[27] When I learn the right term for the shade I can see, namely, the term 'red_{17}', it will be very different from learning about momentum, charm in physics or inertial frames, which do involve acquiring new concepts. It will simply be acquiring a term for something I already grasp. My tagging the shade with the word does not create the concept in me though it

[26] As Christopher Peacocke puts it in *Sense and Content* (Oxford: Oxford University Press, 1983), 7 '[experience] can hardly present the world as being [a certain] way if the subject is incapable of appreciating what that way is'. Peacocke no longer holds this view.

[27] Michael Tye, *Ten Problems of Consciousness*, op. cit., p. 139, suggests that the key point is that to believe that something is F requires having a stored memory representation of F whereas to experience it as F does not. Thus, belief requires possession of the concept F in a way that experience does not. But one can believe that something is F for the very first time, and if the point is merely that one's system needs to have already in place the capacity to categorize something as F, that is equally plausible for both belief and experience. Christopher Peacocke, 'Analogue Content', *Proceedings of the Aristotelian Society*, supp. vol. 15 (1986), 1–17, points out that when we enter a room full of abstract sculptures, we perceive things as having particular shapes but need not have 'in *advance* concepts of these particular shapes' (p. 15, my emphasis). This is true but does not show that we do not have the concepts at the time we see the things as having the shapes.

does give me the wherewithal to *say* that it applies.[28] Any thought to the contrary would appear to conflate the concept of red_{17}—the shade—with the distinct, relational concept of being indistinguishable from the sample labelled 'red_{17}' in some colour chart. It might be objected that this latter concept is the one we have in fact been talking about all along. But if this is the case, the initial datum that we experience red_{17} prior to acquaintance with colour charts is false. Prior to acquaintance with colour charts, we do not experience colours as being the same as such and such a colour on a colour chart.

The same goes for shapes. It is sometimes suggested that when presented with a highly idiosyncratic shape, you may experience it but not have the concept of it. But we need to distinguish two cases. In one, you see something as having the highly idiosyncratic shape but lack a word for it. In this case, you do have the concept. All that is lacking is a word for it, which you can remedy by making one up for yourself or by asking around to find out if there is already one in, say, English.[29] In the second kind of case, you do *not* experience the shape prior to having the word and the concept. There are cases where you see that something has some complex shape or other, where that shape is in fact S, but fail to see it *as* S. You are then told the right word for the shape, acquire the concept it falls under, and thereby acquire the ability to see it *as* S. But then it is false that your experience represented that something is S prior to your mastery of the concept. Your acquisition of the concept changes the perceptual experience.

Of course, what it is to have a concept is disputed territory and one might define concept possession in terms of having a word for that which falls under the concept. But in that case many beliefs lack conceptual content—animals and people have beliefs for which they do not have words. Or, more generally, one might raise the bar on what it is to possess a given concept in a way that, although it is plausible that anyone who believes that something is K has the

---

[28] The talk of tagging the shade should not be understood on the model of a demonstration. According to representationalism, there need be no instance of the colour shade to be demonstrated.

[29] What drives the idea that the lack of words implies a lack of concepts sometimes seems to be the modal claim that it is impossible to have words for all the shapes and colours we represent in experience, together with the plausible thesis that if I have the concept of, e.g., a certain shape, it must be possible for me to have word for it. However, although it is impossible for me to have a word for every shape I discriminate; for any shape I discriminate, it is possible that I have word for it.

concept of K, it is not plausible that anyone whose experience represents that something is K has the concept of K. But it is hard to see how any such reading of what it is to possess a concept could help with our problem. It *adds* to what is takes to believe, and, as we noted earlier, we are looking for something experience has and belief *per se* lacks.

A different way of finding the feel

To find the 'feel', I think representationalists should ask what is special about the representation that takes place when something looks or feels a certain way.[30] It seems to me that there are five distinctive features of cases where our sensory experience represents that things are thus and so.

First, such representation is rich. Visual experience represents how things are here and now in terms of colour, shape, location, extension, orientation and motion. Tactual experience represents how things are in terms of shape, motion, texture, extension, orientation and temperature.

Secondly, it is *inextricably* rich. A sentence that says X is red and round, has a part more concerned with redness and a part more concerned with roundness, and we can use sentences to represent something about colour while being completely silent about shape or motion or position, and conversely. But you cannot prise the colour bit from the shape bit of a visual experience. In representing something about shape, a visual experience *ipso facto* says something about colour (in the wide sense that includes white, black and grey); and a similar point applies to extension, location and motion. Equally, you cannot prise the texture and temperature bits from the shape bit of a tactile representation. Something cannot feel to have some shape or other without feeling to have a texture or a temperature (in the wide sense that includes being neither hotter nor colder than one's limb).

Thirdly, the representation is immediate. Reading from a piece of paper that there is something of such and such a colour, location, *etc.* typically induces a belief that represents that there is, but it does so *via* representing that there is a piece of paper with certain marks on it. Of course, immediacy may vary over time. Someone who uses a stick to feel the shape of an object down a hole will start by

---

[30] I am here following David Armstrong but he should not be held responsible for the details.

working from the feel of the end of the stick in their hand but typically ends up over time in a state that represents immediately the object's shape. The transition will match the transition from having an experience they characterize in terms of how their hand is felt to be to one they characterize in terms of how the object at the end of the stick is being felt to be.

Fourthly, there is a causal element in the content. Perception represents the world as interacting with us. When I hear a sound as being, say, behind and to the left, my experience represents the sound as *coming from* this location. To feel something is to feel in part its *contact with* one's body. Vision represents things as being located where we *see* them as being, as being at the location from which they are affecting us via our sense of sight.

Finally, sensory experience plays a distinctive functional role. Many years ago Armstrong analysed perceptual experience in terms of the acquisition of a disposition to believe as a result of the operation of one's senses.[31] But, as many have objected, the top line in the Müller-Lyer figure looks longer despite the fact that, for experienced customers, there is no tendency whatever to believe that it is. What is, however, true of sensory experience is that it plays a distinctive functional role in mediating between one state of belief and another. It is not itself a state of belief. And it need not move a subject into a state of belief that represents as it does—the subject may know that they are the subject of illusion or hallucination, or may already believe things are as the experience represents them—but it will determine a function that maps states of belief onto states of belief. A subject's posterior state of belief supervenes on their prior state of belief conjoined with their sensory experience.

Obviously, there is much more to say here, both by way of elucidation and by way of defence, but I hope the leading idea is clear. It is that if a representational state's content has inextricably and immediately the requisite richness, and if the state plays the right functional role, we get the phenomenology for free. In such cases, there must be the kind of experience that the blind sighted, the believers in what is written on notes, and the bold guessers lack.

To give a sense of the intuitive appeal of this approach, think of what happens when you summon up a mental image of an event described in a passage of prose. To make it image-like, you *have* to fill in the gaps; you have to include a red shirt kicking the winning goal from some part of the football field with some given trajectory,

[31] D. M. Armstrong, *Perception and the Physical World* (London: Routledge and Kegan Paul, 1961), p. 128.

you have to make the goal scorer some putative size or other, you have to locate the goal somewhere, and so on and so forth. Much can be left indeterminate but you have to put in lots more detail than is delivered in the passage of prose. Also, you need to create a representation that represents inextricably. The 'part' that delivers the size of the scorer is also the 'part' that delivers the putative location of the scorer and the colour of the shirt. And so on. To the extent that you succeed, you create a state with a phenomenology.

Back to Mary on her release

So what is the before and after story about Mary? If feel is a matter of immediacy, inextricability, and richness of representational content, and the right kind of functional role, the difference is that, after her release, Mary has representational states with all those properties. If she makes the mistake of conflating intensional properties with instantiated properties, she will think that she has learnt something new about how things are, but she'll be wrong. Rather, she is in a new kind of representational state from those she was in before. And what is it to know what it is like to be in that kind of state? Presumably, it is to be able to recognize, remember and imagine the state. Once we turn our back on the idea that there is a new property with which she is directly acquainted, knowing what it is like to sense red can only be something about the new kind of representational state she is in, and the obvious candidates for that 'something about' are her ability to recognize, imagine and remember the state. Those who resist accounts in terms of ability acquisition tend to say things like 'Mary acquires a new piece of propositional knowledge, namely, that seeing red is like *this*' but for the representationalist there is nothing suitable to be the referent of the demonstrative.

We have ended up agreeing with Laurence Nemirow and David Lewis on what happens to Mary on her release.[32] But, for the life of me, I cannot see how we could have known they were right without going via representationalism.

[32] Laurence Nemirow, review of T. Nagel, *Mortal Questions*, *Philosophical Review* 89 (1980), 475–6, and 'Physicalism and the Cognitive Role of Acquaintance', *Mind and Cognition*, W. G. Lycan, (ed.) Oxford: Basil Blackwell, 1990, 490–99; David Lewis, 'What Experience Teaches', *Mind and Cognition*, op. cit., 499–19.

Index

Index

DATE DUE

GAYLORD

PRINTED IN U.S.A.

BD418.3 .M553 2003
cop.2
Minds and persons